4.4BSD-Lite
Source CD-ROM

Now in its twentieth year, the USENIX Association, the UNIX and Advanced Computing Systems professional and technical organization, is a not-for-profit membership association of individuals and institutions with an interest in UNIX and UNIX-like systems, and, by extension, C++, X windows, and other advanced tools and technologies.

USENIX and its members are dedicated to:

- fostering innovation and communicating research and technological developments,
- sharing ideas and experience relevant to UNIX, UNIX-related, and advanced computing systems, and
- providing a neutral forum for the exercise of critical thought and airing of technical issues.

USENIX publishes a journal (**Computing Systems**), a newsletter (*;login:*), Proceedings from its frequent Conferences and Symposia, and a Book Series.

SAGE, The Systems Administrators Guild, a Special Technical Group with the USENIX Association, is dedicated to the advancement of system administration as a profession.

SAGE brings together systems managers and administrators to:

- propagate knowledge of good professional practice,
- recruit talented individuals to the profession,
- recognize individuals who attain professional excellence,
- foster technical development and share solutions to technical problems, and
- communicate in an organized voice with users, management, and vendors on system administration topics.

4.4BSD-Lite
Source CD-ROM

Berkeley Software Distribution

April, 1994

Computer Systems Research Group
University of California at Berkeley

A USENIX Association Book
O'Reilly & Associates, Inc.
103 Morris Street, Suite A
Sebastopol, CA 94572

First Printing, 1994

The Institute of Electrical and Electronics Engineers and the American National Standards Committee X3, on Information Processing Systems have given us permission to reprint portions of their documentation.

In the following statement, the phrase ''this text'' refers to portions of the system documentation.

''Portions of this text are reprinted and reproduced in electronic form in 4.4BSD from IEEE Std 1003.1-1988, IEEE Standard Portable Operating System Interface for Computer Environments (POSIX), copyright 1988 by the Institute of Electrical and Electronics Engineers, Inc. In the event of any discrepancy between these versions and the original IEEE Standard, the original IEEE Standard is the referee document.''

In the following statement, the phrase ''This material'' refers to portions of the system documentation.

''This material is reproduced with permission from American National Standards Committee X3, on Information Processing Systems. Computer and Business Equipment Manufacturers Association (CBEMA), 311 First St., NW, Suite 500, Washington, DC 20001-2178. The developmental work of Programming Language C was completed by the X3J11 Technical Committee.''

This book was printed and bound in the United States of America.
Distributed by O'Reilly & Associates, Inc.

[recycle logo]   This book is printed on acid-free paper with 50% recycled content, 10-13% post-consumer waste. O'Reilly & Associates is committed to using paper with the highest recycled content available consistent with high quality.

ꞴN: 1-56592-081-3 (Domestic)
Ɲ: 1-56592-092-9 (International)

Contents

The Computer Systems Research Group
1979 – 1993

CSRG Technical Staff

> Jim Bloom
> Keith Bostic
> Ralph Campbell
> Kevin Dunlap
> William N. Joy
> Michael J. Karels
> Samuel J. Leffler
> Marshall Kirk McKusick
> Miriam Amos Nihart
> Keith Sklower
> Marc Teitelbaum
> Michael Toy

CSRG Administration and Support

> Robert Fabry
> Domenico Ferrari
> Susan L. Graham
> Bob Henry
> Anne Hughes
> Bob Kridle
> David Mosher
> Pauline Schwartz
> Mark Seiden
> Jean Wood

Organizations that funded the CSRG with grants, gifts, personnel, and/or hardware.

> Center for Advanced Aviation System Development, The MITRE Corp.
> Compaq Computer Corporation
> Cray Research Inc.
> Department of Defense Advance Research Projects Agency (DARPA)
> Digital Equipment Corporation
> The Hewlett-Packard Company
> NASA Ames Research Center
> The National Science Foundation
> The Open Software Foundation
> UUNET Technologies Inc.

The following are people and organizations that provided a large subsystem for the BSD releases.

ANSI C library	Chris Torek
ANSI C prototypes	Donn Seeley and John Kohl
Autoconfiguration	Robert Elz
C library documentation	American National Standards Committee X3
CCI 6/32 support	Computer Consoles Inc.
DEC 3000/5000 support	Ralph Campbell
Disklabels	Symmetric Computer Systems
Documentation	Cynthia Livingston and The USENIX Association
Franz Lisp	Richard Fateman, John Foderaro, Keith Sklower, Kevin Layer
GCC, GDB	The Free Software Foundation
Groff	James Clark (The FSF)
HP300 support	Jeff Forys, Mike Hibler, Jay Lepreau, Donn Seeley and the Systems Programming Group; University of Utah Computer Science Department
ISODE	Marshall Rose
Ingres	Mike Stonebraker, Gene Wong, and the Berkeley Ingres Research Group
Intel 386/486 support	Bill Jolitz and TeleMuse
Job control	Jim Kulp
Kerberos	Project Athena and MIT
Kernel support	Bill Shannon and Sun Microsystems Inc.
LFS	Margo Seltzer, Mendel Rosenblum, Carl Staelin
MIPS support	Trent Hein
Math library	K.C. Ng, Zhishun Alex Liu, S. McDonald, P. Tang and W. Kahan
NFS	Rick Macklem
NFS automounter	Jan-Simon Pendry
Network device drivers	Micom-Interlan and Excelan
Omron Luna support	Akito Fujita and Shigeto Mochida
Quotas	Robert Elz
RPC support	Sun Microsystems Inc.
Shared library support	Rob Gingell and Sun Microsystems Inc.
Sony News 3400 support	Kazumasa Utashiro
Sparc I/II support	Computer Systems Engineering Group, Lawrence Berkeley Laboratory
Stackable file systems	John Heidemann
Stdio	Chris Torek
System documentation	The Institute of Electrical and Electronics Engineers, Inc.
TCP/IP	Rob Gurwitz and Bolt Beranek and Newman Inc.
Timezone support	Arthur David Olson
Transport/Network OSI layers	IBM Corporation and the University of Wisconsin
Kernel XNS assistance	William Nesheim, J. Q. Johnson, Chris Torek, and James O'Toole
User level XNS	Cornell University
VAX 3000 support	Mt. Xinu and Tom Ferrin
VAX BI support	Chris Torek
VAX device support	Digital Equipment Corporation and Helge Skrivervik
Versatec printer/plotter support	University of Toronto
Virtual memory implementation	Avadis Tevanian, Jr., Michael Wayne Young, and the Carnegie-Mellon University Mach project
X25	University of British Columbia

The following are people and organizations that provided a specific item, program, library routine or program maintenance for the BSD system. (Their contribution may not be part of the final 4.4BSD release.)

386 device drivers	Carnegie-Mellon University Mach project
386 device drivers	Don Ahn, Sean Fagan and Tim Tucker
HCX device drivers	Harris Corporation
Kernel enhancements	Robert Elz, Peter Ivanov, Ian Johnstone, Piers Lauder,
	John Lions, Tim Long, Chris Maltby, Greg Rose and John Wainwright
ISO-9660 filesystem	Pace Willisson, Atsushi Murai

adventure(6)	Don Woods	log(3)	Peter McIlroy
adventure(6)	Jim Gillogly	look(1)	David Hitz
adventure(6)	Will Crowther	ls(1)	Elan Amir
apply(1)	Rob Pike	ls(1)	Michael Fischbein
apply(1)	Jan-Simon Pendry	lsearch(3)	Roger L. Snyder
ar(1)	Hugh A. Smith	m4(1)	Ozan Yigit
arithmetic(6)	Eamonn McManus	mail(1)	Kurt Schoens
arp(8)	Sun Microsystems Inc.	make(1)	Adam de Boor
at(1)	Steve Wall	me(7)	Eric Allman
atc(6)	Ed James	mergesort(3)	Peter McIlroy
awk(1)	Arnold Robbins	mh(1)	Marshall Rose
awk(1)	David Trueman	mh(1)	The Rand Corporation
backgammon(6)	Alan Char	mille(6)	Ken Arnold
banner(1)	Mark Horton	mknod(8)	Kevin Fall
battlestar(6)	David Riggle	monop(6)	Ken Arnold
bcd(6)	Steve Hayman	more(1)	Eric Shienbrood
bdes(1)	Matt Bishop	more(1)	Mark Nudleman
berknet(1)	Eric Schmidt	mountd(8)	Herb Hasler
bib(1)	Dain Samples	mprof(1)	Ben Zorn
bib(1)	Gary M. Levin	msgs(1)	David Wasley
bib(1)	Timothy A. Budd	multicast	Stephen Deering
bitstring(3)	Paul Vixie	mv(1)	Ken Smith
boggle(6)	Barry Brachman	named/bind(8)	Douglas Terry
bpf(4)	Steven McCanne	named/bind(8)	Kevin Dunlap
btree(3)	Mike Olson	news(1)	Rick Adams (and a cast of thousands)
byte-range locking	Scooter Morris	nm(1)	Hans Huebner
caesar(6)	John Eldridge	pascal(1)	Kirk McKusick
caesar(6)	Stan King	pascal(1)	Peter Kessler
cal(1)	Kim Letkeman	paste(1)	Adam S. Moskowitz
cat(1)	Kevin Fall	patch(1)	Larry Wall
chess(6)	Stuart Cracraft (The FSF)	pax(1)	Keith Muller
ching(6)	Guy Harris	phantasia(6)	C. Robertson
cksum(1)	James W. Williams	phantasia(6)	Edward A. Estes
clri(8)	Rich $alz	ping(8)	Mike Muuss
col(1)	Michael Rendell	pom(6)	Keith E. Brandt
comm(1)	Case Larsen	pr(1)	Keith Muller
compact(1)	Colin L. McMaster	primes(6)	Landon Curt Noll
compress(1)	James A. Woods	qsort(3)	Doug McIlroy
compress(1)	Joseph Orost	qsort(3)	Earl Cohen
compress(1)	Spencer Thomas	qsort(3)	Jon Bentley
courier(1)	Eric Cooper	quad(3)	Chris Torek
cp(1)	David Hitz	quiz(6)	Jim R. Oldroyd
cpio(1)	AT&T	quiz(6)	Keith Gabryelski
crypt(3)	Tom Truscott	radixsort(3)	Dan Bernstein
csh(1)	Christos Zoulas	radixsort(3)	Peter McIlroy
csh(1)	Len Shar	rain(6)	Eric P. Scott
curses(3)	Elan Amir	ranlib(1)	Hugh A. Smith
curses(3)	Ken Arnold	rcs(1)	Walter F. Tichy
cut(1)	Adam S. Moskowitz	rdist(1)	Michael Cooper
cut(1)	Marciano Pitargue	regex(3)	Henry Spencer
dbx(1)	Mark Linton	robots(6)	Ken Arnold
dd(1)	Keith Muller	rogue(6)	Timothy C. Stoehr
dd(1)	Lance Visser	rs(1)	John Kunze
des(1)	Jim Gillogly	sail(6)	David Riggle
des(1)	Phil Karn	sail(6)	Edward Wang
des(1)	Richard Outerbridge	sccs(1)	Eric Allman

dipress(1)	Xerox Corporation	scsiformat(1)	Lawrence Berkeley Laboratory
disklabel(8)	Symmetric Computer Systems	sdb(1)	Howard Katseff
du(1)	Chris Newcomb	sed(1)	Diomidis Spinellis
dungeon(6)	R.M. Supnik	sendmail(8)	Eric Allman
ed(1)	Rodney Ruddock	setmode(3)	Dave Borman
emacs(1)	Richard Stallman	sh(1)	Kenneth Almquist
erf(3)	Peter McIlroy, K.C. Ng	slattach(8)	Rick Adams
error(1)	Robert R. Henry	slip(8)	Rick Adams
ex(1)	Mark Horton	spms(1)	Peter J. Nicklin
factor(6)	Landon Curt Noll	strtod(3)	David M. Gay
file(1)	Ian Darwin	swab(3)	Jeffrey Mogul
find(1)	Cimarron Taylor	sysconf(3)	Sean Eric Fagan
finger(1)	Tony Nardo	sysline(1)	J.K. Foderaro
fish(6)	Muffy Barkocy	syslog(3)	Eric Allman
fmt(1)	Kurt Schoens	systat(1)	Bill Reeves
fnmatch(3)	Guido van Rossum	systat(1)	Robert Elz
fold(1)	Kevin Ruddy	tail(1)	Edward Sze-Tyan Wang
fortune(6)	Ken Arnold	talk(1)	Clem Cole
fpr(1)	Robert Corbett	talk(1)	Kipp Hickman
fsdb(8)	Computer Consoles Inc.	talk(1)	Peter Moore
fsplit(1)	Asa Romberger	telnet(1)	Dave Borman
fsplit(1)	Jerry Berkman	telnet(1)	Paul Borman
gcc/groff integration	UUNET Technologies, Inc.	termcap(5)	John A. Kunze
gcore(1)	Eric Cooper	termcap(5)	Mark Horton
getcap(3)	Casey Leedom	test(1)	Kenneth Almquist
glob(3)	Guido van Rossum	tetris(6)	Chris Torek
gprof(1)	Peter Kessler	tetris(6)	Darren F. Provine
gprof(1)	Robert R. Henry	timed(8)	Riccardo Gusella
hack(6)	Andries Brouwer (and a cast of thousands)	timed(8)	Stefano Zatti
hangman(6)	Ken Arnold	tn3270(1)	Gregory Minshall
hash(3)	Margo Seltzer	tr(1)	Igor Belchinskiy
heapsort(3)	Elmer Yglesias	traceroute(8)	Van Jacobson
heapsort(3)	Kevin Lew	trek(6)	Eric Allman
heapsort(3)	Ronnie Kon	tset(1)	Eric Allman
hunt(6)	Conrad Huang	tsort(1)	Michael Rendell
hunt(6)	Greg Couch	unifdef(1)	Dave Yost
icon(1)	Bill Mitchell	uniq(1)	Case Larsen
icon(1)	Ralph Griswold	uucpd(8)	Rick Adams
indent(1)	David Willcox	uudecode(1)	Mark Horton
indent(1)	Eric Schmidt	uuencode(1)	Mark Horton
indent(1)	James Gosling	uuq(1)	Lou Salkind
indent(1)	Sun Microsystems	uuq(1)	Rick Adams
init(1)	Donn Seeley	uusnap(8)	Randy King
j0(3)	Sun Microsystems, Inc.	uusnap(8)	Rick Adams
j1(3)	Sun Microsystems, Inc.	vacation(1)	Eric Allman
jn(3)	Sun Microsystems, Inc.	vi(1)	Steve Kirkendall
join(1)	David Goodenough	which(1)	Peter Kessler
join(1)	Michiro Hikida	who(1)	Michael Fischbein
join(1)	Steve Hayman	window(1)	Edward Wang
jot(1)	John Kunze	worm(6)	Michael Toy
jove(1)	Jonathon Payne	worms(6)	Eric P. Scott
kermit(1)	Columbia University	write(1)	Craig Leres
kvm(3)	Peter Shipley	write(1)	Jef Poskanzer
kvm(3)	Steven McCanne	wump(6)	Dave Taylor
lam(1)	John Kunze	X25/Ethernet	Univ. of Erlangen-Nuremberg
larn(6)	Noah Morgan	X25/LLC2	Dirk Husemann
lastcomm(1)	Len Edmondson	xargs(1)	John B. Roll Jr.
lex(1)	Vern Paxson	xneko(6)	Masayuki Koba
libm(3)	Peter McIlroy	XNSrouted(1)	Bill Nesheim
libm(3)	UUNET Technologies, Inc.	xroach(6)	J.T. Anderson
locate(1)	James A. Woods	yacc(1)	Robert Paul Corbett
lock(1)	Bob Toxen		

Overview

1. 4.4BSD-Lite Description

This cd-rom contains the source code, manual pages and other documentation, and research papers from the first revision of the University of California, Berkeley's 4.4BSD-Lite distribution.

The 4.4BSD-Lite software is copyrighted by the University of California and others, but may be freely redistributed and used in products without fee, as long as the due credit, copyright notice, and other requirements described in the file /COPYRIGHT are met.

The distribution includes both software developed at Berkeley and much software contributed by authors outside Berkeley. Please see the previous section of this document for a list of the many contributors to the system.

The layout of the 4.4BSD-Lite distribution is described in the *hier*(7) manual page, which follows. A table of contents and permuted index for the 4.4BSD-Lite manual pages follow as well.

The cd-rom is in ISO-9660 format, with Rock Ridge Extensions. For example, to mount on a 4.4BSD-Lite system on which the CD-ROM drive is connected as SCSI unit 1, ensure that the directory /cdrom exists, then enter "mount -r -t cd9660 /dev/sd1a /cdrom". To mount on a Sun, ensure that the directory /cdrom exists, then enter "mount -r -t hsts /dev/sr0 /cdrom".

The 4.4BSD-Lite distribution is a source distribution only, and does not contain program binaries for any architecture. It is not possible to compile or run this software without a pre-existing system that is already installed and running. In addition, the distribution does not include sources for the complete 4.4BSD system. It includes source code and manual pages for the C library, approximately 95% of the utilities distributed in 4.4BSD, and all but a few files from the kernel. The system is almost entirely ANSI C and IEEE POSIX 1003.1 and 1003.2 standards compliant.

2. 4.4BSD-Lite Features

The major new facilities available in the 4.4BSD-Lite release are a new virtual memory system, the addition of ISO/OSI networking support, a new virtual filesystem interface supporting filesystem stacking, a freely redistributable implementation of NFS, a log-structured filesystem, enhancement of the local filesystems to support files and filesystems that are up to 2^{63} bytes in size, enhanced security and system management support, and the conversion to and addition of the IEEE Std1003.1 ("POSIX") facilities and many of the IEEE Std1003.2 facilities. In addition, many new utilities and additions have been made to the C-library. The kernel sources have been reorganized to collect all machine-dependent files for each architecture under one directory, and most of the machine-independent code is now free of code conditional on specific machines. The user structure and process structure have been reorganized to eliminate the statically-mapped user structure and to make most of the process resources shareable by multiple processes. The system and include files have been converted to be compatible with ANSI C, including function prototypes for most of the exported functions. There are numerous other changes throughout the system.

3. Changes in the Kernel

This release includes several important structural kernel changes. The kernel uses a new internal system call convention; the use of global ("u-dot") variables for parameters and error returns has been eliminated, and interrupted system calls no longer abort using non-local goto's (longjmp's). A new sleep interface separates signal handling from scheduling priority, returning characteristic errors to abort or restart the current system call. This sleep call also passes a string describing the process state, which is used by the ps(1) program. The old sleep interface can be used only for non-interruptible sleeps.

Many data structures that were previously statically allocated are now allocated dynamically. These structures include mount entries, file entries, user open file descriptors, the process entries, the vnode table, the name cache, and the quota structures.

The 4.4BSD-Lite distribution adds support for several new architectures including SPARC-based Sparcstations 1 and 2, MIPS-based Decstation 3100 and 5000 and Sony NEWS, 68000-based Hewlett-Packard 9000/300 and Omron Luna, and 386-based Personal Computers. Both the HP300 and SPARC ports feature the ability to run binaries built for the native operating system (HP-UX or SunOS) by emulating their system calls. Though this native operating system compatibility was provided by the developers as needed for their purposes and is by no means complete, it is complete enough to run several non-trivial applications including those that require HP-UX or SunOS shared libraries. For example, the vendor supplied X11 server and windowing environment can be used on both the HP300 and SPARC.

3.1. Virtual memory changes

The new virtual memory implementation is derived from the MACH operating system developed at Carnegie-Mellon, and was ported to the BSD kernel at the University of Utah. The MACH virtual memory system call interface has been replaced with the "mmap"-based interface described in the "Berkeley Software Architecture Manual (4.4 Edition)" (see the UNIX Programmer's Manual, Supplementary Documents, PSD:5). The interface is similar to the interfaces shipped by several commercial vendors such as Sun, USL, and Convex Computer Corp. The integration of the new virtual memory is functionally complete, but, like most MACH-based virtual memory systems, still has serious performance problems under heavy memory load.

3.2. Networking additions and changes

The ISO/OSI Networking consists of a kernel implementation of transport class 4 (TP-4), connectionless networking protocol (CLNP), and 802.3-based link-level support (hardware-compatible with Ethernet*). We also include support for ISO Connection-Oriented Network Service, X.25, and TP-0. The session and presentation layers are provided outside the kernel by the ISO development environment (ISODE). Included in this development environment are file transfer and management (FTAM), virtual terminals (VT), a directory services implementation (X.500), and miscellaneous other utilities.

Several important enhancements have been added to the TCP/IP protocols including TCP header prediction and serial line IP (SLIP) with header compression. The routing implementation has been completely rewritten to use a hierarchical routing tree with a mask per route to support the arbitrary levels of routing found in the ISO protocols. The routing table also stores and caches route characteristics to speed the adaptation of the throughput and congestion avoidance algorithms.

3.3. Additions and changes to filesystems

The 4.4BSD-Lite distribution contains most of the interfaces specified in the IEEE Std1003.1 system interface standard. Filesystem additions include IEEE Std1003.1 FIFOs, byte-range file locking, and saved user and group identifiers.

A new virtual filesystem interface has been added to the kernel to support multiple filesystems. In comparison with other interfaces, the Berkeley interface has been structured for more efficient support of filesystems that maintain state (such as the local filesystem). The interface has been extended with support for stackable filesystems done at UCLA. These extensions allow for filesystems to be layered on top of each other and allow new vnode operations to be added without requiring changes to existing filesystem implementations. For example, the umap filesystem is used to mount a sub-tree of an existing filesystem that uses a different set of uids and gids than the local system. Such a filesystem could be mounted from a remote site via NFS or it could be a filesystem on removable media brought from some foreign location that uses a different password file.

In addition to the local "fast filesystem," we have added an implementation of the network filesystem (NFS) that fully interoperates with the NFS shipped by Sun and its licensees. Because our NFS implementation was implemented using only the publicly available NFS specification, it does not require a license from Sun to use in source or binary form. By default it runs over UDP to be compatible with Sun's implementation. However, it can

---

*Ethernet is a trademark of the Xerox Corporation.

be configured on a per-mount basis to run over TCP. Using TCP allows it to be used quickly and efficiently through gateways and over long-haul networks. Using an extended protocol, it supports Leases to allow a limited callback mechanism that greatly reduces the network traffic necessary to maintain cache consistency between the server and its clients.

A new log-structured filesystem has been added that provides near disk-speed output and fast crash recovery. It is still experimental in the 4.4BSD-Lite release, so we do not recommend it for production use. We have also added a memory-based filesystem that runs in pageable memory, allowing large temporary filesystems without requiring dedicated physical memory.

The local "fast filesystem" has been enhanced to do clustering which allows large pieces of files to be allocated contiguously resulting in near doubling of filesystem throughput. The filesystem interface has been extended to allow files and filesystems to grow to 2^{63} bytes in size. The quota system has been rewritten to support both user and group quotas (simultaneously if desired). Quota expiration is based on time rather than the previous metric of number of logins over quota. This change makes quotas more useful on fileservers onto which users seldom log in.

The system security has been greatly enhanced by the addition of additional file flags that permit a file to be marked as immutable or append only. Once set, these flags can only be cleared by the super-user when the system is running single user. To protect against indiscriminate reading or writing of kernel memory, all writing and most reading of kernel data structures must be done using a new "sysctl" interface. The information to be accessed is described through an extensible "Management Information Base" (MIB).

3.4. POSIX terminal driver changes

The biggest area of change is a new terminal driver. The terminal driver is similar to the System V terminal driver with the addition of the necessary extensions to get the functionality previously available in the 4.3BSD terminal driver. 4.4BSD-Lite also adds the IEEE Std1003.1 job control interface, which is similar to the 4.3BSD job control interface, but adds a security model that was missing in the 4.3BSD job control implementation. A new system call, *setsid*, creates a job-control session consisting of a single process group with one member, the caller, that becomes a session leader. Only a session leader may acquire a controlling terminal. This is done explicitly via a TIOCSCTTY *ioctl* call, not implicitly by an *open* call. The call fails if the terminal is in use.

For backward compatibility, both the old *ioctl* calls and old options to *stty* are emulated.

4. Changes to the utilities

There are several new tools and utilities included in this release. A new version of "make" allows much-simplified makefiles for the system software and allows compilation for multiple architectures from the same source tree (which may be mounted read-only). Notable additions to the libraries include functions to traverse a filesystem hierarchy, database interfaces to btree and hashing functions, a new, fast implementation of stdio, and a radix sort function. The additions to the utility suite include greatly enhanced versions of programs that display system status information, implementations of various traditional tools described in the IEEE Std1003.2 standard, and many others.

We have been tracking the IEEE Std1003.2 shell and utility work and have included prototypes of many of the proposed utilities. Most of the traditional utilities have been replaced with implementations conformant to the POSIX standards. Almost the entire manual suite has been rewritten to reflect the POSIX defined interfaces. In rewriting this software, we have generally been rewarded with significant performance improvements. Most of the libraries and header files have been converted to be compliant with ANSI C. The system libraries and utilities all compile with either ANSI or traditional C.

The Kerberos (version 4) authentication software has been integrated into much of the system (including NFS) to provide the first real network authentication on BSD.

A new implementation of the *ex/vi* text editors is available in this release. It is intended as a bug-for-bug compatible version of the editors. It also has a few new features: 8-bit clean data, lines and files limited only by memory and disk space, split screens, tags stacks and left-right scrolling among them. *Nex/nvi* is not yet production quality; future versions of this software may be retrieved by anonymous ftp from ftp.cs.berkeley.edu, in the directory ucb/4bsd.

The *find* utility has two new options that are important to be aware of if you intend to use NFS. The "fstype" and "prune" options can be used together to prevent find from crossing NFS mount points.

4.1. Additions and changes to the libraries

The *curses* library has been largely rewritten. Important additional features include support for scrolling and *termios*.

An application front-end editing library, named libedit, has been added to the system.

A superset implementation of the SunOS kernel memory interface library, *libkvm*, has been integrated into the system.

Nearly the entire C-library has been rewritten. Some highlights of the changes to the 4.4BSD-Lite C-library:

- The newly added *fts* functions will do either physical or logical traversal of a file hierarchy as well as handle essentially infinite depth filesystems and filesystems with cycles. All the utilities in 4.4BSD-Lite that traverse file hierarchies have been converted to use *fts*. The conversion has always resulted in a significant performance gain, often of four or five to one in system time.

- The newly added *dbopen* functions are intended to be a family of database access methods. Currently, they consist of *hash*, an extensible, dynamic hashing scheme, *btree*, a sorted, balanced tree structure (B+tree's), and *recno*, a flat-file interface for fixed or variable length records referenced by logical record number. Each of the access methods stores associated key/data pairs and uses the same record oriented interface for access. Future versions of this software may be retrieved by anonymous ftp from ftp.cs.berkeley.edu, in the directory ucb/4bsd.

- The *qsort* function has been rewritten for additional performance. In addition, three new types of sorting functions, *heapsort*, *mergesort*, and *radixsort* have been added to the system. The *mergesort* function is optimized for data with pre-existing order, in which case it usually significantly outperforms *qsort*. The *radixsort* functions are variants of most-significant-byte radix sorting. They take time linear to the number of bytes to be sorted, usually significantly outperforming *qsort* on data that can be sorted in this fashion. An implementation of the POSIX 1003.2 standard *sort* based on *radixsort* is included in 4.4BSD-Lite.

- The floating point support in the C-library has been replaced and is now accurate.

- The C functions specified by both ANSI C, POSIX 1003.1 and 1003.2 are now part of the C-library. This includes support for file name matching, shell globbing and both basic and extended regular expressions.

- ANSI C multibyte and wide character support has been integrated. The rune functionality from the Bell Labs' Plan 9 system is provided as well.

- The *termcap* functions have been generalized and replaced with a general purpose interface named *getcap*.

- The *stdio* routines have been replaced, and are usually much faster. In addition, the *funopen* interface permits applications to provide their own I/O stream function support.

5. Acknowledgements

We were greatly assisted by the past employees of the Computer Systems Research Group: Mike Karels, Keith Sklower, and Marc Tietelbaum. Our distribution coordinator, Pauline Schwartz, has reliably managed the finances and the mechanics of shipping distributions for nearly the entire fourteen years of the group's existence. Without the help of lawyers Mary MacDonald, Joel Linzner, and Carla Shapiro, the 4.4BSD-Lite distribution would never have seen the light of day. Much help was provided by Chris Demetriou in getting bug fixes from NetBSD integrated back into the 4.4BSD-Lite distribution.

The vast majority of the 4.4BSD-Lite distribution comes from the numerous people in the UNIX community that provided their time and energy in creating the software contained in this release. We dedicate this distribution to them.

M. K. McKusick
K. Bostic

NAME

`hier` – layout of filesystems

DESCRIPTION

An outline of the filesystem hierarchy.

/   root directory of the system

/COPYRIGHT

system copyright notice

/[a-z]   user filesystems

/altroot/   alternate root filesystem, in case of disaster

/amd/   home directories mount point; see amd(8)

/bin/   utilities used in both single and multi-user environments

/dev/   block, character and other special device files

MAKEDEV

	script for creating device files; see makedev(8)
console	the computer's console device
fd/	file descriptor files; see fd(4)
drum	system swap space; see drum(4)
klog	kernel logging device; see syslog(3)
kmem	kernel virtual memory device; see mem(4)
log	UNIX domain datagram log socket; see syslogd(8)
mem	kernel physical memory device; see mem(4)
stderr	
stdin	
stdout	file descriptor files; see fd(4)
null	the null device; see null(4)
tty	process' controlling terminal device; see tty(4)

/dump/   online dump(8) repository

/etc/   system configuration files and scripts

aliases*	name alias files for sendmail(8)
amd*	configuration files for amd(8)
changelist	files backed up by the security script
crontab	schedule used by the cron(8) daemon
csh.cshrc	
csh.login	
csh.logout	system-wide scripts for csh(1)
daily	script run each day by cron(8)
disklabels/	backup disklabels; see disklabel(8)
disktab	disk description file, see disktab(5)
dm.conf	dungeon master configuration; see dm.conf(5)
dumpdates	dump history; see dump(8)
exports	filesystem export information; see mountd(8)
fstab	filesystem information; see fstab(5) and mount(8)

ftpusers	users denied ftp(1) access; see ftpd(8)
ftpwelcome	ftp(1) initial message; see ftpd(8)
gettytab	terminal configuration database; see gettytab(8)
group	group permissions file; see group(5)
hosts	host name database backup for named(8); see hosts(5)
hosts.equiv	trusted machines with equivalent user ID's
hosts.lpd	trusted machines with printing privileges
inetd.conf	Internet server configuration file; see inetd(8)
kerberosIV/	configuration files for the kerberos version IV; see kerberos(1)
localtime	local timezone information; see ctime(3)
mail.rc	system-wide initialization script for mail(1)
man.conf	configuration file for man(1); see man.conf(5)
master.passwd	
passwd	
pwd.db	
spwd.db	password files and their databases; see pwd_mkdb(8)
monthly	script run each month by cron(8)
motd	system message of the day
mtree/	mtree configuration files; see mtree(1)
named.*	
namedb/	named configuration files and databases; see named(8)
netgroup	network groups; see netgroup(5)
netstart	network startup script
networks	network name data base; see networks(5)
phones	remote host phone number data base; see phones(5)
printcap	system printer configuration; see printcap(5)
protocols	protocol name database; see protocols(5)
rc	
rc.local	system startup files; see rc(8)
remote	remote host description file; see remote(5)
security	daily (in)security script run by cron(8)
sendmail.*	sendmail(8) configuration information
services	service name data base; see services(5)
shells	list of permitted shells; see shells(5)
sliphome	slip login/logout scripts; see slattach(8)
syslog.conf	syslogd(8) configuration file; see syslog.conf(5)
termcap	terminal type database; see termcap(3)
ttys	terminal initialization information; see ttys(5)
weekly	script run each week by cron(8)

/home/   mount point for the automounter; see amd(8)

/mnt/   empty directory commonly used by system administrators as a temporary mount point

/root/   home directory for the super-user

.rhosts	super-user id mapping between machines
.cshrc	super-user start-up file
.login	super-user start-up file
.profile	super-user start-up file

/sbin/   system programs and administration utilities used in both single-user and multi-user environments

/stand/   programs used in a standalone environment

/sys   symbolic link to the operating system source

/tmp/   temporary files, usually a `mfs`(8) memory-based filesystem (the contents of /tmp are usually NOT preserved across a system reboot)

/usr/   contains the majority of the system utilities and files

X11	X11 files	
	bin/	X11 binaries
	include/	X11 include files
	lib/	X11 libraries
bin/	common utilities, programming tools, and applications	
contrib/	packages maintained by groups other than Berkeley	
	bin/	contributed binaries
	include/	contributed include files
	libexec/	contributed daemons
	libdata/	contributed data files
games/	the important stuff	
include/	standard C include files	
	X11/	include files for X11 window system
	arpa/	include files for Internet service protocols
	g++/	include files for the C++ compiler
	kerberosIV/	include files for kerberos authentication package; see `kerberos`(1)
	machine/	machine specific include files
	net/	miscellaneous network include files
	netccitt/	CCITT networking include files
	netinet/	include files for Internet standard protocols; see `inet`(4)
	netiso/	include files for ISO standard protocols; see `iso`(4)
	netns/	include files for XNS standard protocols; see `ns`(4)
	nfs/	include files for NFS (Network File System)
	pascal/	include files for `pc`(1)
	protocols/	include files for Berkeley service protocols
	rpc/	include files for Sun Microsystem's RPC package
	sys/	kernel include files
	ufs/	include files for UFS
	xnscourier/	include files for XNS package
lib/	system C library archives; see `ar`(1)	
	uucp/	UUCP binaries and scripts (historically placed; to be moved)
libdata/	miscellaneous utility data files	

libexec/	system daemons and system utilities (executed by other programs)	
local/	local executables, libraries, etc.	

	bin/	local binaries
	include/	local include files
	libexec/	local daemons
	libdata/	local data files

obj/	architecture-specific target tree produced by building the `/usr/src` tree; normally a symbolic link or mounted filesystem	
old/	programs from past lives of 4BSD which may disappear in future releases	

	bin/	old binaries
	include/	old include files
	libexec/	old daemons
	libdata/	old data files

sbin/	system daemons and system utilities (normally executed by the super-user)	
share/	architecture-independent text files	

	calendar/	a variety of calendar files; see `calendar`(1)
	dict/	word lists; see `look`(1) and `spell`(1)

		words	common words
		web2	words of Webster's 2nd International
		papers/	reference databases; see `refer`(1)
		special/	custom word lists; see `spell`(1)

	doc/	miscellaneous documentation; source for most of the printed 4BSD manuals (available from the USENIX association)
	games/	text files used by various games
	man/	formatted manual pages
	me/	macros for use with the me(7) macro package
	misc/	miscellaneous system-wide text files

		termcap	terminal characteristics database; see `termcap`(5)

	mk/	include files for `make`(1)
	ms/	macros for use with the ms(7) macro package
	skel/	sample initialization files for new user accounts
	tabset/	tab description files for a variety of terminals, used in the termcap file; see `termcap`(5)
	tmac/	text processing macros; see `nroff`(1) and `troff`(1)
	zoneinfo/	timezone configuration information; see `tzfile`(5)

usr.bin/	source for utilities/files in `/usr/bin`	
usr.sbin/	source for utilities/files in `/usr/sbin`	

/usr/src/	4BSD and local source files	

	bin/	source for utilities/files in `/bin`
	contrib/	source for utilities/files in `/usr/contrib`
	etc/	source (usually example files) for files in `/etc`
	games/	source for utilities/files in `/usr/games`
	include/	source for files in `/usr/include`
	kerberosIV/	source for Kerberos version IV utilities and libraries
	lib/	source for libraries in `/usr/lib`

libexec/	source for utilities/files in `/usr/libexec`	
local/	source for utilities/files in `/usr/local`	
old/	source for utilities/files in `/usr/old`	
sbin/	source for utilities/files in `/sbin`	
share/	source for files in `/usr/share`	

    doc/

papers/	source for various Berkeley technical papers
psd/	source for Programmer's Supplementary Documents
smm/	source for System Manager's Manual
usd/	source for User's Supplementary Documents

sys/   kernel source files

compile/	kernel compilation directory
conf/	architecture independent configuration directory
deprecated/	deprecated kernel functionality
dev/	architecture independent device support
hp/	general support for Hewlett-Packard architectures
hp300/	support for the Hewlett-Packard 9000/300 68000-based workstations
i386/	support for the Intel 386/486 workstations
isofs/	support for ISO filesystems

        cd9660/   support for the ISO-9660 filesystem

kern/	support for the high kernel (system calls)
libkern/	C library routines used in the kernel
luna68k/	Omron Luna 68000-based workstations
mips/	general support for MIPS architectures
miscfs/	miscellaneous file systems
net/	miscellaneous networking support
netccitt/	CCITT networking support
netinet/	TCP/IP networking support
netiso/	ISO networking support
netns/	XNS networking support
news3400/	Sony News MIPS-based workstations
nfs/	NFS support
pmax/	DECstation 3100 and 5000 MIPS-based workstations
scripts/	kernel debugging scripts
sparc/	Sparcstation I & II SPARC-based workstations
stand/	kernel standalone support
sys/	kernel (and system) include files
tahoe/	Computer Consoles Inc. Tahoe architecture (obsolete)
tests/	kernel testing
ufs/	local filesystem support

        ffs/   the Berkeley Fast File System
        lfs/   the log-structured file system
        mfs/   the in-memory file system
        ufs/   shared UNIX file system support

vax/	Digital Equipment Corp. VAX architecture (obsolete)
vm/	virtual memory support

/var/   multi-purpose log, temporary, transient, and spool files

    account/   system accounting files

        acct   execution accounting file; see acct(5)

    at/   timed command scheduling files; see at(1)
    backups/   miscellaneous backup files, largely of files found in /etc
    crash/   system crash dumps; see savecore(8)
    db/   miscellaneous automatically generated system-specific database files
    games/   miscellaneous game status and log files
    log/   miscellaneous system log files

amd.*	amd(8) logs
daily.out	output of the last run of the /etc/daily script
ftp.*	ftp(1) logs
kerberos.*	kerberos(1) logs
lastlog	system last time logged in log; see utmp(5)
lpd-errs.*	printer daemon error logs; see lpd(8)
maillog.*	sendmail(8) log files
messages.*	general system information log
monthly.out	output of the last run of the /etc/monthly script
secure	sensitive security information log
sendmail.st	sendmail(8) statistics
timed.*	timed(8) logs
weekly.out	output of the last run of the /etc/weekly script
wtmp	login/logout log; see utmp(5)

    mail/   user system mailboxes
    msgs/   system messages; see msgs(1)
    preserve/   temporary home of files preserved after an accidental death of ex(1) or vi(1)
    quotas/   filesystem quota information
    run/   system information files, rebuilt after each reboot

        utmp   database of current users; see utmp(5)

    rwho/   rwho data files; see rwhod(8), rwho(1), and ruptime(1)
    spool/   miscellaneous printer and mail system spooling directories

ftp/	commonly ''~ftp'', the anonymous ftp root directory; see ftpd(8)
mqueue/	undelivered mail queue; see sendmail(8)
news/	Network news archival and spooling directories
output/	printer spooling directories
secretmail/	secretmail spool directory; see xget(1)
uucp/	uucp spool directory
uucppublic/	commonly ''~uucp'', the uucp public temporary directory; see uucp(1)

    tmp/   temporary files that are not discarded between system reboots

        vi.recover/   recovery directory for nvi(1)

/vmunix   the executable for the operating system

Introduction

The documentation for 4.4BSD is in a format similar to the one used for the 4.2BSD and 4.3BSD manuals. It is divided into three sets; each set consists of one or more volumes. The abbreviations for the volume names are listed in square brackets; the abbreviations for the manual sections are listed in parenthesis.

I. User's Documents
    User's Reference Manual [URM]
        Commands (1)
        Games (6)
        Macro packages and language conventions (7)
    User's Supplementary Documents [USD]
        Getting Started
        Basic Utilities
        Communicating with the World
        Text Editing
        Document Preparation
        Amusements

II. Programmer's Documents
    Programmer's Reference Manual [PRM]
        System calls (2)
        Subroutines (3)
        Special files (4)
        File formats and conventions (5)
    Programmer's Supplementary Documents [PSD]
        Documents of Historic Interest
        Languages in common use
        Programming Tools
        Programming Libraries
        General Reference

III. System Manager's Manual [SMM]
        Maintenance commands (8)
        System Installation and Administration

References to individual documents are given as "volume:document", thus USD:1 refers to the first document in the "User's Supplementary Documents". References to manual pages are given as "*name*(section)" thus *sh*(1) refers to the shell manual entry in section 1.

The manual pages give descriptions of the features of the 4.4BSD system, as developed at the University of California at Berkeley. They do not attempt to provide perspective or tutorial information about the 4.4BSD operating system, its facilities, or its implementation. Various documents on those topics are contained in the "UNIX User's Supplementary Documents" (USD), the "UNIX Programmer's Supplementary Documents" (PSD), and "UNIX System Manager's Manual" (SMM). In particular, for an overview see "The UNIX Time-Sharing System" (PSD:1) by Ritchie and Thompson; for a tutorial see "UNIX for Beginners" (USD:1) by Kernighan, and for an guide to the new features of this latest version, see "Berkeley Software Architecture Manual (4.4 Edition)" (PSD:5).

Within the area it surveys, this volume attempts to be timely, complete and concise. Where the latter two objectives conflict, the obvious is often left unsaid in favor of brevity. It is intended that each program be described as it is, not as it should be. Inevitably, this means that various sections will soon be out of date.

Commands are programs intended to be invoked directly by the user, in contrast to subroutines, that are intended to be called by the user's programs. User commands are described in URM section 1. Commands generally reside in directory */bin* (for *bin* ary programs). Some programs also reside in */usr/bin*, to save space in */bin*. These

directories are searched automatically by the command interpreters. Additional directories that may be of interest include */usr/contrib/bin*, which has contributed software */usr/old/bin*, which has old but sometimes still useful software and */usr/local/bin*, which contains software local to your site.

Games have been relegated to URM section 6 and */usr/games*, to keep them from contaminating the more staid information of URM section 1.

Miscellaneous collection of information necessary for writing in various specialized languages such as character codes, macro packages for typesetting, etc is contained in URM section 7.

System calls are entries into the BSD kernel. The system call interface is identical to a C language procedure call; the equivalent C procedures are described in PRM section 2.

An assortment of subroutines is available; they are described in PRM section 3. The primary libraries in which they are kept are described in *intro*(3). The functions are described in terms of C.

PRM section 4 discusses the characteristics of each system "file" that refers to an I/O device. The names in this section refer to the HP300 device names for the hardware, instead of the names of the special files themselves.

The file formats and conventions (PRM section 5) documents the structure of particular kinds of files; for example, the form of the output of the loader and assembler is given. Excluded are files used by only one command, for example the assembler's intermediate files.

Commands and procedures intended for use primarily by the system administrator are described in SMM section 8. The files described here are almost all kept in the directory */etc*. The system administration binaries reside in */sbin*, and */usr/sbin*.

Each section consists of independent entries of a page or so each. The name of the entry is in the upper corners of its pages, together with the section number. Entries within each section are alphabetized. The page numbers of each entry start at 1; it is infeasible to number consecutively the pages of a document like this that is republished in many variant forms.

All entries are based on a common format; not all subsections always appear.

The *name* subsection lists the exact names of the commands and subroutines covered under the entry and gives a short description of their purpose.

The *synopsis* summarizes the use of the program being described. A few conventions are used, particularly in the Commands subsection:

Boldface words are considered literals, and are typed just as they appear.

Square brackets [ ] around an argument show that the argument is optional. When an argument is given as "name", it always refers to a file name.

Ellipses "..." are used to show that the previous argument-prototype may be repeated.

A final convention is used by the commands themselves. An argument beginning with a minus sign "−" usually means that it is an option-specifying argument, even if it appears in a position where a file name could appear. Therefore, it is unwise to have files whose names begin with "−".

The *description* subsection discusses in detail the subject at hand.

The *files* subsection gives the names of files that are built into the program.

A *see also* subsection gives pointers to related information.

A *diagnostics* subsection discusses the diagnostic indications that may be produced. Messages that are intended to be self-explanatory are not listed.

The *bugs* subsection gives known bugs and sometimes deficiencies. Occasionally the suggested fix is also described.

At the beginning of URM, PRM, and SSM is a List of Manual Pages, organized by section and alphabetically within each section, and a Permuted Index derived from that List. Within each index entry, the title of the writeup to which it refers is followed by the appropriate section number in parentheses. This fact is important because there is considerable name duplication among the sections, arising principally from commands that exist only to exercise a particular system call. Finally, there is a list of documents on the inside back cover of each volume.

List of Manual Pages

1. Commands and Application Programs

intro . . . . introduction to general commands (tools and utilities)
adb . . . . debugger
addftinfo . . . . add information to troff font files for use with groff
afmtodit . . . . create font files for use with groff −Tps
ansitape . . . . ANSI standard tape handler
apply . . . . apply a command to a set of arguments
apropos . . . . locate commands by keyword lookup
ar . . . . create and maintain library archives
at . . . . schedule execution of commands 'at' a given time
atq . . . . display the at(1) job queue
atrm . . . . remove jobs spooled by at(1)
awk . . . . pattern scanning and processing language
basename . . . . return filename or directory portion of pathname
bc . . . . arbitrary-precision arithmetic language and calculator
bdes . . . . encrypt/decrypt using the Data Encryption Standard
bib . . . . bibliographic formatter
biff . . . . be notified if mail arrives and who it is from
cal . . . . displays a calendar
calendar . . . . reminder service
cap_mkdb . . . . create capability database
cat . . . . concatenate and print files
cc . . . . GNU project C and C++ Compiler (v2 preliminary)
cd . . . . change working directory
checknr . . . . check nroff/troff files
chflags . . . . change file flags
chgrp . . . . change group
chkey . . . . change your encryption key
chmod . . . . change file modes
chpass . . . . add or change user database information
ci . . . . check in RCS revisions
cksum . . . . display file checksums and block counts
cmp . . . . compare two files
co . . . . check out RCS revisions
col . . . . filter reverse line feeds from input
colcrt . . . . filter nroff output for CRT previewing
colrm . . . . remove columns from a file
column . . . . columnate lists
comm . . . . select or reject lines common to two files
compact . . . . compress and uncompress files, and cat them
compress . . . . compress and expand data
cp . . . . copy files
cpp . . . . the GNU C-compatible compiler preprocessor
crypt . . . . encode/decode
csh . . . . a shell (command interpreter) with C-like syntax
ctags . . . . create a tags file
cut . . . . select portions of each line of a file
date . . . . display or set date and time
dc . . . . desk calculator
dd . . . . convert and copy a file
deroff . . . . remove nroff, troff, tbl and eqn constructs
df . . . . display free disk space
diction . . . . print wordy sentences; thesaurus for diction
diff . . . . differential file and directory comparator
diff3 . . . . 3-way differential file comparison
dig . . . . send domain name query packets to name servers
du . . . . display disk usage statistics

echo . . . . produce message in a shell script
ed . . . . line oriented text editor
emacs . . . . GNU project Emacs
eqn . . . . format equations for troff
error . . . . analyze and disperse compiler error messages
expand . . . . expand tabs to spaces, and vice versa
expr . . . . evaluate arguments as an expression
false . . . . return false value
file . . . . identify file content
find . . . . walk a file hierarchy
finger . . . . user information lookup program
fmt . . . . simple text formatter
fold . . . . fold long lines for finite width output device
fpr . . . . print Fortran file
from . . . . print names of those who have sent mail
fsplit . . . . split a multi-routine Fortran file into individual files
fstat . . . . file status
ftp . . . . ARPANET file transfer program
g++ . . . . GNU project C++ Compiler (v2 preliminary)
gcore . . . . get core images of running process
gdb . . . . the GNU debugger
gprof . . . . display call graph profile data
graph . . . . draw a graph
grep . . . . file pattern searcher
grodvi . . . . convert groff output to TeX dvi format
groff . . . . front end for the groff document formatting system
grog . . . . guess options for groff command
grops . . . . PostScript driver for groff
grotty . . . . groff driver for typewriter-like devices
groups . . . . show group memberships
gzexe . . . . compress executable files in place
gzip . . . . compress or expand files
head . . . . display first lines of a file
hexdump . . . . ascii, decimal, hexadecimal, octal dump
host . . . . look up host names using domain server
hostname . . . . set or print name of current host system
id . . . . return user identity
ident . . . . identify files
indent . . . . indent and format C program source
indxbib . . . . make inverted index for bibliographic databases
install . . . . install binaries
invert . . . . create and access an inverted index
join . . . . relational database operator
jot . . . . print sequential or random data
kdestroy . . . . destroy Kerberos tickets
kdump . . . . display kernel trace data
kerberos . . . . introduction to the Kerberos system
keylogin . . . . decrypt and store secret key
kill . . . . terminate or signal a process
kinit . . . . Kerberos login utility
klist . . . . list currently held Kerberos tickets
ksrvtgt . . . . fetch and store Kerberos ticket-granting-ticket using a service key
ktrace . . . . enable kernel process tracing
lam . . . . laminate files
last . . . . indicate last logins of users and ttys
lastcomm . . . . show last commands executed in reverse order
ld . . . . link editor
learn . . . . computer aided instruction about
leave . . . . remind you when you have to leave

lex . . . . fast lexical analyzer generator
lkbib . . . . search bibliographic databases
ln . . . . make links
locate . . . . find files
lock . . . . reserve a terminal
logger . . . . make entries in the system log
login . . . . log into the computer
logname . . . . display user's login name
look . . . . display lines beginning with a given string
lookbib . . . . search bibliographic databases
lorder . . . . list dependencies for object files
lpq . . . . spool queue examination program
lpr . . . . off line print
lprm . . . . remove jobs from the line printer spooling queue
lptest . . . . generate lineprinter ripple pattern
ls . . . . list directory contents
m4 . . . . macro language preprocessor for ratfor(1) and pascal(1)
mail . . . . send and receive mail
mailq . . . . print the mail queue
make . . . . maintain program dependencies
man . . . . display the on-line manual pages
merge . . . . three-way file merge
mesg . . . . display (do not display) messages from other users
mh . . . . Message Handler
mkdep . . . . construct Makefile dependency list
mkdir . . . . make directories
mkfifo . . . . make fifos
mklocale . . . . make LC_CTYPE locale files
mkstr . . . . create an error message file by massaging C source
more . . . . file perusal filter for crt viewing
mset . . . . retrieve ASCII to IBM 3270 keyboard map
msgs . . . . system messages and junk mail program
mt . . . . magnetic tape manipulating program
mv . . . . move files
netstat . . . . show network status
newaliases . . . . rebuild the data base for the mail aliases file
nfsstat . . . . display NFS statistics
nice . . . . execute a command at a low scheduling priority
nm . . . . display name list (symbol table)
nohup . . . . invoke a command immune to hangups
nroff . . . . emulate nroff command with groff
od . . . . octal, decimal, hex, ascii dump
pagesize . . . . print system page size
passwd . . . . modify a user's password
paste . . . . merge corresponding or subsequent lines of files
patch . . . . a program for applying a diff file to an original
pax . . . . read and write file archives and copy directory hierarchies
perl . . . . practical extraction and report language
pfbtops . . . . translate a PostScript font in .pfb format to ASCII
pic . . . . compile pictures for troff or TeX
plot . . . . graphics filters
pr . . . . print files
printenv . . . . print out the environment, set and print environment
printf . . . . formatted output
ps . . . . process status
psbb . . . . extract bounding box from PostScript document
ptx . . . . permuted index
pwd . . . . return working directory name
quota . . . . display disk usage and limits

ranlib . . . . table-of-contents for archive libraries
rcp . . . . remote file copy
rcs . . . . change RCS file attributes
rcsclean . . . . clean up working files
rcsdiff . . . . compare RCS revisions
rcsfreeze . . . . freeze a configuration of sources checked in under RCS
rcsintro . . . . introduction to RCS commands
rcsmerge . . . . merge RCS revisions
rdist . . . . remote file distribution program
refer . . . . preprocess bibliographic references for groff
register . . . . register with Kerberos
rev . . . . reverse lines of a file
rlog . . . . print log messages and other information about RCS files
rlogin . . . . remote login
rm . . . . remove directory entries
rmdir . . . . remove directories
rpcgen . . . . an RPC protocol compiler
rs . . . . reshape a data array
rsh . . . . remote shell
rstat . . . . remote status display
ruptime . . . . show host status of local machines
rwho . . . . who is logged in on local machines
sccs . . . . front end for the SCCS subsystem
script . . . . make typescript of terminal session
sed . . . . stream editor
sendbug . . . . mail a system bug report to 4bsd-bugs
sh . . . . command interpreter (shell)
shar . . . . create a shell archive of files
size . . . . display object file segment sizes (text, data and bss)
sleep . . . . suspend execution for an interval of time
soelim . . . . eliminate .so's from nroff input
sort . . . . sort or merge text files
spell . . . . find spelling errors
spline . . . . interpolate smooth curve
split . . . . split a file into pieces
startslip . . . . dial up and login to a slip server
strings . . . . find printable strings in a file
strip . . . . remove unnecessary information from executable files
struct . . . . structure Fortran programs
stty . . . . set the options for a terminal device interface
style . . . . analyze surface characteristics of a document
su . . . . substitute user identity
sum . . . . calculate file checksums and block counts
symorder . . . . rearrange name list
systat . . . . display system statistics on a crt
tail . . . . display the last part of a file
talk . . . . talk to another user
tar . . . . tape archiver
tbl . . . . format tables for troff
tcopy . . . . copy and/or verify mag tapes
tee . . . . pipe fitting
telnet . . . . user interface to the TELNET protocol
test . . . . condition evaluation utility
tfmtodit . . . . create font files for use with groff −Tdvi
tftp . . . . trivial file transfer program
time . . . . time command execution
tip . . . . connect to a remote system
tn3270 . . . . full-screen remote login to IBM VM/CMS
touch . . . . change file access and modification times

tput . . . . terminal capability interface
tr . . . . translate characters
troff . . . . format documents
true . . . . return true value
tset . . . . terminal initialization
tsort . . . . topological sort of a directed graph
tty . . . . return user's terminal name
ul . . . . do underlining
uname . . . . display information about the system
unifdef . . . . remove ifdef'ed lines
uniq . . . . report or filter out repeated lines in a file
units . . . . conversion program
unvis . . . . revert a visual representation of data back to original form
uptime . . . . show how long system has been running
users . . . . list current users
uucp . . . . unix to unix copy
uuencode . . . . encode/decode a binary file
uulog . . . . display UUCP log entries
uuname . . . . list names of UUCP hosts
uuq . . . . examine or manipulate the uucp queue
uusend . . . . send a file to a remote host
uux . . . . unix to unix command execution
vacation . . . . return ''I am not here'' indication
vgrind . . . . grind nice listings of programs
vi . . . . text editors
vis . . . . display non-printable characters in a visual format
w . . . . who present users are and what they are doing
wait . . . . await process completion
wall . . . . write a message to users
wc . . . . word, line, and byte count
what . . . . show what versions of object modules were used to construct a file
whatis . . . . describe what a command is
whereis . . . . locate programs
which . . . . locate a program file including aliases and paths
who . . . . display who is logged in
whoami . . . . display effective user id
whois . . . . Internet user name directory service
window . . . . window environment
write . . . . send a message to another user
xargs . . . . construct argument list(s) and execute utility
xchess . . . . X chess display
xsend . . . . private encrypted mail
xstr . . . . extract strings from C programs to implement shared strings
yacc . . . . an LALR(1) parser generator
yes . . . . be repetitively affirmative
yyfix . . . . extract tables from y.tab.c
zdiff . . . . compare compressed files
zforce . . . . force a '.gz' extension on all gzip files
zgrep . . . . search possibly compressed files for a regular expression
zmore . . . . file perusal filter for crt viewing of compressed text
znew . . . . recompress .Z files to .gz files

2. System Calls

intro . . . . introduction to system calls and error numbers
accept . . . . accept a connection on a socket
access . . . . check access permissions of a file or pathname
acct . . . . enable or disable process accounting
adjtime . . . . correct the time to allow synchronization of the system clock
bind . . . . bind a name to a socket

brk . . . . change data segment size
chdir . . . . change current working directory
chflags . . . . set file flags
chmod . . . . change mode of file
chown . . . . change owner and group of a file
chroot . . . . change root directory
close . . . . delete a descriptor
connect . . . . initiate a connection on a socket
creat . . . . create a new file
dup . . . . duplicate an existing file descriptor
execve . . . . execute a file
_exit . . . . terminate the calling process
fcntl . . . . file control
flock . . . . apply or remove an advisory lock on an open file
fork . . . . create a new process
fsync . . . . synchronize a file's in-core state with that on disk
getdirentries . . . . get directory entries in a filesystem independent format
getdtablesize . . . . get descriptor table size
getfh . . . . get file handle
getfsstat . . . . get list of all mounted filesystems
getgid . . . . get group process identification
getgroups . . . . get group access list
getitimer . . . . get/set value of interval timer
getlogin . . . . get/set login name
getpeername . . . . get name of connected peer
getpgrp . . . . get process group
getpid . . . . get parent or calling process identification
getpriority . . . . get/set program scheduling priority
getrlimit . . . . control maximum system resource consumption
getrusage . . . . get information about resource utilization
getsockname . . . . get socket name
getsockopt . . . . get and set options on sockets
gettimeofday . . . . get/set date and time
getuid . . . . get user identification
ioctl . . . . control device
kill . . . . send signal to a process
killpg . . . . send signal to a process group
ktrace . . . . process tracing
link . . . . make a hard file link
listen . . . . listen for connections on a socket
lseek . . . . reposition read/write file offset
madvise . . . . give advise about use of memory
mincore . . . . get advise about use of memory
mkdir . . . . make a directory file
mkfifo . . . . make a fifo file
mknod . . . . make a special file node
mlock . . . . lock (unlock) physical pages in memory
mmap . . . . map files or devices into memory
mount . . . . mount or dismount a filesystem
mprotect . . . . control the protection of pages
msync . . . . synchronize a mapped region
munmap . . . . remove a mapping
nfssvc . . . . NFS services
open . . . . open or create a file for reading or writing
pathconf . . . . get configurable pathname variables
pipe . . . . create descriptor pair for interprocess communication
profil . . . . control process profiling
ptrace . . . . process trace
quotactl . . . . manipulate filesystem quotas

read . . . . read input
readlink . . . . read value of a symbolic link
reboot . . . . reboot system or halt processor
recv . . . . receive a message from a socket
rename . . . . change the name of a file
revoke . . . . revoke file access
rmdir . . . . remove a directory file
select . . . . synchronous I/O multiplexing
send . . . . send a message from a socket
setgroups . . . . set group access list
setpgid . . . . set process group
setregid . . . . set real and effective group ID
setreuid . . . . set real and effective user ID's
setsid . . . . create session and set process group ID
setuid . . . . set user and group ID
shutdown . . . . shut down part of a full-duplex connection
sigaction . . . . software signal facilities
sigaltstack . . . . set and/or get signal stack context
sigblock . . . . block signals
sigpause . . . . atomically release blocked signals and wait for interrupt
sigpending . . . . get pending signals
sigprocmask . . . . manipulate current signal mask
sigreturn . . . . return from signal
sigsetmask . . . . set current signal mask
sigstack . . . . set and/or get signal stack context
sigsuspend . . . . atomically release blocked signals and wait for interrupt
sigvec . . . . software signal facilities
socket . . . . create an endpoint for communication
socketpair . . . . create a pair of connected sockets
stat . . . . get file status
statfs . . . . get file system statistics
swapon . . . . add a swap device for interleaved paging/swapping
symlink . . . . make symbolic link to a file
sync . . . . synchronize disk block in-core status with that on disk
syscall . . . . indirect system call
truncate . . . . truncate a file to a specified length
umask . . . . set file creation mode mask
unlink . . . . remove directory entry
utimes . . . . set file access and modification times
vfork . . . . spawn new process in a virtual memory efficient way
wait . . . . wait for process termination
write . . . . write output

3. C Library Subroutines

intro . . . . introduction to the C libraries
abort . . . . cause abnormal program termination
abs . . . . integer absolute value function
acl_check . . . . access control list routines
acos . . . . arc cosine function
acosh . . . . inverse hyperbolic cosine function
alarm . . . . set signal timer alarm
alloca . . . . memory allocator
asin . . . . arc sine function
asinh . . . . inverse hyperbolic sine function
assert . . . . expression verification macro
atan . . . . arc tangent function of one variable
atan2 . . . . arc tangent function of two variables
atanh . . . . inverse hyperbolic tangent function
atexit . . . . register a function to be called on exit

atof . . . . convert ASCII string to double
atoi . . . . convert ASCII string to integer
atol . . . . convert ASCII string to long integer
bcmp . . . . compare byte string
bcopy . . . . copy byte string
bitstring . . . . bit-string manipulation macros
bsearch . . . . binary search of a sorted table
bstring . . . . byte string operations
btree . . . . btree database access method
byteorder . . . . convert values between host and network byte order
bzero . . . . write zeroes to a byte string
calloc . . . . allocate clean memory (zero initialized space)
ceil . . . . smallest integral value not greater than x
clock . . . . determine processor time used
confstr . . . . get string-valued configurable variables
cos . . . . cosine function
cosh . . . . hyperbolic cosine function
crypt . . . . DES encryption
ctermid . . . . generate terminal pathname
ctime . . . . transform binary date and time value to ASCII
ctype . . . . character classification macros
curses . . . . screen functions with ''optimal'' cursor motion
daemon . . . . run in the background
dbopen . . . . database access methods
des_crypt . . . . (new) DES encryption
devname . . . . get device name
directory . . . . directory operations
div . . . . return quotient and remainder from division
ecvt . . . . output conversion
end . . . . end boundaries of image segments
erf . . . . error function operators
err . . . . formatted error messages
exec . . . . execute a file
exit . . . . perform normal program termination
exp . . . . exponential, logarithm, power functions
fabs . . . . floating-point absolute value function
fclose . . . . close a stream
ferror . . . . check and reset stream status
fflush . . . . flush a stream
ffs . . . . find first bit set in a bit string
fgetln . . . . get a line from a stream
fgets . . . . get a line from a stream
floor . . . . largest integral value not greater than x
fmod . . . . floating-point remainder function
fnmatch . . . . match filename or pathname
fopen . . . . stream open functions
fputs . . . . output a line to a stream
fread . . . . binary stream input/output
free . . . . free up memory allocated with malloc, calloc or realloc
frexp . . . . convert floating-point number to fractional and integral components
fseek . . . . reposition a stream
ftime . . . . get date and time
fts . . . . traverse a file hierarchy
funopen . . . . open a stream
getbsize . . . . get user block size
getc . . . . get next character or word from input stream
getcap . . . . capability database access routines
getcwd . . . . get working directory pathname
getdiskbyname . . . . get generic disk description by its name

getenv . . . . environment variable functions
getfsent . . . . get file system descriptor file entry
getgrent . . . . group database operations
getgrouplist . . . . calculate group access list
gethostbyname . . . . get network host entry
gethostid . . . . get/set unique identifier of current host
gethostname . . . . get/set name of current host
getloadavg . . . . get system load averages
getmntinfo . . . . get information about mounted file systems
getmntopts . . . . scan mount options
getnetent . . . . get network entry
getnetgrent . . . . netgroup database operations
getopt . . . . get option character from command line argument list
getpagesize . . . . get system page size
getpass . . . . get a password
getprotoent . . . . get protocol entry
getpw . . . . get name from uid
getpwent . . . . password database operations
getservent . . . . get service entry
getsubopt . . . . get sub options from an argument
getttyent . . . . get ttys file entry
getusershell . . . . get legal user shells
glob . . . . generate pathnames matching a pattern
hash . . . . hash database access method
hypot . . . . euclidean distance and complex absolute value functions
ieee . . . . IEEE 754 floating point support
index . . . . locate character in string
inet . . . . Internet address manipulation routines
infnan . . . . signals invalid floating–point operations on a VAX (temporary)
initgroups . . . . initialize group access list
insque . . . . insert/remove element from a queue
isalnum . . . . alphanumeric character test
isalpha . . . . alphabetic character test
isascii . . . . test for ASCII character
isblank . . . . space or tab character test
iscntrl . . . . control character test
isdigit . . . . decimal-digit character test
isgraph . . . . printing character test (space character exclusive)
isinf . . . . test for infinity or not-a-number
islower . . . . lower-case character test
iso_addr . . . . elementary network address conversion routines for Open System Interconnection
isprint . . . . printing character test (space character inclusive)
ispunct . . . . punctuation character test
isspace . . . . white-space character test
isupper . . . . upper-case character test
isxdigit . . . . hexadecimal-digit character test
j0 . . . . bessel functions of first and second kind
krb . . . . Kerberos authentication library
krb_realmofhost . . . . additional Kerberos utility routines
krb_sendauth . . . . Kerberos routines for sending authentication via network stream sockets
krb_set_tkt_string . . . . set Kerberos ticket cache file name
kuserok . . . . Kerberos version of ruserok
kvm . . . . kernel memory interface
kvm_geterr . . . . get error message on kvm descriptor
kvm_getfiles . . . . survey open files
kvm_getloadavg . . . . get error message on kvm descriptor
kvm_getprocs . . . . access user process state
kvm_nlist . . . . retrieve symbol table names from a kernel image
kvm_open . . . . initialize kernel virtual memory access

kvm_read . . . . read or write kernel virtual memory
labs . . . . return the absolute value of a long integer
ldexp . . . . multiply floating-point number by integral power of 2
ldiv . . . . return quotient and remainder from division
lgamma . . . . log gamma function, gamma function
linkaddr . . . . elementary address specification routines for link level access
lsearch . . . . linear searching routines
malloc . . . . general memory allocation function
math . . . . introduction to mathematical library functions
mbrune . . . . multibyte rune support for C
memccpy . . . . copy string until character found
memchr . . . . locate byte in byte string
memcmp . . . . compare byte string
memcpy . . . . copy byte string
memmove . . . . copy byte string
memory . . . . general memory allocation operations
memset . . . . write a byte to byte string
mktemp . . . . make temporary file name (unique)
modf . . . . extract signed integral and fractional values from floating-point number
moncontrol . . . . control execution profile
mp . . . . multiple precision integer arithmetic
mpool . . . . shared memory buffer pool
multibyte . . . . multibyte character support for C
nice . . . . set program scheduling priority
nlist . . . . retrieve symbol table name list from an executable file
ns . . . . Xerox NS Ns (tm) address conversion routines
pause . . . . stop until signal
plot . . . . graphics interface
popen . . . . process I/O
printf . . . . formatted output conversion
psignal . . . . system signal messages
putc . . . . output a character or word to a stream
pwcache . . . . cache password and group entries
qsort . . . . sort functions
queue . . . . implementations of lists, tail queues, and circular queues
radixsort . . . . radix sort
raise . . . . send a signal to the current process
rand . . . . bad random number generator
random . . . . better random number generator; routines for changing generators
rcmd . . . . routines for returning a stream to a remote command
re_comp . . . . regular expression handler
realloc . . . . reallocation of memory function
realpath . . . . returns the canonicalized absolute pathname
recno . . . . record number database access method
regex . . . . regular-expression library
regexp . . . . regular expression handlers
remove . . . . remove directory entry
resolver . . . . resolver routines
rexec . . . . return stream to a remote command
rindex . . . . locate character in string
rint . . . . round-to-closest integer functions
rune . . . . rune support for C
scandir . . . . scan a directory
scanf . . . . input format conversion
setbuf . . . . stream buffering operations
setjmp . . . . non-local jumps
setlocale . . . . natural language formatting for C
setmode . . . . modify mode bits
setruid . . . . set user and group ID

siginterrupt . . . . allow signals to interrupt system calls
signal . . . . simplified software signal facilities
sigsetops . . . . manipulate signal sets
sin . . . . sine function
sinh . . . . hyperbolic sine function
sleep . . . . suspend process execution for interval of seconds
sqrt . . . . cube root and square root functions
stdarg . . . . variable argument lists
stdio . . . . standard input/output library functions
strcasecmp . . . . compare strings, ignoring case
strcat . . . . concatenate strings
strchr . . . . locate character in string
strcmp . . . . compare strings
strcoll . . . . compare strings according to current collation
strcpy . . . . copy strings
strcspn . . . . span the complement of a string
strdup . . . . save a copy of a string
strerror . . . . system error messages
strftime . . . . format date and time
string . . . . string specific functions
strlen . . . . find length of string
strmode . . . . convert inode status information into a symbolic string
strpbrk . . . . locate multiple characters in string
strrchr . . . . locate character in string
strsep . . . . separate strings
strspn . . . . span a string
strstr . . . . locate a substring in a string
strtod . . . . convert ASCII string to double
strtok . . . . string tokens
strtol . . . . convert string value to a long or quad_t integer
strtoul . . . . convert a string to an unsigned long or uquad_t integer
strxfrm . . . . transform a string under locale
stty . . . . set and get terminal state (defunct)
swab . . . . swap adjacent bytes
sysconf . . . . get configurable system variables
sysctl . . . . get or set system information
syslog . . . . control system log
system . . . . pass a command to the shell
tan . . . . tangent function
tanh . . . . hyperbolic tangent function
tcgetpgrp . . . . get foreground process group ID
tcsendbreak . . . . line control functions
tcsetattr . . . . manipulating the termios structure
tcsetpgrp . . . . set foreground process group ID
termcap . . . . terminal independent operation routines
tf_util . . . . routines for manipulating a Kerberos ticket file
time . . . . get time of day
times . . . . process times
timezone . . . . return the timezone abbreviation
tmpnam . . . . temporary file routines
toascii . . . . convert a byte to 7-bit ASCII
tolower . . . . upper case to lower case letter conversion
toupper . . . . lower case to upper case letter conversion
ttyname . . . . get name of associated terminal (tty) from file descriptor
tzset . . . . initialize time conversion information
ualarm . . . . schedule signal after specified time
uname . . . . get system identification
ungetc . . . . un-get character from input stream
unvis . . . . decode a visual representation of characters

usleep . . . . suspend execution for interval of microseconds
utime . . . . set file times
valloc . . . . aligned memory allocation function
vis . . . . visually encode characters
vlimit . . . . control maximum system resource consumption
vtimes . . . . get information about resource utilization

4. Special Files

intro . . . . introduction to special files and hardware support
netintro . . . . introduction to networking facilities
autoconf . . . . diagnostics from the autoconfiguration code
bwtwo . . . . monochromatic frame buffer
cgsix . . . . accelerated 8-bit color frame buffer
cgthree . . . . 8-bit color frame buffer
clnp . . . . Connectionless-Mode Network Protocol
cltp . . . . ISO Connectionless Transport Protocol
cons . . . . HP300 console interface
ct . . . . CS/80 cartridge tape interface
dca . . . . HP 98644A communications interface
dcl . . . . HP 98628A communications link
dcm . . . . HP 98642A communications multiplexer
drum . . . . paging device
dv . . . . HP98730 "DaVinci" device interface
esis . . . . End System to Intermediate System Routing Protocol
euc . . . . EUC encoding of runes
fd . . . . file descriptor files
gb . . . . HP98700 "Gatorbox" device interface
grf . . . . HP graphics frame buffer device interface
hil . . . . Human Interface Link device driver
icmp . . . . Internet Control Message Protocol
idp . . . . Xerox Internet Datagram Protocol
inet . . . . Internet protocol family
ip . . . . Internet Protocol
iso . . . . ISO protocol family
ite . . . . HP Internal Terminal Emulator
le . . . . HP AMD 7990 LANCE Ethernet interface
le . . . . SPARC AMD 7990 LANCE ethernet interface
lo . . . . software loopback network interface
mem . . . . main memory
mem . . . . main memory
ns . . . . Xerox Network Systems(tm) protocol family
nsip . . . . software network interface encapsulating NS packets in IP packets
null . . . . the null device
openprom . . . . OPENPROM and EEPROM interface
ppi . . . . HP-IB printer/plotter interface
pty . . . . pseudo terminal driver
rb . . . . HP98720 "Renaissance" device interface
rd . . . . CS/80 disk interface
route . . . . kernel packet forwarding database
spp . . . . Xerox Sequenced Packet Protocol
st . . . . CCS SCSI tape driver
tc . . . . HP98544 98550 "Topcat" and "Catseye" device interface
tcp . . . . Internet Transmission Control Protocol
termios . . . . general terminal line discipline
tp . . . . ISO Transport Protocol
tty . . . . general terminal interface
udp . . . . Internet User Datagram Protocol
unix . . . . UNIX-domain protocol family
utf2 . . . . Universal character set Transformation Format encoding of runes

5. File Formats

a.out . . . . format of executable binary files
acct . . . . execution accounting file
aliases . . . . aliases file for sendmail
ar.5 . . . . archive (library) file format
core . . . . memory image file format
crontab . . . . chronological services schedule file
dir . . . . directory file format
disklabel.5 . . . . disk pack label
disktab . . . . disk description file
dm.conf . . . . dm configuration file
dump . . . . incremental dump format
exports . . . . define remote mount points for NFS mount requests
fs . . . . format of file system volume
fstab . . . . static information about the filesystems
gettytab . . . . terminal configuration data base
groff_font . . . . format of groff device and font description files
groff_out . . . . groff intermediate output format
group . . . . format of the group permissions file
hosts . . . . host name data base
krb.conf . . . . Kerberos configuration file
krb.realms . . . . host to Kerberos realm translation file
L-devices . . . . UUCP device description file
L-dialcodes . . . . UUCP phone number index file
L.aliases . . . . UUCP hostname alias file
L.cmds . . . . UUCP remote command permissions file
L.sys . . . . UUCP remote host description file
man.conf . . . . configuration file for man(1)
map3270 . . . . database for mapping ascii keystrokes into IBM 3270 keys
netgroup . . . . defines network groups
networks . . . . network name data base
passwd . . . . format of the password file
phones . . . . remote host phone number data base
plot . . . . graphics interface
printcap . . . . printer capability data base
protocols . . . . protocol name data base
publickey . . . . public key database
ranlib.5 . . . . archive (library) table-of-contents format
rcsfile . . . . format of RCS file
remote . . . . remote host description file
resolver . . . . resolver configuration file
rpc . . . . rpc program number data base
services . . . . service name data base
shells . . . . shell database
stab . . . . symbol table types
syslog.conf . . . . syslogd(8) configuration file
tarformat . . . . tape archive file format
termcap . . . . terminal capability data base
ttys . . . . terminal initialization information
types . . . . system data types
tzfile . . . . time zone information
USERFILE . . . . UUCP pathname permissions file
utmp . . . . login records
uuencode.format . . . . format of an encoded uuencode file
vgrindefs . . . . language definition data base for vgrind(1)

6. Games

adventure	an exploration game
arithmetic	quiz on simple arithmetic
atc	air traffic controller game
backgammon	the game of backgammon
banner	print large banner on printer
battlestar	a tropical adventure game
bcd	reformat input as punch cards, paper tape or morse code
boggle	word search game
caesar	decrypt caesar cyphers
canfield	the solitaire card game canfield
chess	GNU chess
ching	thc book of changcs and othcr cookies
cribbage	the card game cribbage
dungeon	Adventures in the Dungeons of Doom
factor	factor a number, generate primes
fish	play ''Go Fish''
fortune	print a random, hopefully interesting, adage
hack	exploring The Dungeons of Doom
hangman	the game of hangman
hunt	a multi-player multi-terminal game
huntd	hunt daemon, back-end for hunt game
larn	exploring the caverns of Larn
mille	play Mille Bornes
monop	Monopoly game
number	convert Arabic numerals to English
phantasia	an interterminal fantasy game
pig	eformatray inputway asway Igpay Atinlay
pom	display the phase of the moon
quiz	random knowledge tests
rain	animated raindrops display
random	random lines from a file or random numbers
robots	fight off villainous robots
rogue	exploring The Dungeons of Doom
sail	multi-user wooden ships and iron men
snake	display chase game
tetris	the game of tetris
trek	trekkie game
worm	play the growing worm game
worms	animate worms on a display terminal
wump	hunt the wumpus in an underground cave
xneko	cat-and-mouse chase in an X window
xroach	cockroaches hide under your windows

7. Miscellaneous

intro	miscellaneous information pages
ascii	octal, hexadecimal and decimal ASCII character sets
environ	user environment
eqnchar	special character definitions for eqn
groff_char	groff character names
hier	layout of filesystems
hostname	host name resolution description
mailaddr	mail addressing description
man	(deprecated) macros to typeset manual
mdoc	quick reference guide for the −mdoc macro package
mdoc.samples	tutorial sampler for writing manuals with −mdoc
me	macros for formatting papers
mm	groff mm macros

ms . . . . text formatting macros
operator . . . . C operator precedence and order of evaluation
re_format . . . . POSIX 1003.2 regular expressions
symlink . . . . symbolic link handling
term . . . . conventional names for terminals

8. System Maintenance

intro . . . . introduction to system maintenance and operation commands
ac . . . . display connect time accounting
acucntrl . . . . turn around tty line between dialin and dialout
adduser . . . . procedure for adding new users
amd . . . . automatically mount file systems
amq . . . . automounter query tool
arp . . . . address resolution display and control
bad144 . . . . read/write dec standard 144 bad sector information
badsect . . . . create files to contain bad sectors
boot_hp300 . . . . system bootstrapping procedures
boot_sparc . . . . UNIX bootstrapping procedures
bugfiler . . . . file bug reports in folders automatically
chown . . . . change file owner and group
chroot . . . . change root directory
clri . . . . clear an inode
comsat . . . . biff server
config . . . . build system configuration files
config.new . . . . build kernel compilation directories
crash . . . . UNIX system failures
cron . . . . clock daemon
dev_mkdb . . . . create /dev database
disklabel . . . . read and write disk pack label
diskpart . . . . calculate default disk partition sizes
dm . . . . dungeon master
dmesg . . . . display the system message buffer
dump . . . . filesystem backup
dumpfs . . . . dump file system information
dumplfs . . . . dump file system information
edquota . . . . edit user quotas
eeprom . . . . openprom control utility
ext_srvtab . . . . extract service key files from Kerberos key distribution center database
fastboot . . . . reboot/halt the system without checking the disks
fingerd . . . . remote user information server
format . . . . how to format disks and tapes
fsck . . . . filesystem consistency check and interactive repair
fsdb . . . . file system debugger
fsinfo . . . . co-ordinate site-wide filesystem information
ftpd . . . . Internet File Transfer Protocol server
getty . . . . set terminal mode
icheck . . . . file system storage consistency check
ifconfig . . . . configure network interface parameters
inetd . . . . internet super-server
init . . . . process control initialization
iostat . . . . report I/O statistics
kdb_destroy . . . . destroy Kerberos key distribution center database
kdb_edit . . . . Kerberos key distribution center database editing utility
kdb_init . . . . initialize Kerberos key distribution center database
kdb_util . . . . Kerberos key distribution center database utility
kgmon . . . . generate a dump of the operating system's profile buffers
kpasswdd . . . . Kerberos password changing daemon
kstash . . . . stash Kerberos key distribution center database master key
kvm_mkdb . . . . create kernel database

lfs_cleanerd . . . . garbage collect a log-structured file system
lpc . . . . line printer control program
lpd . . . . line printer spooler daemon
mail.local . . . . store mail in a mailbox
make_keypair . . . . generate Kerberos host key pair
makedev . . . . make system special files
MAKEDEV . . . . create system and device special files
makekey . . . . make encrypted keys or passwords
makemap . . . . create database maps for sendmail
mh-gen . . . . generating the MH system
mk-amd-map . . . . create database maps for Amd
mknod . . . . build special file
mkproto . . . . construct a prototype file system
mount . . . . mount file systems
mount_cd9660 . . . . mount an ISO-9660 filesystem
mount_fdesc . . . . mount the file-descriptor file system
mount_kernfs . . . . mount the /kern file system
mount_lfs . . . . mount a log-structured file system
mount_nfs . . . . mount nfs file systems
mount_null . . . . demonstrate the use of a null file system layer
mount_portal . . . . mount the portal daemon
mount_procfs . . . . mount the process file system
mount_umap . . . . sample file system layer
mount_union . . . . mount union filesystems
mountd . . . . service remote NFS mount requests
mtree . . . . map a directory hierarchy
named . . . . Internet domain name server
named-xfer . . . . ancillary agent for inbound zone transfers
named.reload . . . . cause the name server to synchronize its database
named.restart . . . . stop and restart the name server
ncheck . . . . generate names from i-numbers
newfs . . . . construct a new file system
newlfs . . . . construct a new LFS file system
nfsd . . . . remote NFS server
nfsiod . . . . local NFS asynchronous I/O server
nologin . . . . politely refuse a login
nslookup . . . . query Internet name servers interactively
pac . . . . printer/plotter accounting information
ping . . . . send ICMP ECHO_REQUEST packets to network hosts
portmap . . . . DARPA port to RPC program number mapper
pstat . . . . display system data structures
pwd_mkdb . . . . generate the password databases
quot . . . . display total block usage per user for a file system
quotacheck . . . . filesystem quota consistency checker
quotaon . . . . turn filesystem quotas on and off
rbootd . . . . HP remote boot server
rc . . . . command script for auto–reboot and daemons
reboot . . . . stopping and restarting the system
registerd . . . . Kerberos registration daemon
renice . . . . alter priority of running processes
repquota . . . . summarize quotas for a file system
restore . . . . restore files or file systems from backups made with dump
rexecd . . . . remote execution server
rlogind . . . . remote login server
rmail . . . . handle remote mail received via uucp
rmt . . . . remote magtape protocol module
route . . . . manually manipulate the routing tables.
routed . . . . network routing daemon
rshd . . . . remote shell server

rwhod . . . . system status server
sa . . . . system accounting
savecore . . . . save a core dump of the operating system
scsiformat . . . . format SCSI disks and show SCSI parameters
sendmail . . . . send mail over the internet
showmount . . . . show remote nfs mounts on host
shutdown . . . . close down the system at a given time
slattach . . . . attach serial lines as network interfaces
sliplogin . . . . attach a serial line network interface
sticky . . . . sticky text and append-only directories
swapon . . . . specify additional device for paging and swapping
sync . . . . force completion of pending disk writes (flush cache)
sysctl . . . . get or set kernel state
syslogd . . . . log systems messages
talkd . . . . remote user communication server
telnetd . . . . DARPA TELNET protocol server
tftpd . . . . Internet Trivial File Transfer Protocol server
timed . . . . time server daemon
timedc . . . . timed control program
traceroute . . . . print the route packets take to network host
trpt . . . . transliterate protocol trace
trsp . . . . transliterate sequenced packet protocol trace
tunefs . . . . tune up an existing file system
umount . . . . unmount file systems
update . . . . flush internal filesystem caches to disk frequently
uucico . . . . transfer files queued by uucp or uux
uuclean . . . . uucp spool directory clean-up
uupoll . . . . poll a remote UUCP site
uusnap . . . . show snapshot of the UUCP system
uuxqt . . . . UUCP execution file interpreter
vipw . . . . edit the password file
vmstat . . . . report virtual memory statistics
XNSrouted . . . . NS Routing Information Protocol daemon
zic . . . . time zone compiler

Permuted Index

@: arithmetic on shell variables. . . . . csh(1)
re_format: POSIX 1003.2 regular expressions. . . . . re_format(7)
mset: retrieve ASCII to IBM 3270 keyboard map. . . . . mset(1)
database for mapping ascii keystrokes into IBM 3270 keys. map3270: . . . . map3270(5)
diff3: 3-way differential file comparison. . . . . diff3(1)
sendbug: mail a system bug report to 4bsd-bugs. sendbug(1)
copysign, drem, finite, logb, scalb: IEEE 754 floating point support. . . . . ieee(3)
le: HP AMD 7990 LANCE Ethernet interface. . . . . le(4)
le: SPARC AMD 7990 LANCE ethernet interface. . . . . le(4)
toascii: convert a byte to 7-bit ASCII. . . . . toascii(3)
cgsix: accelerated 8-bit color frame buffer. . . . . cgsix(4)
cgthree: 8-bit color frame buffer. . . . . cgthree(4)
tc: HP98544 98550 "Topcat" and "Catseye" device interface. . . . . . . tc(4)
dcl: HP 98628A communications link. . . . . dcl(4)
dcm: HP 98642A communications multiplexer. . . . . dcm(4)
dca: HP 98644A communications interface. . . . . dca(4)
timezone: return the timezone abbreviation. . . . . timezone(3)
abort: cause abnormal program termination. . . . . abort(3)
abort: cause abnormal program termination. . . . . abort(3)
abs: integer absolute value function. . . . . abs(3)
realpath: returns the canonicalized absolute pathname. . . . . realpath(3)
abs: integer absolute value function. . . . . abs(3)
fabs: floating-point absolute value function. . . . . fabs(3)
hypot, cabs: euclidean distance and complex absolute value functions. . . . . hypot(3)
labs: return the absolute value of a long integer. . . . . labs(3)
ac: display connect time accounting. ac(8)
cgsix: accelerated 8-bit color frame buffer. . . . . cgsix(4)
accept: accept a connection on a socket. . . . . accept(2)
accept: accept a connection on a socket. . . . . accept(2)
kvm_close: initialize kernel virtual memory access. kvm_open, kvm_openfiles. . . . . kvm_open(3)
address specification routines for link level access. link_addr, link_ntoa: elementary . . . . . . linkaddr(3)
revoke: revoke file access. . . . . revoke(2)
invert, lookup: create and access an inverted index. . . . . invert(1)
touch: change file access and modification times. . . . . touch(1)
utimes: set file access and modification times. . . . . utimes(2)
pathname. access: check access permissions of a file or . . . . . access(2)
acl_add, acl_delete, acl_initialize: access control list routines. /acl_exact_match, ... acl_check(3)
getgrouplist: calculate group access list. getgrouplist(3)
getgroups: get group access list. getgroups(2)
initgroups: initialize group access list. initgroups(3)
setgroups: set group access list. setgroups(2)
btree: btree database access method. . . . . btree(3)
hash: hash database access method. . . . . hash(3)
recno: record number database access method. . . . . recno(3)
dbopen: database access methods. . . . . dbopen(3)
access: check access permissions of a file or pathname. . . . . access(2)
cgetfirst, cgetnext, cgetclose: capability database access routines. /cgetnum, cgetstr, cgetustr, ... getcap(3)
kvm_getprocs, kvm_getargv, kvm_getenvv: access user process state. . . . . kvm_getprocs(3)
strcoll: compare strings according to current collation. . . . . strcoll(3)
ac: display connect time accounting. ac(8)
acct: enable or disable process accounting. acct(2)
sa, accton: system accounting. sa(8)
acct: execution accounting file. . . . . acct(5)
pac: printer/plotter accounting information. . . . . pac(8)
acct: enable or disable process accounting. . . . . acct(2)
acct: execution accounting file. . . . . acct(5)
sa, accton: system accounting. . . . . sa(8)
list routines. /acl_check, acl_exact_match, acl_add, acl_delete, acl_initialize: access control . . . . . acl_check(3)
acl_exact_match, acl_add, acl_delete,/ acl_canonicalize_principal, acl_check, ... acl_check(3)
acl_initialize: access/ acl_canonicalize_principal, acl_check, acl_exact_match, acl_add, acl_delete, ... acl_check(3)
routines. /acl_check, acl_exact_match, acl_add, acl_delete, acl_initialize: access control list . . . . acl_check(3)
acl_canonicalize_principal, acl_check, acl_exact_match, acl_add, acl_delete,/ . . . . acl_check(3)
/acl_check, acl_exact_match, acl_add, acl_delete, acl_initialize: access control list routines. . . . . acl_check(3)
acos: arc cosine function. . . . . acos(3)
acosh: inverse hyperbolic cosine function. . . . . acosh(3)
dialout. acucntrl: turn around tty line between dialin and . . . . . . acucntrl(8)
fortune: print a random, hopefully interesting, adage. . . . . fortune(6)

adb: debugger. adb(1)
swapon: add a swap device for interleaved paging/swapping. . . . . swapon(2)
groff. addftinfo: add information to troff font files for use with . . . . . . addftinfo(1)
chpass: add or change user database information. . . . . chpass(1)
use with groff. addftinfo: add information to troff font files for . . . . . . addftinfo(1)
adduser: procedure for adding new users. . . . . adduser(8)
swapon: specify additional device for paging and swapping. . . . . swapon(8)
/krb_get_krbhst, krb_get_admhst, krb_get_lrealm: additional Kerberos utility routines. . . . . krb_realmofhost(3)
ns_addr, ns_ntoa: Xerox NS Ns (tm) address conversion routines. . . . . ns(3)
iso_addr, iso_ntoa: elementary network address conversion routines for Open System/ . . . . iso_addr(3)
inet_makeaddr, inet_lnaof, inet_netof: Internet address manipulation routines. /inet_ntoa, ... inet(3)
arp: address resolution display and control. . . . . arp(8)
access. link_addr, link_ntoa: elementary address specification routines for link level . . . . linkaddr(3)
mailaddr: mail addressing description. . . . . mailaddr(7)
adduser: procedure for adding new users. . . . . adduser(8)
swab: swap adjacent bytes. . . . . swab(3)
of the system clock. adjtime: correct the time to allow synchronization . . . . . adjtime(2)
adventure: an exploration game. . . . . adventure(6)
battlestar: a tropical adventure game. . . . . battlestar(6)
dungeon: Adventures in the Dungeons of Doom. . . . . dungeon(6)
madvise: give advise about use of memory. . . . . madvise(2)
mincore: get advise about use of memory. . . . . mincore(2)
flock: apply or remove an advisory lock on an open file. . . . . flock(2)
yes: be repetitively affirmative. . . . . yes(1)
−Tps. afmtodit: create font files for use with groff . . . . . afmtodit(1)
named-xfer: ancillary agent for inbound zone transfers. . . . . named-xfer(8)
learn: computer aided instruction about. . . . . learn(1)
atc: air traffic controller game. . . . . atc(6)
alarm: set signal timer alarm. . . . . alarm(3)
alarm: set signal timer alarm. . . . . alarm(3)
L.aliases: UUCP hostname alias file. . . . . L.aliases(5)
alias: shell macros. . . . . csh(1)
unalias: remove aliases. . . . . csh(1)
aliases: aliases file for sendmail. . . . . aliases(5)
which: locate a program file including aliases and paths. . . . . which(1)
newaliases: rebuild the data base for the mail aliases file. . . . . newaliases(1)
aliases: aliases file for sendmail. . . . . aliases(5)
L. aliases: UUCP hostname alias file. . . . . L.aliases(5)
valloc: aligned memory allocation function. . . . . valloc(3)
malloc, free, realloc, calloc, alloca: general memory allocation operations. . . . . memory(3)
alloca: memory allocator. . . . . alloca(3)
calloc: allocate clean memory (zero initialized space). . . . . . . calloc(3)
free: free up memory allocated with malloc, calloc or realloc. . . . . free(3)
malloc,: general memory allocation function. . . . . malloc(3)
valloc: aligned memory allocation function. . . . . valloc(3)
free, realloc, calloc, alloca: general memory allocation operations. malloc, ... memory(3)
alloca: memory allocator. alloca(3)
isalpha: alphabetic character test. . . . . isalpha(3)
isalnum: alphanumeric character test. . . . . isalnum(3)
scandir, alphasort: scan a directory. . . . . scandir(3)
limit: alter per-process resource limitations. . . . . csh(1)
renice: alter priority of running processes. . . . . renice(8)
else: alternative commands. . . . . csh(1)
mk-amd-map: create database maps for Amd. . . . . mk-amd-map(8)
le: HP AMD 7990 LANCE Ethernet interface. . . . . le(4)
le: SPARC AMD 7990 LANCE ethernet interface. . . . . le(4)
amd: automatically mount file systems. . . . . amd(8)
amq: automounter query tool. . . . . amq(8)
error: analyze and disperse compiler error messages. . . . . error(1)
style: analyze surface characteristics of a document. . . . . . . style(1)
lex: fast lexical analyzer generator. . . . . lex(1)
named-xfer: ancillary agent for inbound zone transfers. . . . . named-xfer(8)
worms: animate worms on a display terminal. . . . . worms(6)
rain: animated raindrops display. . . . . rain(6)
ansitape: ANSI standard tape handler. . . . . ansitape(1)
ansitape: ANSI standard tape handler. . . . . ansitape(1)
sticky: sticky text and append-only directories. . . . . sticky(8)
apply: apply a command to a set of arguments. . . . . apply(1)
apply: apply a command to a set of arguments. . . . . apply(1)
flock: apply or remove an advisory lock on an open file. . . . . . . flock(2)
patch: a program for applying a diff file to an original. . . . . patch(1)
apropos: locate commands by keyword lookup. . . . . apropos(1)

ar: archive (library) file format. . . . . ar.5(5)
ar: create and maintain library archives. . . . . ar(1)
number: convert Arabic numerals to English. . . . . number(6)
calculator. bc: arbitrary-precision arithmetic language and . . . . . bc(1)
acos: arc cosine function. . . . . acos(3)
graphics/ plot: openpl, erase, label, line, circle, arc, move, cont, point, linemod, space, closepl: . . . plot(3)
asin: arc sine function. . . . . asin(3)
atan: arc tangent function of one variable. . . . . . . atan(3)
atan2: arc tangent function of two variables. . . . . . . atan2(3)
tar: tape archive file format. . . . . tarformat(5)
ranlib: table-of-contents for archive libraries. . . . . ranlib(1)
ar: archive (library) file format. . . . . ar.5(5)
ranlib: archive (library) table-of-contents format. . . . . ranlib.5(5)
shar: create a shell archive of files. . . . . shar(1)
tar: tape archiver. . . . . tar(1)
ar: create and maintain library archives. . . . . ar(1)
pax: read and write file archives and copy directory hierarchies. . . . . . . pax(1)
getsubopt: get sub options from an argument. . . . . getsubopt(3)
glob: filename expand argument list. . . . . csh(1)
shift: manipulate argument list. . . . . csh(1)
getopt: get option character from command line argument list. . . . . getopt(3)
stdarg: variable argument lists. . . . . stdarg(3)
xargs: construct argument list(s) and execute utility. . . . . xargs(1)
apply: apply a command to a set of arguments. apply(1)
echo: echo arguments. . . . . csh(1)
expr: evaluate arguments as an expression. . . . . expr(1)
arithmetic: quiz on simple arithmetic. arithmetic(6)
omout, pow, rpow, sdiv,: multiple precision integer arithmetic. /mout, move, msqrt, msub, mult, omin, ... mp(3)
bc: arbitrary-precision arithmetic language and calculator. . . . . bc(1)
@: arithmetic on shell variables. . . . . csh(1)
arithmetic: quiz on simple arithmetic. . . . . arithmetic(6)
acucntrl: turn around tty line between dialin and dialout. . . . . . acucntrl(8)
arp: address resolution display and control. . . . . arp(8)
ftp: ARPANET file transfer program. . . . . ftp(1)
rs: reshape a data array. . . . . rs(1)
biff: be notified if mail arrives and who it is from. . . . . biff(1)
expr: evaluate arguments as an expression. . . . . expr(1)
slattach: attach serial lines as network interfaces. . . . . slattach(8)
bcd, ppt, morse: reformat input as punch cards, paper tape or morse code. . . . . . . bcd(6)
mktime: transform binary date and time value to ASCII. /ctime, difftime, gmtime, localtime, ... ctime(3)
translate a PostScript font in .pfb format to ASCII. pfbtops: . . . . pfbtops(1)
toascii: convert a byte to 7-bit ASCII. . . . . toascii(3)
isascii: test for ASCII character. . . . . isascii(3)
ascii: octal, hexadecimal and decimal ASCII character sets. . . . . ascii(7)
hexdump: ascii, decimal, hexadecimal, octal dump. . . . . hexdump(1)
od: octal, decimal, hex, ascii dump. od(1)
map3270: database for mapping ascii keystrokes into IBM 3270 keys. . . . . map3270(5)
character sets. ascii: octal, hexadecimal and decimal ASCII . . . . ascii(7)
atof: convert ASCII string to double. . . . . atof(3)
strtod: convert ASCII string to double. . . . . strtod(3)
atoi: convert ASCII string to integer. . . . . atoi(3)
atol: convert ASCII string to long integer. . . . . atol(3)
mset: retrieve ASCII to IBM 3270 keyboard map. . . . . mset(1)
mktime: transform binary date and time value to/ asctime, ctime, difftime, gmtime, localtime, ... ctime(3)
asin: arc sine function. . . . . asin(3)
asinh: inverse hyperbolic sine function. . . . . asinh(3)
assert: expression verification macro. . . . . assert(3)
ttyname, isatty, ttyslot: get name of associated terminal (tty) from file descriptor. . . . . . . ttyname(3)
pig: eformatray inputway asway Igpay Atinlay. . . . . pig(6)
nfsiod: local NFS asynchronous I/O server. . . . . nfsiod(8)
at: schedule execution of commands 'at' a given time. . . . . at(1)
shutdown: close down the system at a given time. . . . . shutdown(8)
nice: execute a command at a low scheduling priority. . . . . nice(1)
time. at: schedule execution of commands 'at' a given . . . . . . at(1)
atrm: remove jobs spooled by at(1). . . . . atrm(1)
atq: display the at(1) job queue. . . . . atq(1)
atan: arc tangent function of one variable. . . . . atan(3)
atan2: arc tangent function of two variables. . . . . atan2(3)
atanh: inverse hyperbolic tangent function. . . . . atanh(3)
atc: air traffic controller game. . . . . atc(6)
atexit: register a function to be called on exit. . . . . . atexit(3)
pig: eformatray inputway asway Igpay Atinlay. . . . . pig(6)

	atof: convert ASCII string to double.	atof(3)
	atoi: convert ASCII string to integer.	atoi(3)
	atol: convert ASCII string to long integer.	atol(3)
interrupt. sigpause:	atomically release blocked signals and wait for	sigpause(2)
interrupt. sigsuspend:	atomically release blocked signals and wait for	sigsuspend(2)
	atq: display the at(1) job queue.	atq(1)
	atrm: remove jobs spooled by at(1).	atrm(1)
sliplogin:	attach a serial line network interface.	sliplogin(8)
slattach:	attach serial lines as network interfaces.	slattach(8)
rcs: change RCS file	attributes.	rcs(1)
krb_mk_err, krb_rd_err, krb_ck_repl: Kerberos	authentication library. /krb_mk_safe, krb_rd_safe, ...	krb(3)
/krb_net_read: Kerberos routines for sending	authentication via network stream sockets.	krb_sendauth(3)
code. autoconf: diagnostics from the autoconfiguration	autoconf: diagnostics from the autoconfiguration	autoconf(4)
autoconf: diagnostics from the	autoconfiguration code.	autoconf(4)
bugfiler: file bug reports in folders	automatically.	bugfiler(1)
amd:	automatically mount file systems.	amd(8)
amq:	automounter query tool.	amq(8)
rc: command script for	auto–reboot and daemons.	rc(8)
getloadavg: get system load	averages.	getloadavg(3)
wait:	await process completion.	wait(1)
	awk: pattern scanning and processing language.	awk(1)
huntd: hunt daemon,	back-end for hunt game.	huntd(6)
backgammon: the game of	backgammon.	backgammon(6)
	backgammon: the game of backgammon.	backgammon(6)
bg: place job in	background.	csh(1)
daemon: run in the	background.	daemon(3)
wait: wait for	background processes to complete.	csh(1)
dump: filesystem	backup.	dump(8)
restore: restore files or file systems from	backups made with dump.	restore(8)
rand, srand:	bad random number generator.	rand(3)
bad144: read/write dec standard 144	bad sector information.	bad144(8)
badsect: create files to contain	bad sectors.	badsect(8)
information.	bad144: read/write dec standard 144 bad sector	bad144(8)
	badsect: create files to contain bad sectors.	badsect(8)
banner: print large	banner on printer.	banner(6)
	banner: print large banner on printer.	banner(6)
gettytab: terminal configuration data	base.	gettytab(5)
hosts: host name data	base.	hosts(5)
networks: network name data	base.	networks(5)
phones: remote host phone number data	base.	phones(5)
printcap: printer capability data	base.	printcap(5)
protocols: protocol name data	base.	protocols(5)
rpc: rpc program number data	base.	rpc(5)
services: service name data	base.	services(5)
termcap: terminal capability data	base.	termcap(5)
newaliases: rebuild the data	base for the mail aliases file.	newaliases(1)
vgrindefs: language definition data	base for vgrind(1).	vgrindefs(5)
portion of pathname.	basename, dirname: return filename or directory	basename(1)
	battlestar: a tropical adventure game.	battlestar(6)
calculator.	bc: arbitrary-precision arithmetic language and	bc(1)
paper tape or morse code.	bcd, ppt, morse: reformat input as punch cards, ...	bcd(6)
memcpy, memmove, memset: byte string operations.	bcmp, bcopy, bzero, memccpy, memchr, memcmp, ...	bstring(3)
	bcmp: compare byte string.	bcmp(3)
memmove, memset: byte string operations. bcmp,	bcopy, bzero, memccpy, memchr, memcmp, memcpy, . . .	bstring(3)
	bcopy: copy byte string.	bcopy(3)
Standard.	bdes: encrypt/decrypt using the Data Encryption	bdes(1)
look: display lines	beginning with a given string.	look(1)
j0, j1, jn, y0, y1, yn:	bessel functions of first and second kind.	j0(3)
changing/ random, srandom, initstate, setstate:	better random number generator; routines for	random(3)
	bg: place job in background.	csh(1)
formatter.	bib, listrefs, bibinc, bib2tib: bibliographic	bib(1)
bib, listrefs, bibinc,	bib2tib: bibliographic formatter.	bib(1)
bib, listrefs,	bibinc, bib2tib: bibliographic formatter.	bib(1)
indxbib: make inverted index for	bibliographic databases.	indxbib(1)
lkbib: search	bibliographic databases.	lkbib(1)
lookbib: search	bibliographic databases.	lookbib(1)
bib, listrefs, bibinc, bib2tib:	bibliographic formatter.	bib(1)
refer: preprocess	bibliographic references for groff.	refer(1)
from.	biff: be notified if mail arrives and who it is	biff(1)
comsat:	biff server.	comsat(8)
install: install	binaries.	install(1)
difftime, gmtime, localtime, mktime: transform	binary date and time value to ASCII. /ctime, ...	ctime(3)

uuencode, uudecode: encode/decode a	binary file.	uuencode(1)
a.out: format of executable	binary files.	a.out(5)
bsearch:	binary search of a sorted table.	bsearch(3)
fread, fwrite:	binary stream input/output.	fread(3)
bind:	bind a name to a socket.	bind(2)
	bind: bind a name to a socket.	bind(2)
ffs: find first	bit set in a bit string.	ffs(3)
ffs: find first bit set in a	bit string.	ffs(3)
bit_nclear, bit_nset, bit_set, bitstr_size,/	bit_alloc, bit_clear, bit_decl, bit_ffs,	bitstring(3)
bit_set, bitstr_size, bit_test:/ bit_alloc,	bit_clear, bit_decl, bit_ffs, bit_nclear, bit_nset,	bitstring(3)
bitstr_size, bit_test:/ bit_alloc, bit_clear,	bit_decl, bit_ffs, bit_nclear, bit_nset, bit_set,	bitstring(3)
bitstr_size,/ bit_alloc, bit_clear, bit_decl,	bit_ffs, bit_nclear, bit_nset, bit_set,	bitstring(3)
bit_test:/ bit_alloc, bit_clear, bit_decl, bit_ffs,	bit_nclear, bit_nset, bit_set, bitstr_size,	bitstring(3)
/bit_clear, bit_decl, bit_ffs, bit_nclear,	bit_nset, bit_set, bitstr_size, bit_test:/	bitstring(3)
/bit_clear, bit_decl, bit_ffs, bit_nclear, bit_nset,	bit_set, bitstr_size, bit_test: bit-string/	bitstring(3)
bit_nset, bit_set, bitstr_size, bit_test:	bit-string manipulation macros. /bit_nclear,	bitstring(3)
/bit_decl, bit_ffs, bit_nclear, bit_nset, bit_set,	bitstr_size, bit_test: bit-string manipulation/	bitstring(3)
bit_nclear, bit_nset, bit_set, bitstr_size,	bit_test: bit-string manipulation macros. /bit_ffs,	bitstring(3)
cksum: display file checksums and	block counts.	cksum(1)
sum: calculate file checksums and	block counts.	sum(1)
sync: synchronize disk	block in-core status with that on disk.	sync(2)
sigblock:	block signals.	sigblock(2)
getbsize: get user	block size.	getbsize(3)
quot: display total	block usage per user for a file system.	quot(8)
sigpause: atomically release	blocked signals and wait for interrupt.	sigpause(2)
sigsuspend: atomically release	blocked signals and wait for interrupt.	sigsuspend(2)
	boggle: word search game.	boggle(6)
ching: the	book of changes and other cookies.	ching(6)
rbootd: HP remote	boot server.	rbootd(8)
	boot: system bootstrapping procedures.	boot_hp300(8)
boot: system	bootstrapping procedures.	boot_hp300(8)
reboot: UNIX	bootstrapping procedures.	boot_sparc(8)
mille: play Mille	Bornes.	mille(6)
end, etext, edata: end	boundaries of image segments.	end(3)
psbb: extract	bounding box from PostScript document.	psbb(1)
psbb: extract bounding	box from PostScript document.	psbb(1)
switch: multi-way command	branch.	csh(1)
	break: exit while/foreach loop.	csh(1)
	breaksw: exit from switch.	csh(1)
fg:	bring job into foreground.	csh(1)
	brk, sbrk: change data segment size.	brk(2)
	bsearch: binary search of a sorted table.	bsearch(3)
display object file segment sizes (text, data and	bss). size:	size(1)
	btree: btree database access method.	btree(3)
btree:	btree database access method.	btree(3)
bwtwo: monochromatic frame	buffer.	bwtwo(4)
cgsix: accelerated 8-bit color frame	buffer.	cgsix(4)
cgthree: 8-bit color frame	buffer.	cgthree(4)
dmesg: display the system message	buffer.	dmesg(8)
grf: HP graphics frame	buffer device interface.	grf(4)
mpool: shared memory	buffer pool.	mpool(3)
setbuf, setbuffer, setlinebuf, setvbuf: stream	buffering operations.	setbuf(3)
generate a dump of the operating system's profile	buffers. kgmon:	kgmon(8)
sendbug: mail a system	bug report to 4bsd-bugs.	sendbug(1)
bugfiler: file	bug reports in folders automatically.	bugfiler(8)
automatically. bugfiler: file bug reports in folders		bugfiler(8)
config.new:	build kernel compilation directories.	config.new(8)
mknod:	build special file.	mknod(8)
config:	build system configuration files.	config(8)
	bwtwo: monochromatic frame buffer.	bwtwo(4)
wc: word, line, and	byte count.	wc(1)
memchr: locate	byte in byte string.	memchr(3)
ntohs: convert values between host and network	byte order. htonl, htons, ntohl,	byteorder(3)
bcmp: compare	byte string.	bcmp(3)
bcopy: copy	byte string.	bcopy(3)
bzero: write zeroes to a	byte string.	bzero(3)
memchr: locate byte in	byte string.	memchr(3)
memcmp: compare	byte string.	memcmp(3)
memcpy: copy	byte string.	memcpy(3)
memmove: copy	byte string.	memmove(3)
memset: write a byte to	byte string.	memset(3)
memccpy, memchr, memcmp, memcpy, memmove, memset:	byte string operations. bcmp, bcopy, bzero,	bstring(3)

```
           toascii: convert a  byte to 7-bit ASCII. . . . . . . . . . . . . . . . .  toascii(3)
          memset: write a  byte to byte string. . . . . . . . . . . . . . . . .  memset(3)
           swab: swap adjacent  bytes. . . . . . . . . . . . . . . . . . . . . . . .  swab(3)
memset: byte string operations. bcmp, bcopy,  bzero, memccpy, memchr, memcmp, memcpy, memmove,  . .  bstring(3)
                                 bzero: write zeroes to a byte string. . . . . . . . . .  bzero(3)
  mbrune, mbrrune, mbmb: multibyte rune support for  C. . . . . . . . . . . . . . . . . . . . . . . . .  mbrune(3)
wcstombs, wctomb: multibyte character support for  C. mblen, mbstowcs, mbtowc, . . . . . . . . . . . .  multibyte(3)
     sgetrune, sputrune: rune support for  C. setrunelocale, setinvalidrune, . . . . . . . . . . . .  rune(3)
    localeconv: natural language formatting for  C. setlocale, . . . . . . . . . . . . . . . . . . .  setlocale(3)
       yyfix: extract tables from y.tab.  c. . . . . . . . . . . . . . . . . . . . . . . . . .  yyfix(1)
         cc, g++: GNU project  C and C++ Compiler (v2 preliminary). . . . . . . . . . .  cc(1)
    cc, g++: GNU project C and  C++ Compiler (v2 preliminary). . . . . . . . . . . . .  cc(1)
       g++: GNU project  C++ Compiler (v2 preliminary). . . . . . . . . . . . . .  g++(1)
      intro: introduction to the  C libraries. . . . . . . . . . . . . . . . . . . . . . . .  intro(3)
                      operator:  C operator precedence and order of evaluation. . . . . . .  operator(7)
    indent: indent and format  C program source. . . . . . . . . . . . . . . . . . . .  indent(1)
        xstr: extract strings from  C programs to implement shared strings. . . . . . . . .  xstr(1)
mkstr: create an error message file by massaging  C source. . . . . . . . . . . . . . . . . . . . . . . .  mkstr(1)
             functions. hypot,  cabs: euclidean distance and complex absolute value . . . . .  hypot(3)
force completion of pending disk writes (flush  cache). sync: . . . . . . . . . . . . . . . . . . . . .  sync(8)
     krb_set_tkt_string: set Kerberos ticket  cache file name. . . . . . . . . . . . . . . . . . . . .  krb_set_tkt_string(3)
                       pwcache:  cache password and group entries. . . . . . . . . . . .  pwcache(3)
   update: flush internal filesystem  caches to disk frequently. . . . . . . . . . . . . . . .  update(8)
               caesar: decrypt  caesar cyphers. . . . . . . . . . . . . . . . . . . . .  caesar(6)
                                 caesar: decrypt caesar cyphers. . . . . . . . . . . . .  caesar(6)
                                 cal: displays a calendar. . . . . . . . . . . . . . . . .  cal(1)
                      diskpart:  calculate default disk partition sizes. . . . . . . . . . .  diskpart(8)
                          sum:  calculate file checksums and block counts. . . . . . . . .  sum(1)
                   getgrouplist:  calculate group access list. . . . . . . . . . . . . . . .  getgrouplist(3)
bc: arbitrary-precision arithmetic language and  calculator. . . . . . . . . . . . . . . . . . . . . . .  bc(1)
                 dc: desk  calculator. . . . . . . . . . . . . . . . . . . . . . . .  dc(1)
              cal: displays a  calendar. . . . . . . . . . . . . . . . . . . . . . . . .  cal(1)
                                 calendar: reminder service. . . . . . . . . . . . . . . .  calendar(1)
    syscall, __syscall: indirect system  call. . . . . . . . . . . . . . . . . . . . . . . . . . .  syscall(2)
            gprof: display  call graph profile data. . . . . . . . . . . . . . . . .  gprof(1)
    atexit: register a function to be  called on exit. . . . . . . . . . . . . . . . . . . . . .  atexit(3)
            _exit: terminate the  calling process. . . . . . . . . . . . . . . . . . . . .  _exit(2)
    getpid, getppid: get parent or  calling process identification. . . . . . . . . . . . . .  getpid(2)
  operations. malloc, free, realloc,  calloc, alloca: general memory allocation . . . . . . . .  memory(3)
               space).  calloc: allocate clean memory (zero initialized . . . . . .  calloc(3)
free: free up memory allocated with malloc,  calloc or realloc. . . . . . . . . . . . . . . . . . . .  free(3)
siginterrupt: allow signals to interrupt system  calls. . . . . . . . . . . . . . . . . . . . . . . . . .  siginterrupt(3)
   intro: introduction to system  calls and error numbers. . . . . . . . . . . . . . . .  intro(2)
 canfield, cfscores: the solitaire card game  canfield. . . . . . . . . . . . . . . . . . . . . . . . .  canfield(6)
                       canfield.  canfield, cfscores: the solitaire card game . . . . . . . .  canfield(6)
           realpath: returns the  canonicalized absolute pathname. . . . . . . . . . . . .  realpath(3)
              printcap: printer  capability data base. . . . . . . . . . . . . . . . . . .  printcap(5)
             termcap: terminal  capability data base. . . . . . . . . . . . . . . . . . .  termcap(5)
              cap_mkdb: create  capability database. . . . . . . . . . . . . . . . . . .  cap_mkdb(1)
cgetstr, cgetustr, cgetfirst, cgetnext, cgetclose:  capability database access routines. /cgetnum, . . . . . . .  getcap(3)
                 tput: terminal  capability interface. . . . . . . . . . . . . . . . . . .  tput(1)
                                 cap_mkdb: create capability database. . . . . . . . . . .  cap_mkdb(1)
   canfield, cfscores: the solitaire  card game canfield. . . . . . . . . . . . . . . . . . .  canfield(6)
             cribbage: the  card game cribbage. . . . . . . . . . . . . . . . . . .  cribbage(6)
bcd, ppt, morse: reformat input as punch  cards, paper tape or morse code. . . . . . . . . . . .  bcd(6)
                 ct: CS/80  cartridge tape interface. . . . . . . . . . . . . . . . .  ct(4)
   strcasecmp: compare strings, ignoring  case. . . . . . . . . . . . . . . . . . . . . . . . . . .  strcasecmp(3)
      tolower: upper case to lower  case letter conversion. . . . . . . . . . . . . . . . .  tolower(3)
      toupper: lower case to upper  case letter conversion. . . . . . . . . . . . . . . . .  toupper(3)
                                 case: selector in switch. . . . . . . . . . . . . . . . .  csh(1)
         tolower: upper  case to lower case letter conversion. . . . . . . . . . .  tolower(3)
         toupper: lower  case to upper case letter conversion. . . . . . . . . . .  toupper(3)
                                 cat: concatenate and print files. . . . . . . . . . . . .  cat(1)
uncompact, ccat: compress and uncompress files, and  cat them. compact, . . . . . . . . . . . . . . . . . .  compact(1)
                       xneko:  cat-and-mouse chase in an X window. . . . . . . . . . .  xneko(6)
                      default:  catchall clause in switch. . . . . . . . . . . . . . . . .  csh(1)
     tc: HP98544 98550 ''Topcat'' and  ''Catseye'' device interface. . . . . . . . . . . . . . .  tc(4)
                       abort:  cause abnormal program termination. . . . . . . . . . .  abort(3)
              named.reload:  cause the name server to synchronize its database. . . . . .  named.reload(8)
wump: hunt the wumpus in an underground  cave. . . . . . . . . . . . . . . . . . . . . . . . . .  wump(6)
           larn: exploring the  caverns of Larn. . . . . . . . . . . . . . . . . . . . .  larn(6)
                                 cbrt, sqrt: cube root and square root functions. . . . . . .  sqrt(3)
```

preliminary). cc, g++: GNU project C and C++ Compiler (v2 . . . . cc(1)
compact, uncompact, ccat: compress and uncompress files, and cat them. . . . . . compact(1)
preprocessor. cccp, cpp: the GNU C-compatible compiler . . . . cpp(1)
cccp, cpp: the GNU C-compatible compiler preprocessor. . . . . cpp(1)
st: CCS SCSI tape driver. . . . . st(4)
cd: change directory. . . . . csh(1)
cd: change working directory. . . . . cd(1)
ceil: smallest integral value not greater than x. . . . . ceil(3)
service key files from Kerberos key distribution center database. ext_srvtab: extract . . . . . ext_srvtab(8)
kdb_destroy: destroy Kerberos key distribution center database. . . . . kdb_destroy(8)
kdb_init: initialize Kerberos key distribution center database. . . . . kdb_init(8)
kdb_edit: Kerberos key distribution center database editing utility. . . . . kdb_edit(8)
kstash: stash Kerberos key distribution center database master key. . . . . kstash(8)
kdb_util: Kerberos key distribution center database utility. . . . . kdb_util(8)
cfsetspeed, cfmakeraw, tcgetattr, tcsetattr:/ cfgetispeed, cfsetispeed, cfgetospeed, cfsetospeed, ... tcsetattr(3)
tcgetattr, tcsetattr:/ cfgetispeed, cfsetispeed, cfgetospeed, cfsetospeed, cfsetspeed, cfmakeraw, ... tcsetattr(3)
/cfsetspeed, cfgetospeed, cfsetospeed, cfsetspeed, cfmakeraw, tcgetattr, tcsetattr: manipulating the/ . . . . . . tcsetattr(3)
canfield, cfscores: the solitaire card game canfield. . . . . canfield(6)
cfmakeraw, tcgetattr, tcsetattr:/ cfgetispeed, cfsetispeed, cfgetospeed, cfsetospeed, cfsetspeed, ... tcsetattr(3)
tcsetattr:/ cfgetispeed, cfsetispeed, cfgetospeed, cfsetospeed, cfsetspeed, cfmakeraw, tcgetattr, ... tcsetattr(3)
cfgetispeed, cfsetispeed, cfgetospeed, cfsetospeed, cfsetspeed, cfmakeraw, tcgetattr, tcsetattr:/ . . . . . . tcsetattr(3)
cgetnext, cgetclose:/ cgetent, cgetset, cgetmatch, cgetcap, cgetnum, cgetstr, cgetustr, cgetfirst, ... getcap(3)
/cgetnum, cgetstr, cgetustr, cgetfirst, cgetnext, cgetclose: capability database access routines. . . . . . . getcap(3)
cgetstr, cgetustr, cgetfirst, cgetnext, cgetclose:/ cgetent, cgetset, cgetmatch, cgetcap, cgetnum, ... getcap(3)
/cgetmatch, cgetcap, cgetnum, cgetstr, cgetustr, cgetfirst, cgetnext, cgetclose: capability database/ . . . . . . getcap(3)
cgetfirst, cgetnext, cgetclose:/ cgetent, cgetset, cgetmatch, cgetcap, cgetnum, cgetstr, cgetustr, ... getcap(3)
/cgetcap, cgetnum, cgetstr, cgetustr, cgetfirst, cgetnext, cgetclose: capability database access/ . . . . . . getcap(3)
cgetclose:/ cgetent, cgetset, cgetmatch, cgetcap, cgetnum, cgetstr, cgetustr, cgetfirst, cgetnext, ... getcap(3)
cgetustr, cgetfirst, cgetnext, cgetclose:/ cgetent, cgetset, cgetmatch, cgetcap, cgetnum, cgetstr, ... getcap(3)
cgetent, cgetset, cgetmatch, cgetcap, cgetnum, cgetstr, cgetustr, cgetfirst, cgetnext, cgetclose:/ . . . . . . getcap(3)
cgetset, cgetmatch, cgetcap, cgetnum, cgetstr, cgetustr, cgetfirst, cgetnext, cgetclose:/ cgetent, ... getcap(3)
cgsix: accelerated 8-bit color frame buffer. . . . . cgsix(4)
cgthree: 8-bit color frame buffer. . . . . cgthree(4)
chdir, fchdir: change current working directory. . . . . chdir(2)
brk, sbrk: change data segment size. . . . . brk(2)
cd: change directory. . . . . csh(1)
chdir: change directory. . . . . csh(1)
touch: change file access and modification times. . . . . touch(1)
chflags: change file flags. . . . . chflags(1)
chmod: change file modes. . . . . chmod(1)
chown: change file owner and group. . . . . chown(8)
chgrp: change group. . . . . chgrp(1)
chmod, fchmod: change mode of file. . . . . chmod(2)
umask: change or display file creation mask. . . . . csh(1)
chown, fchown: change owner and group of a file. . . . . chown(2)
rcs: change RCS file attributes. . . . . rcs(1)
chroot: change root directory. . . . . chroot(2)
chroot: change root directory. . . . . chroot(8)
rename: change the name of a file. . . . . rename(2)
chpass: add or change user database information. . . . . chpass(1)
set: change value of shell variable. . . . . csh(1)
cd: change working directory. . . . . cd(1)
chkey: change your encryption key. . . . . chkey(1)
ching: the book of changes and other cookies. . . . . ching(6)
kpasswdd: Kerberos password changing daemon. . . . . kpasswdd(8)
better random number generator; routines for changing generators. /srandom, initstate, setstate: . . . . . . random(3)
isascii: test for ASCII character. . . . . isascii(3)
isupper, isxdigit, toascii tolower, toupper,: character classification macros. /ispunct, isspace, ... ctype(3)
eqnchar: special character definitions for eqn. . . . . eqnchar(7)
isgraph: printing character test (space character exclusive). . . . . isgraph(3)
memccpy: copy string until character found. . . . . memccpy(3)
getopt: get option character from command line argument list. . . . . . getopt(3)
ungetc: un-get character from input stream. . . . . ungetc(3)
index: locate character in string. . . . . index(3)
rindex: locate character in string. . . . . rindex(3)
strchr: locate character in string. . . . . strchr(3)
strrchr: locate character in string. . . . . strrchr(3)
isprint: printing character test (space character inclusive). . . . . isprint(3)
groff_char: groff character names. . . . . groff_char(7)
fgetc, getc, getchar, getw: get next character or word from input stream. . . . . getc(3)
fputc, putc, putchar, putw: output a character or word to a stream. . . . . putc(3)
runes. UTF2: Universal character set Transformation Format encoding of . . . . . . utf2(4)

ascii: octal, hexadecimal and decimal ASCII   character sets. ascii(7)
mbstowcs, mbtowc, wcstombs, wctomb: multibyte   character support for C. mblen, ... multibyte(3)
isalnum: alphanumeric   character test. . . . . isalnum(3)
isalpha: alphabetic   character test. . . . . isalpha(3)
isblank: space or tab   character test. . . . . isblank(3)
iscntrl: control   character test. . . . . iscntrl(3)
isdigit: decimal-digit   character test. . . . . isdigit(3)
islower: lower-case   character test. . . . . islower(3)
ispunct: punctuation   character test. . . . . ispunct(3)
isspace: white-space   character test. . . . . isspace(3)
isupper: upper-case   character test. . . . . isupper(3)
isxdigit: hexadecimal-digit   character test. . . . . isxdigit(3)
isgraph: printing   character test (space character exclusive). . . . . isgraph(3)
isprint: printing   character test (space character inclusive). . . . . isprint(3)
style: analyze surface   characteristics of a document. . . . . style(1)
tr: translate   characters. . . . . tr(1)
unvis, strunvis: decode a visual representation of   characters. . . . . unvis(3)
vis: visually encode   characters. . . . . vis(3)
vis: display non-printable   characters in a visual format. . . . . vis(1)
strpbrk: locate multiple   characters in string. . . . . strpbrk(3)
snake, snscore: display   chase game. . . . . snake(6)
xneko: cat-and-mouse   chase in an X window. . . . . xneko(6)
chdir: change directory. . . . . csh(1)
chdir, fchdir: change current working directory. . . . . . . chdir(2)
icheck: file system storage consistency   check. . . . . icheck(8)
access: check access permissions of a file or pathname. . . . . access(2)
fsck: filesystem consistency   check and interactive repair. . . . . fsck(8)
clearerr, feof, ferror, fileno: check and reset stream status. . . . . ferror(3)
ci: check in RCS revisions. . . . . ci(1)
checknr: check nroff/troff files. . . . . checknr(1)
co: check out RCS revisions. . . . . co(1)
rcsfreeze: freeze a configuration of sources   checked in under RCS. . . . . rcsfreeze(1)
quotacheck: filesystem quota consistency   checker. . . . . quotacheck(8)
fastboot, fasthalt: reboot/halt the system without   checking the disks. . . . . fastboot(8)
checknr: check nroff/troff files. . . . . checknr(1)
cksum: display file   checksums and block counts. . . . . cksum(1)
sum: calculate file   checksums and block counts. . . . . sum(1)
chess: GNU   chess. . . . . chess(6)
xchess: X   chess display. . . . . xchess(1)
chess: GNU chess. . . . . chess(6)
chflags: change file flags. . . . . chflags(1)
chflags, fchflags: set file flags. . . . . chflags(2)
chgrp: change group. . . . . chgrp(1)
ching: the book of changes and other cookies. . . . . . . ching(6)
chkey: change your encryption key. . . . . chkey(1)
chmod: change file modes. . . . . chmod(1)
chmod, fchmod: change mode of file. . . . . chmod(2)
chown: change file owner and group. . . . . chown(8)
chown, fchown: change owner and group of a file. . . . . chown(2)
chpass: add or change user database information. . . . . . chpass(1)
crontab: chronological services schedule file. . . . . crontab(5)
chroot: change root directory. . . . . chroot(2)
chroot: change root directory. . . . . chroot(8)
ci: check in RCS revisions. . . . . ci(1)
closepl:/ plot: openpl, erase, label, line,   circle, arc, move, cont, point, linemod, space, ... plot(3)
cksum: display file checksums and block counts. . . . . . cksum(1)
isxdigit, toascii tolower, toupper,: character   classification macros. /ispunct, isspace, isupper, ... ctype(3)
default: catchall   clause in switch. . . . . csh(1)
calloc: allocate   clean memory (zero initialized space). . . . . calloc(3)
rcsclean: clean up working files. . . . . rcsclean(1)
uuclean: uucp spool directory   clean-up. . . . . uuclean(8)
clri: clear an inode. . . . . clri(8)
stream status.   clearerr, feof, ferror, fileno: check and reset . . . . . ferror(3)
csh: a shell (command interpreter) with   C-like syntax. . . . . csh(1)
clnp: Connectionless-Mode Network Protocol. . . . . . . clnp(4)
the time to allow synchronization of the system   clock. adjtime: correct . . . . adjtime(2)
cron: clock daemon. . . . . cron(8)
clock: determine processor time used. . . . . clock(3)
fclose: close a stream. . . . . fclose(3)
close: delete a descriptor. . . . . close(2)
shutdown: close down the system at a given time. . . . . shutdown(8)
opendir, readdir, telldir, seekdir, rewinddir,   closedir, dirfd: directory operations. . . . . directory(3)

syslog, vsyslog, openlog, closelog, setlogmask: control system log. . . . . syslog(3)
circle, arc, move, cont, point, linemod, space, closepl: graphics interface. /erase, label, line, ... plot(3)
clri: clear an inode. . . . . clri(8)
cltp: ISO Connectionless Transport Protocol. . . . . . . cltp(4)
L. cmds: UUCP remote command permissions file. . . . . . L.cmds(5)
cmp: compare two files. . . . . cmp(1)
co: check out RCS revisions. . . . . co(1)
xroach: cockroaches hide under your windows. . . . . xroach(6)
autoconf: diagnostics from the autoconfiguration code. autoconf(4)
reformat input as punch cards, paper tape or morse code. bcd, ppt, morse: . . . . bcd(6)
col: filter reverse line feeds from input. . . . . col(1)
colcrt: filter nroff output for CRT previewing. . . . . . . colcrt(1)
strcoll: compare strings according to current collation. . . . . strcoll(3)
lfs_cleanerd: garbage collect a log-structured file system. . . . . lfs_cleanerd(8)
cgsix: accelerated 8-bit color frame buffer. . . . . cgsix(4)
cgthree: 8-bit color frame buffer. . . . . cgthree(4)
colrm: remove columns from a file. . . . . colrm(1)
column: columnate lists. . . . . column(1)
column: columnate lists. . . . . column(1)
colrm: remove columns from a file. . . . . colrm(1)
comm: select or reject lines common to two files. . . . . . comm(1)
exec: overlay shell with specified command. . . . . csh(1)
time: time command. csh(1)
grog: guess options for groff command. grog(1)
routines for returning a stream to a remote command. rcmd, rresvport, ruserok: . . . . rcmd(3)
rexec: return stream to a remote command. . . . . rexec(3)
nice: execute a command at a low scheduling priority. . . . . nice(1)
switch: multi-way command branch. . . . . csh(1)
time: time command execution. . . . . time(1)
uux: unix to unix command execution. . . . . uux(1)
rehash: recompute command hash table. . . . . csh(1)
unhash: discard command hash table. . . . . csh(1)
hashstat: print command hashing statistics. . . . . csh(1)
nohup: run command immune to hangups. . . . . csh(1)
nohup: invoke a command immune to hangups. . . . . nohup(1)
sh: command interpreter (shell). . . . . sh(1)
csh: a shell (command interpreter) with C-like syntax. . . . . csh(1)
whatis: describe what a command is. . . . . whatis(1)
getopt: get option character from command line argument list. . . . . getopt(3)
L.cmds: UUCP remote command permissions file. . . . . L.cmds(5)
repeat: execute command repeatedly. . . . . csh(1)
rc: command script for auto-reboot and daemons. . . . . . . rc(8)
onintr: process interrupts in command scripts. . . . . csh(1)
apply: apply a command to a set of arguments. . . . . apply(1)
system: pass a command to the shell. . . . . system(3)
goto: command transfer. . . . . csh(1)
nroff: emulate nroff command with groff. . . . . nroff(1)
else: alternative commands. csh(1)
introduction to system maintenance and operation commands. intro: . . . . intro(8)
rcsintro: introduction to RCS commands. rcsintro(1)
at: schedule execution of commands 'at' a given time. . . . . at(1)
apropos: locate commands by keyword lookup. . . . . apropos(1)
while: repeat commands conditionally. . . . . csh(1)
lastcomm: show last commands executed in reverse order. . . . . lastcomm(1)
source: read commands from file. . . . . csh(1)
intro: introduction to general commands (tools and utilities). . . . . intro(1)
comm: select or reject lines common to two files. . . . . comm(1)
pipe: create descriptor pair for interprocess communication. pipe(2)
socket: create an endpoint for communication. socket(2)
talkd: remote user communication server. . . . . talkd(8)
dca: HP 98644A communications interface. . . . . dca(4)
dcl: HP 98628A communications link. . . . . dcl(4)
dcm: HP 98642A communications multiplexer. . . . . dcm(4)
files, and cat them. compact, uncompact, ccat: compress and uncompress . . . . compact(1)
diff: differential file and directory comparator. . . . . diff(1)
bcmp: compare byte string. . . . . bcmp(3)
memcmp: compare byte string. . . . . memcmp(3)
zcmp, zdiff: compare compressed files. . . . . zdiff(1)
rcsdiff: compare RCS revisions. . . . . rcsdiff(1)
strcmp: compare strings. . . . . strcmp(3)
strcoll: compare strings according to current collation. . . . . . . strcoll(3)
strcasecmp: compare strings, ignoring case. . . . . strcasecmp(3)

cmp:	compare two files.	cmp(1)
diff3: 3-way differential file	comparison.	diff3(1)
config.new: build kernel	compilation directories.	config.new(8)
pic:	compile pictures for troff or TeX.	pic(1)
rpcgen: an RPC protocol	compiler.	rpcgen(1)
zic: time zone	compiler.	zic(8)
error: analyze and disperse	compiler error messages.	error(1)
cccp, cpp: the GNU C-compatible	compiler preprocessor.	cpp(1)
cc, g++: GNU project C and C++	Compiler (v2 preliminary).	cc(1)
g++: GNU project C++	Compiler (v2 preliminary).	g++(1)
strcspn: span the	complement of a string.	strcspn(3)
wait: wait for background processes to	complete.	csh(1)
wait: await process	completion.	wait(1)
sync: force	completion of pending disk writes (flush cache).	sync(8)
hypot, cabs: euclidean distance and	complex absolute value functions.	hypot(3)
floating-point number to fractional and integral	components. frexp: convert	frexp(3)
compress, uncompress, zcat:	compress and expand data.	compress(1)
compact, uncompact, ccat:	compress and uncompress files, and cat them.	compact(1)
gzexe:	compress executable files in place.	gzexe(1)
gzip, gunzip, zcat:	compress or expand files.	gzip(1)
data.	compress, uncompress, zcat: compress and expand	compress(1)
zcmp, zdiff: compare	compressed files.	zdiff(1)
zgrep: search possibly	compressed files for a regular expression.	zgrep(1)
zmore: file perusal filter for crt viewing of	compressed text.	zmore(1)
login: log into the	computer.	login(1)
learn:	computer aided instruction about.	learn(1)
comsat: biff server.		comsat(8)
cat:	concatenate and print files.	cat(1)
strcat:	concatenate strings.	strcat(3)
test:	condition evaluation utility.	test(1)
endif: terminate	conditional.	csh(1)
if:	conditional statement.	csh(1)
while: repeat commands	conditionally.	csh(1)
man.	conf: configuration file for man(1).	man.conf(5)
dm.	conf: dm configuration file.	dm.conf(5)
/etc/kerberosIV/krb.	conf: Kerberos configuration file.	krb.conf(5)
syslog.	conf: syslogd(8) configuration file.	syslog.conf(5)
	config: build system configuration files.	config(8)
	config.new: build kernel compilation directories.	config.new(8)
pathconf, fpathconf: get	configurable pathname variables.	pathconf(2)
sysconf: get	configurable system variables.	sysconf(3)
confstr: get string-valued	configurable variables.	confstr(3)
gettytab: terminal	configuration data base.	gettytab(5)
dm.conf: dm	configuration file.	dm.conf(5)
/etc/kerberosIV/krb.conf: Kerberos	configuration file.	krb.conf(5)
resolver: resolver	configuration file.	resolver(5)
syslog.conf: syslogd(8)	configuration file.	syslog.conf(5)
man.conf:	configuration file for man(1).	man.conf(5)
config: build system	configuration files.	config(8)
rcsfreeze: freeze a	configuration of sources checked in under RCS.	rcsfreeze(1)
ifconfig:	configure network interface parameters.	ifconfig(8)
	confstr: get string-valued configurable variables.	confstr(3)
	connect: initiate a connection on a socket.	connect(2)
ac: display	connect time accounting.	ac(8)
tip, cu:	connect to a remote system.	tip(1)
getpeername: get name of	connected peer.	getpeername(2)
socketpair: create a pair of	connected sockets.	socketpair(2)
shutdown: shut down part of a full-duplex	connection.	shutdown(2)
accept: accept a	connection on a socket.	accept(2)
connect: initiate a	connection on a socket.	connect(2)
cltp: ISO	Connectionless Transport Protocol.	cltp(4)
clnp:	Connectionless-Mode Network Protocol.	clnp(4)
listen: listen for	connections on a socket.	listen(2)
	cons: HP300 console interface.	cons(4)
icheck: file system storage	consistency check.	icheck(8)
fsck: filesystem	consistency check and interactive repair.	fsck(8)
quotacheck: filesystem quota	consistency checker.	quotacheck(8)
cons: HP300	console interface.	cons(4)
show what versions of object modules were used to	construct a file. what:	what(1)
newfs, mfs:	construct a new file system.	newfs(8)
newlfs:	construct a new LFS file system.	newlfs(8)
mkproto:	construct a prototype file system.	mkproto(8)

xargs: construct argument list(s) and execute utility. . . . . . . xargs(1)
mkdep: construct Makefile dependency list. . . . . mkdep(1)
deroff: remove nroff, troff, tbl and eqn constructs. . . . . deroff(1)
setrlimit: control maximum system resource consumption. getrlimit, ... getrlimit(2)
vlimit: control maximum system resource consumption. . . . . vlimit(3)
/openpl, erase, label, line, circle, arc, move, cont, point, linemod, space, closepl: graphics/ . . . . plot(3)
badsect: create files to contain bad sectors. . . . . badsect(8)
file: identify file content. . . . . file(1)
ls: list directory contents. . . . . ls(1)
sigaltstack: set and/or get signal stack context. . . . . sigaltstack(2)
sigstack: set and/or get signal stack context. . . . . sigstack(2)
continue: cycle in loop. . . . . csh(1)
arp: address resolution display and control. . . . . arp(8)
fcntl: file control. . . . . fcntl(2)
iscntrl: control character test. . . . . iscntrl(3)
ioctl: control device. . . . . ioctl(2)
moncontrol, monstartup: control execution profile. . . . . moncontrol(3)
tcsendbreak, tcdrain, tcflush, tcflow: line control functions. . . . . tcsendbreak(3)
init: process control initialization. init(8)
acl_add, acl_delete, acl_initialize: access control list routines. /acl_check, acl_exact_match, ... acl_check(3)
getrlimit, setrlimit: control maximum system resource consumption. . . . . . . getrlimit(2)
vlimit: control maximum system resource consumption. . . . . . . vlimit(3)
icmp: Internet Control Message Protocol. . . . . icmp(4)
profil: control process profiling. . . . . profil(2)
lpc: line printer control program. . . . . lpc(8)
timedc: timed control program. . . . . timedc(8)
tcp: Internet Transmission Control Protocol. tcp(4)
syslog, vsyslog, openlog, closelog, setlogmask: control system log. . . . . syslog(3)
mprotect: control the protection of pages. . . . . mprotect(2)
eeprom: openprom control utility. . . . . eeprom(8)
atc: air traffic controller game. . . . . atc(6)
term: conventional names for terminals. . . . . term(7)
ecvt, fcvt, gcvt: output conversion. . . . . ecvt(3)
vfprintf, vsprintf, vsnprintf: formatted output conversion. /fprintf, sprintf, snprintf, vprintf, ... printf(3)
sscanf, vscanf, vsscanf, vfscanf: input format conversion. scanf, fscanf, ... scanf(3)
tolower: upper case to lower case letter conversion. . . . . tolower(3)
toupper: lower case to upper case letter conversion. . . . . toupper(3)
tzset, tzsetwall: initialize time conversion information. . . . . tzset(3)
units: conversion program. . . . . units(1)
ns_addr, ns_ntoa: Xerox NS Ns (tm) address conversion routines. . . . . ns(3)
iso_addr, iso_ntoa: elementary network address conversion routines for Open System/ . . . . iso_addr(3)
toascii: convert a byte to 7-bit ASCII. . . . . toascii(3)
integer. strtoul, strtouq: convert a string to an unsigned long or uquad_t . . . . . strtoul(3)
dd: convert and copy a file. . . . . dd(1)
number: convert Arabic numerals to English. . . . . number(6)
atof: convert ASCII string to double. . . . . atof(3)
strtod: convert ASCII string to double. . . . . strtod(3)
atoi: convert ASCII string to integer. . . . . atoi(3)
atol: convert ASCII string to long integer. . . . . atol(3)
integral components. frexp: convert floating-point number to fractional and . . . . frexp(3)
grodvi: convert groff output to TeX dvi format. . . . . grodvi(1)
string. strmode: convert inode status information into a symbolic . . . . . strmode(3)
strtol, strtoq: convert string value to a long or quad_t integer. . . . . . . strtol(3)
htonl, htons, ntohl, ntohs: convert values between host and network byte order. . . . . byteorder(3)
ching: the book of changes and other cookies. . . . . ching(6)
fsinfo: co-ordinate site-wide filesystem information. . . . . fsinfo(8)
rcp: remote file copy. . . . . rcp(1)
uucp: unix to unix copy. . . . . uucp(1)
dd: convert and copy a file. . . . . dd(1)
tcopy: copy and/or verify mag tapes. . . . . tcopy(1)
bcopy: copy byte string. . . . . bcopy(3)
memcpy: copy byte string. . . . . memcpy(3)
memmove: copy byte string. . . . . memmove(3)
pax: read and write file archives and copy directory hierarchies. . . . . pax(1)
cp: copy files. . . . . cp(1)
strdup: save a copy of a string. . . . . strdup(3)
memccpy: copy string until character found. . . . . memccpy(3)
strcpy: copy strings. . . . . strcpy(3)
floating point support. copysign, drem, finite, logb, scalb: IEEE 754 . . . . ieee(3)
savecore: save a core dump of the operating system. . . . . savecore(8)
gcore: get core images of running process. . . . . gcore(1)
core: memory image file format. . . . . core(5)

```
          system clock.  adjtime:  correct the time to allow synchronization of the  . . . . . . .  adjtime(2)
                 paste: merge  corresponding or subsequent lines of files. . . . . . . . .  paste(1)
                              cos: cosine function.   . . . . . . . . . . . . . .  cos(3)
                    cosh: hyperbolic cosine function.   . . . . . . . . . . . . .  cosh(3)
             acos: arc  cosine function.   . . . . . . . . . . . . . . . . . .  acos(3)
    acosh: inverse hyperbolic  cosine function.   . . . . . . . . . . . . . . . .  acosh(3)
                     cos:  cosine function.   . . . . . . . . . . . . . . . . . .  cos(3)
          cosh: hyperbolic  cosine function.   . . . . . . . . . . . . . . . . . .  cosh(3)
     wc: word, line, and byte  count.  . . . . . . . . . . . . . . . . . . . .  wc(1)
 cksum: display file checksums and block  counts.  . . . . . . . . . . . . . . . . . . . .  cksum(1)
   sum: calculate file checksums and block  counts.  . . . . . . . . . . . . . . . . . . . .  sum(1)
                              cp: copy files.  . . . . . . . . . . . . . . . . . .  cp(1)
                    cccp,  cpp: the GNU C-compatible compiler preprocessor.  . . . . .  cpp(1)
                              crash: UNIX system failures.  . . . . . . . . . . . .  crash(8)
                              creat: create a new file.  . . . . . . . . . . . . .  creat(2)
           open: open or  create a file for reading or writing.  . . . . . . . . .  open(2)
                   creat:  create a new file.  . . . . . . . . . . . . . . . . . .  creat(2)
                    fork:  create a new process.  . . . . . . . . . . . . . . . .  fork(2)
              socketpair:  create a pair of connected sockets.  . . . . . . . . . .  socketpair(2)
                    shar:  create a shell archive of files.  . . . . . . . . . . . .  shar(1)
                   ctags:  create a tags file.  . . . . . . . . . . . . . . . . . .  ctags(1)
                  socket:  create an endpoint for communication.  . . . . . . . . . .  socket(2)
                   mkstr:  create an error message file by massaging C source.  . . . . .  mkstr(1)
           invert, lookup:  create and access an inverted index.  . . . . . . . . . .  invert(1)
                      ar:  create and maintain library archives.  . . . . . . . . . .  ar(1)
               cap_mkdb:  create capability database.  . . . . . . . . . . . . . .  cap_mkdb(1)
             mk-amd-map:  create database maps for Amd.  . . . . . . . . . . . . .  mk-amd-map(8)
                makemap:  create database maps for sendmail.  . . . . . . . . . . .  makemap(8)
      communication. pipe:  create descriptor pair for interprocess  . . . . . . . . .  pipe(2)
               dev_mkdb:  create /dev database.  . . . . . . . . . . . . . . . .  dev_mkdb(8)
                 badsect:  create files to contain bad sectors.  . . . . . . . . . . .  badsect(8)
                tfmtodit:  create font files for use with groff −Tdvi.  . . . . . . . .  tfmtodit(1)
                afmtodit:  create font files for use with groff −Tps.  . . . . . . . .  afmtodit(1)
               kvm_mkdb:  create kernel database.  . . . . . . . . . . . . . . . .  kvm_mkdb(8)
                   setsid:  create session and set process group ID.  . . . . . . . . .  setsid(2)
                MAKEDEV:  create system and device special files.  . . . . . . . . . .  MAKEDEV(8)
  umask: change or display file  creation mask.  . . . . . . . . . . . . . . . . . .  csh(1)
          umask: set file  creation mode mask.  . . . . . . . . . . . . . . . . .  umask(2)
    cribbage: the card game  cribbage.  . . . . . . . . . . . . . . . . . . . . .  cribbage(6)
                              cribbage: the card game cribbage.  . . . . . . . . . . .  cribbage(6)
                              cron: clock daemon.  . . . . . . . . . . . . . . . .  cron(8)
                              crontab: chronological services schedule file.  . . . . . . .  crontab(5)
 systat: display system statistics on a  crt.  . . . . . . . . . . . . . . . . . . . . . .  systat(1)
    colcrt: filter nroff output for  CRT previewing. . . . . . . . . . . . . . . . . .  colcrt(1)
    more: file perusal filter for  crt viewing.  . . . . . . . . . . . . . . . . . .  more(1)
   zmore: file perusal filter for  crt viewing of compressed text.  . . . . . . . . . .  zmore(1)
                              crypt: encode/decode.  . . . . . . . . . . . . . . .  crypt(1)
            encryption.  crypt, setkey, encrypt, des_setkey, des_cipher: DES  . . . . .  crypt(3)
                      ct:  CS/80 cartridge tape interface.  . . . . . . . . . . . . .  ct(4)
                      rd:  CS/80 disk interface.  . . . . . . . . . . . . . . . .  rd(4)
                 syntax.  csh: a shell (command interpreter) with C-like  . . . . . . .  csh(1)
                              ct: CS/80 cartridge tape interface.  . . . . . . . . . . .  ct(4)
                              ctags: create a tags file.  . . . . . . . . . . . . . .  ctags(1)
                              ctermid: generate terminal pathname.  . . . . . . . . . .  ctermid(3)
 transform binary date and time value to/  asctime,  ctime, difftime, gmtime, localtime, mktime:  . . . . . . . .  ctime(3)
                     tip:  cu: connect to a remote system.  . . . . . . . . . . . .  tip(1)
               cbrt, sqrt:  cube root and square root functions.  . . . . . . . . . .  sqrt(3)
   strcoll: compare strings according to  current collation.  . . . . . . . . . . . . . . . . .  strcoll(3)
 gethostid, sethostid: get/set unique identifier of  current host.  . . . . . . . . . . . . . . . . . . .  gethostid(3)
 gethostname, sethostname: get/set name of  current host.  . . . . . . . . . . . . . . . . . . .  gethostname(3)
  hostname: set or print name of  current host system.  . . . . . . . . . . . . . . .  hostname(1)
               jobs: print  current job list.  . . . . . . . . . . . . . . . . . .  csh(1)
      raise: send a signal to the  current process.  . . . . . . . . . . . . . . . . .  raise(3)
      sigprocmask: manipulate  current signal mask.  . . . . . . . . . . . . . . . .  sigprocmask(2)
       sigsetmask: set  current signal mask.  . . . . . . . . . . . . . . . .  sigsetmask(2)
              users: list  current users.  . . . . . . . . . . . . . . . . . . .  users(1)
      chdir, fchdir: change  current working directory.  . . . . . . . . . . . . . .  chdir(2)
  klist: list  currently held Kerberos tickets.  . . . . . . . . . . .  klist(1)
                 motion.  curses: screen functions with "optimal" cursor  . . . . . .  curses(3)
 curses: screen functions with "optimal"  cursor motion.  . . . . . . . . . . . . . . . . .  curses(3)
      spline: interpolate smooth  curve.  . . . . . . . . . . . . . . . . . . . . .  spline(1)
                              cut: select portions of each line of a file.  . . . . . . . . .  cut(1)
```

```
                continue:  cycle in loop. . . . . . . . . . . . . . . . . . . . . . .  csh(1)
         caesar: decrypt caesar  cyphers. . . . . . . . . . . . . . . . . . . . . . .  caesar(6)
                cron: clock  daemon. . . . . . . . . . . . . . . . . . . . . . . .  cron(8)
  kpasswdd: Kerberos password changing  daemon. . . . . . . . . . . . . . . . . .  kpasswdd(8)
         lpd: line printer spooler  daemon. . . . . . . . . . . . . . . . . . . .  lpd(8)
    mount_portal: mount the portal  daemon. . . . . . . . . . . . . . . . . . .  mount_portal(8)
    registerd: Kerberos registration  daemon. . . . . . . . . . . . . . . . . .  registerd(8)
         routed: network routing  daemon. . . . . . . . . . . . . . . . . . . .  routed(8)
          timed: time server  daemon. . . . . . . . . . . . . . . . . . . . . .  timed(8)
 XNSrouted: NS Routing Information Protocol  daemon. . . . . . . . . . . . . . .  XNSrouted(8)
         huntd: hunt  daemon, back-end for hunt game. . . . . . . . . . . . .  huntd(6)
                  daemon: run in the background. . . . . . . . . . . . . . .  daemon(3)
 rc: command script for auto–reboot and  daemons. . . . . . . . . . . . . . . .  rc(8)
                portmap:  DARPA port to RPC program number mapper. . . . . . .  portmap(8)
                telnetd:  DARPA TELNET protocol server. . . . . . . . . . . . .  telnetd(8)
 compress, uncompress, zcat: compress and expand  data. . . . . . . . . . . .  compress(1)
         eval: re-evaluate shell  data. . . . . . . . . . . . . . . . . . . . .  csh(1)
    gprof: display call graph profile  data. . . . . . . . . . . . . . . . . .  gprof(1)
     jot: print sequential or random  data. . . . . . . . . . . . . . . . . .  jot(1)
        kdump: display kernel trace  data. . . . . . . . . . . . . . . . . . .  kdump(1)
 size: display object file segment sizes (text,  data and bss). . . . . . . . .  size(1)
            rs: reshape a  data array. . . . . . . . . . . . . . . . . . . . .  rs(1)
 unvis: revert a visual representation of  data back to original form. . . . .  unvis(1)
    gettytab: terminal configuration  data base. . . . . . . . . . . . . . . .  gettytab(5)
         hosts: host name  data base. . . . . . . . . . . . . . . . . . . . . .  hosts(5)
     networks: network name  data base. . . . . . . . . . . . . . . . . . . . .  networks(5)
  phones: remote host phone number  data base. . . . . . . . . . . . . . . . .  phones(5)
     printcap: printer capability  data base. . . . . . . . . . . . . . . . . .  printcap(5)
     protocols: protocol name  data base. . . . . . . . . . . . . . . . . . . .  protocols(5)
    rpc: rpc program number  data base. . . . . . . . . . . . . . . . . . . . .  rpc(5)
       services: service name  data base. . . . . . . . . . . . . . . . . . . .  services(5)
     termcap: terminal capability  data base. . . . . . . . . . . . . . . . . .  termcap(5)
    newaliases: rebuild the  data base for the mail aliases file. . . . . . . .  newaliases(1)
   vgrindefs: language definition  data base for vgrind(1). . . . . . . . . . .  vgrindefs(5)
 bdes: encrypt/decrypt using the  Data Encryption Standard. . . . . . . . . . .  bdes(1)
      brk, sbrk: change  data segment size. . . . . . . . . . . . . . . . . . .  brk(2)
    pstat: display system  data structures. . . . . . . . . . . . . . . . . . .  pstat(8)
          types: system  data types. . . . . . . . . . . . . . . . . . . . . .  types(5)
    cap_mkdb: create capability  database. . . . . . . . . . . . . . . . . . .  cap_mkdb(1)
         dev_mkdb: create /dev  database. . . . . . . . . . . . . . . . . . . .  dev_mkdb(8)
 key files from Kerberos key distribution center  database. ext_srvtab: extract service  . . . . .  ext_srvtab(8)
 destroy Kerberos key distribution center  database. kdb_destroy: . . . . . . .  kdb_destroy(8)
 initialize Kerberos key distribution center  database. kdb_init: . . . . . . .  kdb_init(8)
      kvm_mkdb: create kernel  database. . . . . . . . . . . . . . . . . . . .  kvm_mkdb(8)
 cause the name server to synchronize its  database. named.reload: . . . . . .  named.reload(8)
    publickey: public key  database. . . . . . . . . . . . . . . . . . . . . .  publickey(5)
 route: kernel packet forwarding  database. . . . . . . . . . . . . . . . . . .  route(4)
        shells: shell  database. . . . . . . . . . . . . . . . . . . . . . . .  shells(5)
       btree: btree  database access method. . . . . . . . . . . . . . . . . .  btree(3)
        hash: hash  database access method. . . . . . . . . . . . . . . . . . .  hash(3)
 recno: record number  database access method. . . . . . . . . . . . . . . . .  recno(3)
             dbopen:  database access methods. . . . . . . . . . . . . . . . .  dbopen(3)
 cgetfirst, cgetnext, cgetclose: capability  database access routines. /cgetstr, cgetustr, . . . . . . .  getcap(3)
 kdb_edit: Kerberos key distribution center  database editing utility. . . . .  kdb_edit(8)
 keys. map3270:  database for mapping ascii keystrokes into IBM 3270 . . . .  map3270(5)
 chpass: add or change user  database information. . . . . . . . . . . . . . .  chpass(1)
 mk-amd-map: create  database maps for Amd. . . . . . . . . . . . . . . . . . .  mk-amd-map(8)
  makemap: create  database maps for sendmail. . . . . . . . . . . . . . . . .  makemap(8)
 kstash: stash Kerberos key distribution center  database master key. . . . .  kstash(8)
 .Nm setgrfile, setgrent, endgrent: group  database operations. /getgrgid, setgroupent, . . . . . .  getgrent(3)
 innetgr, setnetgrent, endnetgrent: netgroup  database operations. getnetgrent, . . . . . .  getnetgrent(3)
 getpwuid, setpassent, setpwent, endpwent: password  database operations. getpwent, getpwnam, . . . . . .  getpwent(3)
    join: relational  database operator. . . . . . . . . . . . . . . . . . . .  join(1)
 kdb_util: Kerberos key distribution center  database utility. . . . . . . . .  kdb_util(8)
 indxbib: make inverted index for bibliographic  databases. . . . . . . . . .  indxbib(1)
 lkbib: search bibliographic  databases. . . . . . . . . . . . . . . . . . . .  lkbib(1)
 lookbib: search bibliographic  databases. . . . . . . . . . . . . . . . . . .  lookbib(1)
 pwd_mkdb: generate the password  databases. . . . . . . . . . . . . . . . . .  pwd_mkdb(8)
    idp: Xerox Internet  Datagram Protocol. . . . . . . . . . . . . . . . . . .  idp(4)
    udp: Internet User  Datagram Protocol. . . . . . . . . . . . . . . . . . .  udp(4)
    date: display or set  date and time. . . . . . . . . . . . . . . . . . . .  date(1)
        ftime: get  date and time. . . . . . . . . . . . . . . . . . . . . . .  ftime(3)
```

gettimeofday, settimeofday: get/set date and time. gettimeofday(2)
strftime: format date and time. . . . . strftime(3)
gmtime, localtime, mktime: transform binary date and time value to ASCII. /ctime, difftime, ... ctime(3)
date: display or set date and time. . . . . date(1)
dv: HP98730 ''DaVinci'' device interface. . . . . dv(4)
time: get time of day. . . . . time(3)
dbopen: database access methods. . . . . dbopen(3)
dc: desk calculator. . . . . dc(1)
dca: HP 98644A communications interface. . . . . dca(4)
dcl: HP 98628A communications link. . . . . dcl(4)
dcm: HP 98642A communications multiplexer. . . . . dcm(4)
dd: convert and copy a file. . . . . dd(1)
adb: debugger. . . . . adb(1)
fsdb: file system debugger. . . . . fsdb(8)
gdb: the GNU debugger. . . . . gdb(1)
bad144: read/write dec standard 144 bad sector information. . . . . bad144(8)
ascii: octal, hexadecimal and decimal ASCII character sets. . . . . ascii(7)
od: octal, decimal, hex, ascii dump. . . . . od(1)
hexdump: ascii, decimal, hexadecimal, octal dump. . . . . hexdump(1)
isdigit: decimal-digit character test. . . . . isdigit(3)
unvis, strunvis: decode a visual representation of characters. . . . . unvis(3)
keylogin: decrypt and store secret key. . . . . keylogin(1)
caesar: decrypt caesar cyphers. . . . . caesar(6)
default: catchall clause in switch. . . . . csh(1)
diskpart: calculate default disk partition sizes. . . . . diskpart(8)
exports: define remote mount points for NFS mount requests. . . . . exports(5)
netgroup: defines network groups. . . . . netgroup(5)
vgrindefs: language definition data base for vgrind(1). . . . . vgrindefs(5)
eqnchar: special character definitions for eqn. . . . . eqnchar(7)
stty, gtty: set and get terminal state (defunct). . . . . stty(3)
close: delete a descriptor. . . . . close(2)
mount_null: demonstrate the use of a null file system layer. . . . . . . mount_null(8)
make: maintain program dependencies. . . . . make(1)
lorder: list dependencies for object files. . . . . lorder(1)
mkdep: construct Makefile dependency list. . . . . mkdep(1)
man: (deprecated) macros to typeset manual. . . . . man(7)
constructs. deroff: remove nroff, troff, tbl and eqn . . . . deroff(1)
crypt, setkey, encrypt, des_setkey, des_cipher: DES encryption. . . . . crypt(3)
des_cbc_cksum, des_quad_cksum,: (new) DES encryption. /des_cbc_encrypt, des_pcbc_encrypt, . . . des_crypt(3)
/des_ecb_encrypt, des_cbc_encrypt, des_pcbc_encrypt, des_cbc_cksum, des_quad_cksum,: (new) DES/ . . . des_crypt(3)
/des_random_key, des_set_key, des_ecb_encrypt, des_cbc_encrypt, des_pcbc_encrypt, des_cbc_cksum,/ . . . . des_crypt(3)
crypt, setkey, encrypt, des_setkey, des_cipher: DES encryption. . . . . crypt(3)
whatis: describe what a command is. . . . . whatis(1)
hostname: host name resolution description. . . . . hostname(7)
mailaddr: mail addressing description. . . . . mailaddr(7)
getdiskbyname: get generic disk description by its name. . . . . getdiskbyname(3)
disktab: disk description file. . . . . disktab(5)
L-devices: UUCP device description file. . . . . L-devices(5)
L.sys: UUCP remote host description file. . . . . L.sys(5)
remote: remote host description file. . . . . remote(5)
groff_font: format of groff device and font description files. groff_font(5)
close: delete a descriptor. . . . . close(2)
dup, dup2: duplicate an existing file descriptor. . . . . dup(2)
kvm_geterr: get error message on kvm descriptor. . . . . kvm_geterr(3)
kvm_getloadavg: get error message on kvm descriptor. . . . . kvm_getloadavg(3)
get name of associated terminal (tty) from file descriptor. ttyname, isatty, ttyslot: . . . . ttyname(3)
getfsfile, setfsent, endfsent: get file system descriptor file entry. getfsent, getfsspec, ... getfsent(3)
fd, stdin, stdout, stderr: file descriptor files. . . . . fd(4)
pipe: create descriptor pair for interprocess communication. . . . . . . pipe(2)
getdtablesize: get descriptor table size. . . . . getdtablesize(2)
/des_string_to_key, des_random_key, des_set_key, des_ecb_encrypt, des_cbc_encrypt, des_pcbc_encrypt,/ . . . des_crypt(3)
dc: desk calculator. . . . . dc(1)
/des_set_key, des_ecb_encrypt, des_cbc_encrypt, des_pcbc_encrypt, des_cbc_cksum, des_quad_cksum,:/ . . . des_crypt(3)
/des_cbc_encrypt, des_pcbc_encrypt, des_cbc_cksum, des_quad_cksum,: (new) DES encryption. . . . . . des_crypt(3)
des_read_password, des_string_to_key, des_random_key, des_set_key, des_ecb_encrypt,/ . . . . des_crypt(3)
des_random_key, des_set_key, des_ecb_encrypt,/ des_read_password, des_string_to_key, ... des_crypt(3)
crypt, setkey, encrypt, des_setkey, des_cipher: DES encryption. . . . . crypt(3)
/des_string_to_key, des_random_key, des_set_key, des_ecb_encrypt, des_cbc_encrypt,/ . . . . . . des_crypt(3)
des_ecb_encrypt,/ des_read_password, des_string_to_key, des_random_key, des_set_key, ... des_crypt(3)
kdb_destroy: destroy Kerberos key distribution center database. . . . . . . kdb_destroy(8)
kdestroy: destroy Kerberos tickets. . . . . kdestroy(1)
clock: determine processor time used. . . . . clock(3)

dev_mkdb: create /dev database. . . . . dev_mkdb(8)
drum: paging device. . . . . drum(4)
fold: fold long lines for finite width output device. . . . . fold(1)
ioctl: control device. . . . . ioctl(2)
null: the null device. . . . . null(4)
groff_font: format of groff device and font description files. . . . . groff_font(5)
L-devices: UUCP device description file. . . . . L-devices(5)
hil: Human Interface Link device driver. . . . . hil(4)
swapon: add a swap device for interleaved paging/swapping. . . . . swapon(2)
swapon: specify additional device for paging and swapping. . . . . swapon(8)
dv: HP98730 "DaVinci" device interface. . . . . dv(4)
gb: HP98700 "Gatorbox" device interface. . . . . gb(4)
grf: HP graphics frame buffer device interface. . . . . grf(4)
rb: HP98720 "Renaissance" device interface. . . . . rb(4)
stty: set the options for a terminal device interface. . . . . stty(1)
tc: HP98544 98550 "Topcat" and "Catseye" device interface. . . . . tc(4)
devname: get device name. . . . . devname(3)
MAKEDEV: create system and device special files. . . . . MAKEDEV(8)
grotty: groff driver for typewriter-like devices. . . . . grotty(1)
mmap: map files or devices into memory. . . . . mmap(2)
dev_mkdb: create /dev database. . . . . dev_mkdb(8)
devname: get device name. . . . . devname(3)
df: display free disk space. . . . . df(1)
autoconf: diagnostics from the autoconfiguration code. . . . . autoconf(4)
startslip: dial up and login to a slip server. . . . . startslip(1)
acucntrl: turn around tty line between dialin and dialout. . . . . acucntrl(8)
acucntrl: turn around tty line between dialin and dialout. acucntrl(8)
explain: print wordy sentences; thesaurus for diction. diction, ... diction(1)
for diction. diction, explain: print wordy sentences; thesaurus . . . . . . diction(1)
diff: differential file and directory comparator. . . . . diff(1)
patch: a program for applying a diff file to an original. . . . . patch(1)
diff3: 3-way differential file comparison. . . . . diff3(1)
diff: differential file and directory comparator. . . . . diff(1)
diff3: 3-way differential file comparison. . . . . diff3(1)
binary date and time value to/ asctime, ctime, difftime, gmtime, localtime, mktime: transform . . . . . . ctime(3)
servers. dig: send domain name query packets to name . . . . . . dig(1)
dir, dirent: directory file format. . . . . dir(5)
tsort: topological sort of a directed graph. . . . . tsort(1)
config.new: build kernel compilation directories. . . . . config.new(8)
mkdir: make directories. . . . . mkdir(1)
rmdir: remove directories. . . . . rmdir(1)
sticky: sticky text and append-only directories. . . . . sticky(8)
cd: change working directory. . . . . cd(1)
chdir, fchdir: change current working directory. . . . . chdir(2)
chroot: change root directory. . . . . chroot(2)
chroot: change root directory. . . . . chroot(8)
cd: change directory. . . . . csh(1)
chdir: change directory. . . . . csh(1)
scandir, alphasort: scan a directory. . . . . scandir(3)
uuclean: uucp spool directory clean-up. . . . . uuclean(8)
diff: differential file and directory comparator. . . . . diff(1)
ls: list directory contents. . . . . ls(1)
rm: remove directory entries. . . . . rm(1)
format. getdirentries: get directory entries in a filesystem independent . . . . getdirentries(2)
remove: remove directory entry. remove(3)
unlink: remove directory entry. unlink(2)
mkdir: make a directory file. . . . . mkdir(2)
rmdir: remove a directory file. . . . . rmdir(2)
dir, dirent: directory file format. . . . . dir(5)
pax: read and write file archives and copy directory hierarchies. . . . . pax(1)
mtree: map a directory hierarchy. . . . . mtree(8)
pwd: return working directory name. pwd(1)
telldir, seekdir, rewinddir, closedir, dirfd: directory operations. opendir, readdir, ... directory(3)
getcwd: get working directory pathname. . . . . getcwd(3)
basename, dirname: return filename or directory portion of pathname. . . . . basename(1)
whois: Internet user name directory service. whois(1)
popd: pop shell directory stack. csh(1)
pushd: push shell directory stack. csh(1)
dir, dirent: directory file format. . . . . dir(5)
readdir, telldir, seekdir, rewinddir, closedir, dirfd: directory operations. opendir, ... directory(3)
pathname. basename, dirname: return filename or directory portion of . . . . . . basename(1)
acct: enable or disable process accounting. . . . . acct(2)

unhash:	discard command hash table.	csh(1)
unset:	discard shell variables.	csh(1)
termios: general terminal line	discipline.	termios(4)
synchronize a file's in-core state with that on	disk. fsync:	fsync(2)
synchronize disk block in-core status with that on	disk. sync:	sync(2)
sync: synchronize	disk block in-core status with that on disk.	sync(2)
getdiskbyname: get generic	disk description by its name.	getdiskbyname(3)
disktab:	disk description file.	disktab(5)
update: flush internal filesystem caches to	disk frequently.	update(8)
rd: CS/80	disk interface.	rd(4)
disklabel:	disk pack label.	disklabel.5(5)
disklabel: read and write	disk pack label.	disklabel(8)
diskpart: calculate default	disk partition sizes.	diskpart(8)
df: display free	disk space.	df(1)
quota: display	disk usage and limits.	quota(1)
du: display	disk usage statistics.	du(1)
sync: force completion of pending	disk writes (flush cache).	sync(8)
	disklabel: disk pack label.	disklabel.5(5)
	disklabel: read and write disk pack label.	disklabel(8)
	diskpart: calculate default disk partition sizes.	diskpart(8)
reboot/halt the system without checking the	disks. fastboot, fasthalt:	fastboot(8)
scsiformat: format SCSI	disks and show SCSI parameters.	scsiformat(8)
format: how to format	disks and tapes.	format(8)
	disktab: disk description file.	disktab(5)
mount, unmount: mount or	dismount a filesystem.	mount(2)
error: analyze and	disperse compiler error messages.	error(1)
rain: animated raindrops	display.	rain(6)
rstat: remote status	display.	rstat(1)
xchess: X chess	display.	xchess(1)
arp: address resolution	display and control.	arp(8)
gprof:	display call graph profile data.	gprof(1)
snake, snscore:	display chase game.	snake(6)
ac:	display connect time accounting.	ac(8)
quota:	display disk usage and limits.	quota(1)
du:	display disk usage statistics.	du(1)
mesg:	display (do not display) messages from other users.	mesg(1)
whoami:	display effective user id.	whoami(1)
cksum:	display file checksums and block counts.	cksum(1)
umask: change or	display file creation mask.	csh(1)
head:	display first lines of a file.	head(1)
df:	display free disk space.	df(1)
uname:	display information about the system.	uname(1)
kdump:	display kernel trace data.	kdump(1)
look:	display lines beginning with a given string.	look(1)
mesg: display (do not	display) messages from other users.	mesg(1)
nm:	display name list (symbol table).	nm(1)
nfsstat:	display NFS statistics.	nfsstat(1)
format. vis:	display non-printable characters in a visual	vis(1)
bss). size:	display object file segment sizes (text, data and	size(1)
date:	display or set date and time.	date(1)
pstat:	display system data structures.	pstat(8)
systat:	display system statistics on a crt.	systat(1)
worms: animate worms on a	display terminal.	worms(6)
atq:	display the at(1) job queue.	atq(1)
tail:	display the last part of a file.	tail(1)
man:	display the on-line manual pages.	man(1)
pom:	display the phase of the moon.	pom(6)
dmesg:	display the system message buffer.	dmesg(8)
system. quot:	display total block usage per user for a file	quot(8)
logname:	display user's login name.	logname(1)
uulog:	display UUCP log entries.	uulog(1)
who:	display who is logged in.	who(1)
cal:	displays a calendar.	cal(1)
hypot, cabs: euclidean	distance and complex absolute value functions.	hypot(3)
extract service key files from Kerberos key	distribution center database. ext_srvtab:	ext_srvtab(8)
kdb_destroy: destroy Kerberos key	distribution center database.	kdb_destroy(8)
kdb_init: initialize Kerberos key	distribution center database.	kdb_init(8)
kdb_edit: Kerberos key	distribution center database editing utility.	kdb_edit(8)
kstash: stash Kerberos key	distribution center database master key.	kstash(8)
kdb_util: Kerberos key	distribution center database utility.	kdb_util(8)
rdist: remote file	distribution program.	rdist(1)
	div: return quotient and remainder from division.	div(3)

div: return quotient and remainder from   division.   . . . .   div(3)
ldiv: return quotient and remainder from   division.   . . . .   ldiv(3)
                               dm.conf: dm configuration file.   . . . .   dm.conf(5)
                                            dm: dungeon master.   . . . .   dm(8)
                                            dm.conf: dm configuration file.   . . . .   dm.conf(5)
                                            dmesg: display the system message buffer.   . . . . .   dmesg(8)
res_search, res_mkquery, res_send, res_init,   dn_comp, dn_expand: resolver routines. res_query, ...   resolver(3)
res_mkquery, res_send, res_init, dn_comp,   dn_expand: resolver routines. /res_search, ...   resolver(3)
                            mesg: display   (do not display) messages from other users.   . . . .   mesg(1)
psbb: extract bounding box from PostScript   document.   . . . .   psbb(1)
style: analyze surface characteristics of a   document.   . . . .   style(1)
      groff: front end for the groff   document formatting system.   . . . .   groff(1)
                          troff: format   documents.   . . . .   troff(1)
w: who present users are and what they are   doing.   . . . .   w(1)
                               dig: send   domain name query packets to name servers.   . . . . . .   dig(1)
                      named: Internet   domain name server.   . . . .   named(8)
        rhost: look up host names using   domain server.   . . . .   host(1)
  dungeon: Adventures in the Dungeons of   Doom.   . . . .   dungeon(6)
     hack: exploring The Dungeons of   Doom.   . . . .   hack(6)
    rogue: exploring The Dungeons of   Doom.   . . . .   rogue(6)
          atof: convert ASCII string to   double.   . . . .   atof(3)
        strtod: convert ASCII string to   double.   . . . .   strtod(3)
                     shutdown: shut   down part of a full-duplex connection.   . . . .   shutdown(2)
                    shutdown: close   down the system at a given time.   . . . .   shutdown(8)
                            graph: draw a graph.   . . . .   graph(1)
            support. copysign,   drem, finite, logb, scalb: IEEE 754 floating point   . . . . . .   ieee(3)
    hil: Human Interface Link device   driver.   . . . .   hil(4)
             pty: pseudo terminal   driver.   . . . .   pty(4)
                  st: CCS SCSI tape   driver.   . . . .   st(4)
           grops: PostScript   driver for groff.   . . . .   grops(1)
             grotty: groff   driver for typewriter-like devices.   . . . .   grotty(1)
                                            drum: paging device.   . . . .   drum(4)
                                            du: display disk usage statistics.   . . . .   du(1)
hexdump: ascii, decimal, hexadecimal, octal   dump.   . . . .   hexdump(1)
        od: octal, decimal, hex, ascii   dump.   . . . .   od(1)
files or file systems from backups made with   dump. restore: restore   . . . .   restore(8)
                                            dump, dumpdates: incremental dump format.   . . . . . .   dump(5)
                        dumpfs: dump file system information.   . . . .   dumpfs(8)
                       dumplfs: dump file system information.   . . . .   dumplfs(8)
                                            dump: filesystem backup.   . . . .   dump(8)
      dump, dumpdates: incremental   dump format.   . . . .   dump(5)
       savecore: save a core   dump of the operating system.   . . . .   savecore(8)
       kgmon: generate a   dump of the operating system's profile buffers.   . . . .   kgmon(8)
                        dump,   dumpdates: incremental dump format.   . . . .   dump(5)
                                            dumpfs: dump file system information.   . . . .   dumpfs(8)
                                            dumplfs: dump file system information.   . . . .   dumplfs(8)
                                            dungeon: Adventures in the Dungeons of Doom.   . . . . . .   dungeon(6)
                            dm: dungeon master.   . . . .   dm(8)
   dungeon: Adventures in the   Dungeons of Doom.   . . . .   dungeon(6)
      hack: exploring The   Dungeons of Doom.   . . . .   hack(6)
     rogue: exploring The   Dungeons of Doom.   . . . .   rogue(6)
                                            dup, dup2: duplicate an existing file descriptor.   . . . . . .   dup(2)
                     dup,   dup2: duplicate an existing file descriptor.   . . . .   dup(2)
             dup, dup2:   duplicate an existing file descriptor.   . . . .   dup(2)
                                            dv: HP98730 "DaVinci" device interface.   . . . .   dv(4)
     grodvi: convert groff output to TeX   dvi format.   . . . .   grodvi(1)
           cut: select portions of   each line of a file.   . . . .   cut(1)
                           echo: echo arguments.   . . . .   csh(1)
                                            echo: echo arguments.   . . . .   csh(1)
                                            echo: produce message in a shell script.   . . . .   echo(1)
                   ping: send ICMP   ECHO_REQUEST packets to network hosts.   . . . .   ping(8)
                                            ecvt, fcvt, gcvt: output conversion.   . . . .   ecvt(3)
                                            ed: line oriented text editor.   . . . .   ed(1)
                 end, etext,   edata: end boundaries of image segments.   . . . .   end(3)
                       vipw: edit the password file.   . . . .   vipw(8)
                    edquota: edit user quotas.   . . . .   edquota(8)
kdb_edit: Kerberos key distribution center database   editing utility.   . . . .   kdb_edit(8)
          ed: line oriented text   editor.   . . . .   ed(1)
                   ld: link   editor.   . . . .   ld(1)
                 sed: stream   editor.   . . . .   sed(1)
         ex, vi, view: text   editors.   . . . .   vi(1)
                                            edquota: edit user quotas.   . . . .   edquota(8)

openprom: OPENPROM and EEPROM interface. . . . . openprom(4)
eeprom: openprom control utility. . . . . eeprom(8)
setregid: set real and effective group ID. . . . . setregid(2)
whoami: display effective user id. . . . . whoami(1)
setreuid: set real and effective user ID's. . . . . setreuid(2)
vfork: spawn new process in a virtual memory efficient way. . . . . vfork(2)
pig: eformatray inputway asway Igpay Atinlay. . . . . pig(6)
insque, remque: insert/remove element from a queue. . . . . insque(3)
level access. link_addr, link_ntoa: elementary address specification routines for link . . . . . linkaddr(3)
Open System Interconnection. iso_addr, iso_ntoa: elementary network address conversion routines for . . . . iso_addr(3)
soelim: eliminate .so's from nroff input. . . . . soelim(1)
else: alternative commands. . . . . csh(1)
emacs: GNU project Emacs. . . . . emacs(1)
emacs: GNU project Emacs. . . . . emacs(1)
nroff: emulate nroff command with groff. . . . . nroff(1)
ite: HP Internal Terminal Emulator. . . . . ite(4)
ktrace: enable kernel process tracing. . . . . ktrace(1)
acct: enable or disable process accounting. . . . . acct(2)
nsip: software network interface encapsulating NS packets in IP packets. . . . . nsip(4)
vis: visually encode characters. vis(3)
uuencode: format of an encoded uuencode file. . . . . uuencode.format(5)
crypt: encode/decode. crypt(1)
uuencode, uudecode: encode/decode a binary file. . . . . uuencode(1)
EUC: EUC encoding of runes. euc(4)
UTF2: Universal character set Transformation Format encoding of runes. . . . . utf2(4)
crypt, setkey, encrypt, des_setkey, des_cipher: DES encryption. . . . . . crypt(3)
bdes: encrypt/decrypt using the Data Encryption Standard. . . . . bdes(1)
makekey: make encrypted keys or passwords. . . . . makekey(8)
xsend, xget, enroll: private encrypted mail. . . . . xsend(1)
crypt, setkey, encrypt, des_setkey, des_cipher: DES encryption. . . . . crypt(3)
des_cbc_cksum, des_quad_cksum,: (new) DES encryption. /des_cbc_encrypt, des_pcbc_encrypt, ... des_crypt(3)
chkey: change your encryption key. . . . . chkey(1)
bdes: encrypt/decrypt using the Data Encryption Standard. . . . . bdes(1)
end, etext, edata: end boundaries of image segments. . . . . end(3)
segments. end, etext, edata: end boundaries of image . . . . end(3)
groff: front end for the groff document formatting system. . . . . groff(1)
sccs: front end for the SCCS subsystem. . . . . sccs(1)
logout: end session. . . . . csh(1)
es-is: End System to Intermediate System Routing Protocol. . . . . esis(4)
end: terminate loop. . . . . csh(1)
getfsent, getfsspec, getfsfile, setfsent, endfsent: get file system descriptor file entry. . . . . getfsent(3)
getgrgid, setgroupent, .Nm setgrfile, setgrent, endgrent: group database operations. /getgrnam, ... getgrent(3)
/gethostbyaddr, gethostent, sethostent, endhostent, herror: get network host entry. . . . . gethostbyname(3)
endif: terminate conditional. . . . . csh(1)
getnetent, getnetbyaddr, getnetbyname, setnetent, endnetent: get network entry. . . . . getnetent(3)
getnetgrent, innetgr, setnetgrent, endnetgrent: netgroup database operations. . . . . getnetgrent(3)
socket: create an endpoint for communication. . . . . socket(2)
getprotobynumber, getprotobyname, setprotoent, endprotoent: get protocol entry. getprotoent, ... getprotoent(3)
getpwent, getpwnam, getpwuid, setpassent, setpwent, endpwent: password database operations. . . . . getpwent(3)
getservbyport, getservbyname, setservent, endservent: get service entry. getservent, ... getservent(3)
endsw: terminate switch. . . . . csh(1)
getttyent, getttynam, setttyent, endttyent: get ttys file entry. . . . . getttyent(3)
getusershell, setusershell, endusershell: get legal user shells. . . . . getusershell(3)
number: convert Arabic numerals to English. . . . . number(6)
xsend, xget, enroll: private encrypted mail. . . . . xsend(1)
pwcache: cache password and group entries. . . . . pwcache(3)
rm: remove directory entries. . . . . rm(1)
uulog: display UUCP log entries. . . . . uulog(1)
getdirentries: get directory entries in a filesystem independent format. . . . . getdirentries(2)
logger: make entries in the system log. . . . . logger(1)
setfsent, endfsent: get file system descriptor file entry. getfsent, getfsspec, getfsfile, ... getfsent(3)
sethostent, endhostent, herror: get network host entry. gethostbyname, gethostbyaddr, gethostent, ... gethostbyname(3)
getnetbyname, setnetent, endnetent: get network entry. getnetent, getnetbyaddr, ... getnetent(3)
setprotoent, endprotoent: get protocol entry. /getprotobynumber, getprotobyname, ... getprotoent(3)
getservbyname, setservent, endservent: get service entry. getservent, getservbyport, ... getservent(3)
getttynam, setttyent, endttyent: get ttys file entry. getttyent, ... getttyent(3)
remove: remove directory entry. . . . . remove(3)
unlink: remove directory entry. . . . . unlink(2)
environment. printenv: env: print out the environment, set and print . . . . . . printenv(1)
environ: user environment. . . . . environ(7)
setenv: set variable in environment. . . . . csh(1)
environ: user environment. environ(7)

env: print out the environment, set and print environment. printenv, ... printenv(1)
window: window environment. window(1)
printenv, env: print out the environment, set and print environment. . . . . printenv(1)
getenv, putenv, setenv, unsetenv: environment variable functions. . . . . getenv(3)
unsetenv: remove environment variables. . . . . csh(1)
eqnchar: special character definitions for eqn. . . . . eqnchar(7)
deroff: remove nroff, troff, tbl and eqn constructs. deroff(1)
eqn: format equations for troff. . . . . eqn(1)
eqnchar: special character definitions for eqn. . . . . . . eqnchar(7)
eqn: format equations for troff. . . . . eqn(1)
linemod, space, closepl: graphics/ plot: openpl, erase, label, line, circle, arc, move, cont, point, ... plot(1)
erf, erfc: error function operators. . . . . erf(3)
formatted error messages. err, verr, errx, verrx, warn, vwarn, warnx, vwarnx: . . . . . err(3)
messages. error: analyze and disperse compiler error . . . . error(1)
erf, erfc: error function operators. . . . . erf(3)
mkstr: create an error message file by massaging C source. . . . . mkstr(1)
kvm_geterr: get error message on kvm descriptor. . . . . kvm_geterr(3)
kvm_getloadavg: get error message on kvm descriptor. . . . . kvm_getloadavg(3)
errx, verrx, warn, vwarn, warnx, vwarnx: formatted error messages. err, verr, ... err(3)
error: analyze and disperse compiler error messages. . . . . error(1)
perror, strerror, sys_errlist, sys_nerr: system error messages. . . . . strerror(3)
intro: introduction to system calls and error numbers. . . . . intro(2)
spell, spellin, spellout: find spelling errors. . . . . spell(1)
error messages. err, verr, errx, verrx, warn, vwarn, warnx, vwarnx: formatted . . . . . . err(3)
Protocol. es-is: End System to Intermediate System Routing . . . . esis(4)
file. /etc/kerberosIV/krb.conf: Kerberos configuration . . . . krb.conf(5)
translation file. /etc/kerberosIV/krb.realms: host to Kerberos realm . . . . krb.realms(5)
end, etext, edata: end boundaries of image segments. . . . . end(3)
le: HP AMD 7990 LANCE Ethernet interface. . . . . le(4)
le: SPARC AMD 7990 LANCE ethernet interface. . . . . le(4)
EUC: EUC encoding of runes. . . . . euc(4)
EUC: EUC encoding of runes. . . . . euc(4)
functions. hypot, cabs: euclidean distance and complex absolute value . . . . hypot(3)
eval: re-evaluate shell data. . . . . csh(1)
expr: evaluate arguments as an expression. . . . . expr(1)
operator: C operator precedence and order of evaluation. . . . . operator(7)
test: condition evaluation utility. . . . . test(1)
history: print history event list. . . . . csh(1)
ex, vi, view: text editors. . . . . vi(1)
lpq: spool queue examination program. . . . . lpq(1)
uuq: examine or manipulate the uucp queue. . . . . uuq(1)
isgraph: printing character test (space character exclusive). . . . . isgraph(3)
exec: overlay shell with specified command. . . . . csh(1)
execute a file. execl, execlp, execle, exect, execv, execvp: . . . . exec(3)
execl, execlp, execle, exect, execv, execvp: execute a file. . . . . exec(3)
file. execl, execlp, execle, exect, execv, execvp: execute a . . . . exec(3)
execl, execlp, execle, exect, execv, execvp: execute a file. . . . . exec(3)
a.out: format of executable binary files. . . . . a.out(5)
nlist: retrieve symbol table name list from an executable file. . . . . nlist(3)
strip: remove unnecessary information from executable files. strip(1)
gzexe: compress executable files in place. . . . . gzexe(1)
nice: execute a command at a low scheduling priority. . . . . . . nice(1)
execl, execlp, execle, exect, execv, execvp: execute a file. . . . . exec(3)
execve: execute a file. . . . . execve(2)
repeat: execute command repeatedly. . . . . csh(1)
xargs: construct argument list(s) and execute utility. . . . . xargs(1)
lastcomm: show last commands executed in reverse order. . . . . lastcomm(1)
time: time command execution. . . . . time(1)
uux: unix to unix command execution. . . . . uux(1)
acct: execution accounting file. . . . . acct(5)
uuxqt: UUCP execution file interpreter. . . . . uuxqt(8)
sleep: suspend execution for an interval of time. . . . . sleep(1)
usleep: suspend execution for interval of microseconds. . . . . usleep(3)
sleep: suspend process execution for interval of seconds. . . . . sleep(3)
at: schedule execution of commands 'at' a given time. . . . . at(1)
moncontrol, monstartup: control execution profile. moncontrol(3)
rexecd: remote execution server. . . . . rexecd(8)
execl, execlp, execle, exect, execv, execvp: execute a file. . . . . exec(3)
execve: execute a file. . . . . execve(2)
execl, execlp, execle, exect, execv, execvp: execute a file. . . . . exec(3)
dup, dup2: duplicate an existing file descriptor. . . . . dup(2)

tunefs: tune up an	existing file system.	tunefs(8)
atexit: register a function to be called on	exit.	atexit(3)
breaksw:	exit from switch.	csh(1)
	exit: leave shell.	csh(1)
	exit: perform normal program termination.	exit(3)
	_exit: terminate the calling process.	_exit(2)
break:	exit while/foreach loop.	csh(1)
logarithm, power functions.	exp, expm1, log, log10, log1p, pow: exponential,	exp(3)
glob: filename	expand argument list.	csh(1)
compress, uncompress, zcat: compress and	expand data.	compress(1)
gzip, gunzip, zcat: compress or	expand files.	gzip(1)
expand, unexpand:	expand tabs to spaces, and vice versa.	expand(1)
versa.	expand, unexpand: expand tabs to spaces, and vice	expand(1)
diction. diction.	explain: print wordy sentences; thesaurus for	diction(1)
adventure: an	exploration game.	adventure(6)
larn:	exploring the caverns of Larn.	larn(6)
hack:	exploring The Dungeons of Doom.	hack(6)
rogue:	exploring The Dungeons of Doom.	rogue(6)
logarithm, power functions. exp,	expm1, log, log10, log1p, pow: exponential,	exp(3)
exp, expm1, log, log10, log1p, pow:	exponential, logarithm, power functions.	exp(3)
requests.	exports: define remote mount points for NFS mount	exports(5)
	expr: evaluate arguments as an expression.	expr(1)
expr: evaluate arguments as an	expression.	expr(1)
search possibly compressed files for a regular	expression. zgrep:	zgrep(1)
re_comp, re_exec: regular	expression handler.	re_comp(3)
regcomp, regexec, regsub, regerror: regular	expression handlers.	regexp(3)
assert:	expression verification macro.	assert(3)
re_format: POSIX 1003.2 regular	expressions.	re_format(7)
zforce: force a '.gz'	extension on all gzip files.	zforce(1)
psbb:	extract bounding box from PostScript document.	psbb(1)
distribution center database. ext_srvtab:	extract service key files from Kerberos key	ext_srvtab(8)
floating-point number. modf:	extract signed integral and fractional values from	modf(3)
strings. xstr:	extract strings from C programs to implement shared	xstr(1)
yyfix:	extract tables from y.tab.c.	yyfix(1)
perl: practical	extraction and report language.	perl(1)
key distribution center database.	ext_srvtab: extract service key files from Kerberos	ext_srvtab(8)
	fabs: floating-point absolute value function.	fabs(3)
networking: introduction to networking	facilities.	netintro(4)
sigaction: software signal	facilities.	sigaction(2)
signal: simplified software signal	facilities.	signal(3)
sigvec: software signal	facilities.	sigvec(2)
factor, primes:	factor a number, generate primes.	factor(6)
	factor, primes: factor a number, generate primes.	factor(6)
crash: UNIX system	failures.	crash(8)
	false: return false value.	false(1)
false: return	false value.	false(1)
inet: Internet protocol	family.	inet(4)
iso: ISO protocol	family.	iso(4)
ns: Xerox Network Systems(tm) protocol	family.	ns(4)
unix: UNIX-domain protocol	family.	unix(4)
phantasia: an interterminal	fantasy game.	phantasia(6)
lex:	fast lexical analyzer generator.	lex(1)
checking the disks.	fastboot, fasthalt: reboot/halt the system without	fastboot(8)
the disks. fastboot,	fasthalt: reboot/halt the system without checking	fastboot(8)
chdir,	fchdir: change current working directory.	chdir(2)
chflags,	fchflags: set file flags.	chflags(2)
chmod,	fchmod: change mode of file.	chmod(2)
chown,	fchown: change owner and group of a file.	chown(2)
	fclose: close a stream.	fclose(3)
	fcntl: file control.	fcntl(2)
ecvt,	fcvt, gcvt: output conversion.	ecvt(3)
	fd, stdin, stdout, stderr: file descriptor files.	fd(4)
fopen,	fdopen, freopen: stream open functions.	fopen(3)
status. clearerr,	feof, ferror, fileno: check and reset stream	ferror(3)
clearerr, feof,	ferror, fileno: check and reset stream status.	ferror(3)
using a service key. ksrvtgt:	fetch and store Kerberos ticket-granting-ticket	ksrvtgt(1)
	fflush, fpurge: flush a stream.	fflush(3)
	ffs: find first bit set in a bit string.	ffs(3)
	fg: bring job into foreground.	csh(1)
word from input stream.	fgetc, getc, getchar, getw: get next character or	getc(3)
	fgetln: get a line from a stream.	fgetln(3)
a stream.	fgetpos, fseek, fsetpos, ftell, rewind: reposition	fseek(3)

fgets, gets: get a line from a stream. . . . . fgets(3)
mkfifo: make a   fifo file. . . . . mkfifo(2)
mkfifo: make   fifos. . . . . mkfifo(1)
robots: fight off villainous robots. . . . . robots(6)
acct: execution accounting   file. . . . . acct(5)
chmod, fchmod: change mode of   file. . . . . chmod(2)
chown, fchown: change owner and group of a   file. . . . . chown(2)
colrm: remove columns from a   file. . . . . colrm(1)
creat: create a new   file. . . . . creat(2)
crontab: chronological services schedule   file. . . . . crontab(5)
source: read commands from   file. . . . . csh(1)
ctags: create a tags   file. . . . . ctags(1)
cut: select portions of each line of a   file. . . . . cut(1)
dd: convert and copy a   file. . . . . dd(1)
disktab: disk description   file. . . . . disktab(5)
dm.conf: dm configuration   file. . . . . dm.conf(5)
execlp, execle, exect, execv, execvp: execute a   file. execl, ... exec(3)
execve: execute a   file. . . . . execve(2)
flock: apply or remove an advisory lock on an open   file. . . . . flock(2)
fpr: print Fortran   file. . . . . fpr(1)
group: format of the group permissions   file. . . . . group(5)
head: display first lines of a   file. . . . . head(1)
/etc/kerberosIV/krb.conf: Kerberos configuration   file. . . . . krb.conf(5)
host to Kerberos realm translation   file. /etc/kerberosIV/krb.realms: . . . . krb.realms(5)
L.aliases: UUCP hostname alias   file. . . . . L.aliases(5)
L.cmds: UUCP remote command permissions   file. . . . . L.cmds(5)
L-devices: UUCP device description   file. . . . . L-devices(5)
L-dialcodes: UUCP phone number index   file. . . . . L-dialcodes(5)
L.sys: UUCP remote host description   file. . . . . L.sys(5)
mkdir: make a directory   file. . . . . mkdir(2)
mkfifo: make a fifo   file. . . . . mkfifo(2)
mknod: build special   file. . . . . mknod(8)
rebuild the data base for the mail aliases   file. newaliases: . . . . newaliases(1)
retrieve symbol table name list from an executable   file. nlist: . . . . nlist(3)
passwd: format of the password   file. . . . . passwd(5)
rcsfile: format of RCS   file. . . . . rcsfile(5)
remote: remote host description   file. . . . . remote(5)
rename: change the name of a   file. . . . . rename(2)
resolver: resolver configuration   file. . . . . resolver(5)
rev: reverse lines of a   file. . . . . rev(1)
rmdir: remove a directory   file. . . . . rmdir(2)
strings: find printable strings in a   file. . . . . strings(1)
symlink: make symbolic link to a   file. . . . . symlink(2)
syslog.conf: syslogd(8) configuration   file. . . . . syslog.conf(5)
tail: display the last part of a   file. . . . . tail(1)
routines for manipulating a Kerberos ticket   file. /tf_get_pinst, tf_get_cred, tf_close: . . . . . . tf_util(3)
uniq: report or filter out repeated lines in a   file. . . . . uniq(1)
USERFILE: UUCP pathname permissions   file. . . . . USERFILE(5)
uuencode, uudecode: encode/decode a binary   file. . . . . uuencode(1)
uuencode: format of an encoded uuencode   file. . . . . uuencode.format(5)
vipw: edit the password   file. . . . . vipw(8)
versions of object modules were used to construct a   file. what: show what . . . . what(1)
revoke: revoke   file access. revoke(2)
touch: change   file access and modification times. . . . . touch(1)
utimes: set   file access and modification times. . . . . utimes(2)
diff: differential   file and directory comparator. . . . . diff(1)
pax: read and write   file archives and copy directory hierarchies. . . . . pax(1)
rcs: change RCS   file attributes. . . . . rcs(1)
bugfiler: file bug reports in folders automatically. . . . . . . bugfiler(8)
mkstr: create an error message   file by massaging C source. . . . . mkstr(1)
cksum: display   file checksums and block counts. . . . . cksum(1)
sum: calculate   file checksums and block counts. . . . . sum(1)
diff3: 3-way differential   file comparison. . . . . diff3(1)
file: identify   file content. file(1)
fcntl: file control. fcntl(2)
rcp: remote   file copy. . . . . rcp(1)
umask: change or display   file creation mask. . . . . csh(1)
umask: set   file creation mode mask. . . . . umask(2)
dup, dup2: duplicate an existing   file descriptor. . . . . dup(2)
ttyslot: get name of associated terminal (tty) from   file descriptor. ttyname, isatty, ... ttyname(3)
fd, stdin, stdout, stderr: file descriptor files. . . . . fd(4)
rdist: remote   file distribution program. . . . . rdist(1)

setsent, endfsent: get file system descriptor file entry. getfsent, getfsspec, getfsfile, ... getfsent(3)
getttynam, setttyent, endttyent: get ttys file entry. getttyent, ... getttyent(3)
chflags: change file flags. . . . . chflags(1)
chflags, fchflags: set file flags. . . . . chflags(2)
man.conf: configuration file for man(1). . . . . man.conf(5)
open: open or create a file for reading or writing. . . . . open(2)
aliases: aliases file for sendmail. . . . . aliases(5)
ar: archive (library) file format. . . . . ar.5(5)
core: memory image file format. . . . . core(5)
dir, dirent: directory file format. . . . . dir(5)
tar: tape archive file format. . . . . tarformat(5)
getfh: get file handle. . . . . getfh(2)
find: walk a file hierarchy. . . . . find(1)
fts: traverse a file hierarchy. . . . . fts(3)
file: identify file content. . . . . file(1)
which: locate a program file including aliases and paths. . . . . which(1)
uuxqt: UUCP execution file interpreter. . . . . uuxqt(8)
fsplit: split a multi-routine Fortran file into individual files. . . . . fsplit(1)
split: split a file into pieces. . . . . split(1)
link: make a hard file link. . . . . link(2)
merge: three-way file merge. . . . . merge(1)
chmod: change file modes. . . . . chmod(1)
krb_set_tkt_string: set Kerberos ticket cache file name. . . . . krb_set_tkt_string(3)
mktemp: make temporary file name (unique). . . . . mktemp(3)
mknod: make a special file node. . . . . mknod(2)
lseek: reposition read/write file offset. . . . . lseek(2)
access: check access permissions of a file or pathname. . . . . access(2)
random: random lines from a file or random numbers. . . . . random(6)
chown: change file owner and group. . . . . chown(8)
grep: file pattern searcher. . . . . grep(1)
more: file perusal filter for crt viewing. . . . . more(1)
text. zmore: file perusal filter for crt viewing of compressed . . . . . . zmore(1)
tempnam, tmpfile, tmpnam: temporary file routines. . . . . tmpnam(3)
size: display object file segment sizes (text, data and bss). . . . . size(1)
fstat: file status. . . . . fstat(1)
stat, lstat, fstat: get file status. . . . . stat(2)
lfs_cleanerd: garbage collect a log-structured file system. . . . . lfs_cleanerd(8)
mkproto: construct a prototype file system. . . . . mkproto(8)
mount_fdesc: mount the file-descriptor file system. . . . . mount_fdesc(8)
mount_kernfs: mount the /kern file system. . . . . mount_kernfs(8)
mount_lfs: mount a log-structured file system. . . . . mount_lfs(8)
mount_procfs: mount the process file system. . . . . mount_procfs(8)
newfs, mfs: construct a new file system. . . . . newfs(8)
newlfs: construct a new LFS file system. . . . . newlfs(8)
quot: display total block usage per user for a file system. . . . . quot(8)
repquota: summarize quotas for a file system. . . . . repquota(8)
tunefs: tune up an existing file system. . . . . tunefs(8)
fsdb: file system debugger. . . . . fsdb(8)
getfsspec, getfsfile, setfsent, endfsent: get file system descriptor file entry. getfsent, ... getfsent(3)
dumpfs: dump file system information. . . . . dumpfs(8)
dumplfs: dump file system information. . . . . dumplfs(8)
mount_null: demonstrate the use of a null file system layer. . . . . mount_null(8)
mount_umap: sample file system layer. . . . . mount_umap(8)
statfs: get file system statistics. . . . . statfs(2)
icheck: file system storage consistency check. . . . . icheck(8)
fs, inode: format of file system volume. . . . . fs(5)
amd: automatically mount file systems. . . . . amd(8)
getmntinfo: get information about mounted file systems. . . . . getmntinfo(3)
mount: mount file systems. . . . . mount(8)
mount_nfs: mount nfs file systems. . . . . mount_nfs(8)
umount: unmount file systems. . . . . umount(8)
restore: restore files or file systems from backups made with dump. . . . . restore(8)
utime: set file times. . . . . utime(3)
uusend: send a file to a remote host. . . . . uusend(1)
truncate, ftruncate: truncate a file to a specified length. . . . . truncate(2)
patch: a program for applying a diff file to an original. . . . . patch(1)
ftp: ARPANET file transfer program. . . . . ftp(1)
tftp: trivial file transfer program. . . . . tftp(1)
ftpd: Internet File Transfer Protocol server. . . . . ftpd(8)
tftpd: Internet Trivial File Transfer Protocol server. . . . . tftpd(8)
mount_fdesc: mount the file-descriptor file system. . . . . mount_fdesc(8)
glob: filename expand argument list. . . . . csh(1)

basename, dirname: return filename or directory portion of pathname. . . . . basename(1)
fnmatch: match filename or pathname. . , ... fnmatch(3)
clearerr, feof, ferror, fileno: check and reset stream status. . . . . ferror(3)
a.out: format of executable binary files. . . . . a.out(5)
cat: concatenate and print files. . . . . cat(1)
checknr: check nroff/troff files. . . . . checknr(1)
cmp: compare two files. . . . . cmp(1)
comm: select or reject lines common to two files. . . . . comm(1)
config: build system configuration files. . . . . config(8)
cp: copy files. . . . . cp(1)
fd, stdin, stdout, stderr: file descriptor files. . . . . fd(4)
split a multi-routine Fortran file into individual files. fsplit: . . . . fsplit(1)
format of groff device and font description files. groff_font: . . . . groff_font(5)
gzip, gunzip, zcat: compress or expand files. . . . . gzip(1)
ident: identify files. . . . . ident(1)
kvm_getfiles: survey open files. . . . . kvm_getfiles(3)
lam: laminate files. . . . . lam(1)
locate: find files. . . . . locate(1)
lorder: list dependencies for object files. . . . . lorder(1)
MAKEDEV: create system and device special files. . . . . MAKEDEV(8)
makedev: make system special files. . . . . makedev(8)
mklocale: make LC_CTYPE locale files. . . . . mklocale(1)
mv: move files. . . . . mv(1)
paste: merge corresponding or subsequent lines of files. . . . . paste(1)
pr: print files. . . . . pr(1)
rcsclean: clean up working files. . . . . rcsclean(1)
print log messages and other information about RCS files. rlog: . . . . rlog(1)
shar: create a shell archive of files. . . . . shar(1)
sort: sort or merge text files. . . . . sort(1)
remove unnecessary information from executable files. strip: . . . . strip(1)
zcmp, zdiff: compare compressed files. . . . . zdiff(1)
zforce: force a '.gz' extension on all gzip files. . . . . zforce(1)
znew: recompress .Z files to .gz files. . . . . znew(1)
compact, uncompact, ccat: compress and uncompress files, and cat them. . . . . compact(1)
intro: introduction to special files and hardware support. . . . . intro(4)
zgrep: search possibly compressed files for a regular expression. . . . . zgrep(1)
addftinfo: add information to troff font files for use with groff. . . . . addftinfo(1)
tfmtodit: create font files for use with groff −Tdvi. . . . . tfmtodit(1)
afmtodit: create font files for use with groff −Tps. . . . . afmtodit(1)
database. ext_srvtab: extract service key files from Kerberos key distribution center . . . . ext_srvtab(8)
gzexe: compress executable files in place. . . . . gzexe(1)
fsync: synchronize a file's in-core state with that on disk. . . . . fsync(2)
mmap: map files or devices into memory. . . . . mmap(2)
restore: restore files or file systems from backups made with dump. . . . . . restore(8)
uucico, uucpd: transfer files queued by uucp or uux. . . . . uucico(8)
badsect: create files to contain bad sectors. . . . . badsect(8)
znew: recompress .Z files to .gz files. . . . . znew(1)
mount, unmount: mount or dismount a filesystem. . . . . mount(2)
mount_cd9660: mount an ISO-9660 filesystem. . . . . mount_cd9660(8)
dump: filesystem backup. . . . . dump(8)
update: flush internal filesystem caches to disk frequently. . . . . update(8)
repair. fsck: filesystem consistency check and interactive . . . . . fsck(8)
getdirentries: get directory entries in a filesystem independent format. . . . . getdirentries(2)
fsinfo: co-ordinate site-wide filesystem information. . . . . fsinfo(8)
quotacheck: filesystem quota consistency checker. . . . . quotacheck(8)
quotactl: manipulate filesystem quotas. . . . . quotactl(2)
quotaon, quotaoff: turn filesystem quotas on and off. . . . . quotaon(8)
fstab: static information about the filesystems. . . . . fstab(5)
getfsstat: get list of all mounted filesystems. . . . . getfsstat(2)
hier: layout of filesystems. . . . . hier(7)
mount_union: mount union filesystems. . . . . mount_union(8)
more: file perusal filter for crt viewing. . . . . more(1)
zmore: file perusal filter for crt viewing of compressed text. . . . . zmore(1)
colcrt: filter nroff output for CRT previewing. . . . . colcrt(1)
uniq: report or filter out repeated lines in a file. . . . . uniq(1)
col: filter reverse line feeds from input. . . . . col(1)
plot: graphics filters. . . . . plot(1)
locate: find files. . . . . locate(1)
ffs: find first bit set in a bit string. . . . . ffs(3)
strlen: find length of string. . . . . strlen(3)
strings: find printable strings in a file. . . . . strings(1)
spell, spellin, spellout: find spelling errors. . . . . spell(1)

find: walk a file hierarchy. . . . . find(1)
finger: user information lookup program. . . . . finger(1)
fingerd: remote user information server. . . . . fingerd(8)
support. copysign, drem, finite, logb, scalb: IEEE 754 floating point . . . . ieee(3)
fold: fold long lines for finite width output device. . . . . fold(1)
j0, j1, jn, y0, y1, yn: bessel functions of first and second kind. . . . . j0(3)
ffs: find first bit set in a bit string. . . . . ffs(3)
head: display first lines of a file. . . . . head(1)
fish: play "Go Fish". . . . . fish(6)
fish: play "Go Fish". . . . . fish(6)
chflags: change file flags. . . . . chflags(1)
chflags, fchflags: set file flags. . . . . chflags(2)
copysign, drem, finite, logb, scalb: IEEE 754 floating point support. . . . . ieee(3)
fabs: floating-point absolute value function. . . . . fabs(3)
extract signed integral and fractional values from floating-point number. modf: . . . . modf(3)
ldexp: multiply floating-point number by integral power of 2. . . . . . . ldexp(3)
components. frexp: convert floating-point number to fractional and integral . . . . . frexp(3)
infnan: signals invalid floating-point operations on a VAX (temporary). . . . . . infnan(3)
fmod: floating-point remainder function. . . . . fmod(3)
file. flock: apply or remove an advisory lock on an open . . . . flock(2)
floor: largest integral value not greater than x. . . . . . . floor(3)
fflush, fpurge: flush a stream. fflush(3)
sync: force completion of pending disk writes (flush cache). . . . . sync(8)
frequently. update: flush internal filesystem caches to disk . . . . update(8)
mcmp, mdiv, min, mout, move, msqrt, msub, mult,/ fmin, fmout, gcd, invert, itom m_in, m_out, madd, ... mp(3)
fmod: floating-point remainder function. . . . . fmod(3)
mdiv, min, mout, move, msqrt, msub, mult,/ fmin, fmout, gcd, invert, itom m_in, m_out, madd, mcmp, ... mp(3)
fmt: simple text formatter. . . . . fmt(1)
fnmatch: match filename or pathname. . . . . fnmatch(3)
device. fold: fold long lines for finite width output . . . . fold(1)
fold: fold long lines for finite width output device. . . . . fold(1)
bugfiler: file bug reports in folders automatically. . . . . bugfiler(8)
groff_font: format of groff device and font description files. . . . . groff_font(5)
addftinfo: add information to troff font files for use with groff. . . . . addftinfo(1)
tfmtodit: create font files for use with groff -Tdvi. . . . . tfmtodit(1)
afmtodit: create font files for use with groff -Tps. . . . . afmtodit(1)
pfbtops: translate a PostScript font in .pfb format to ASCII. . . . . pfbtops(1)
fopen, fdopen, freopen: stream open functions. . . . . fopen(3)
zforce: force a '.gz' extension on all gzip files. . . . . zforce(1)
cache). sync: force completion of pending disk writes (flush . . . . . . sync(8)
foreach: loop over list of names. . . . . csh(1)
fg: bring job into foreground. . . . . csh(1)
tcgetpgrp: get foreground process group ID. . . . . tcgetpgrp(3)
tcsetpgrp: set foreground process group ID. . . . . tcsetpgrp(3)
fork: create a new process. . . . . fork(2)
a visual representation of data back to original form. unvis: revert . . . . unvis(1)
ar: archive (library) file format. . . . . ar.5(5)
core: memory image file format. . . . . core(5)
dir, dirent: directory file format. . . . . dir(5)
dump, dumpdates: incremental dump format. . . . . dump(5)
get directory entries in a filesystem independent format. getdirentries: . . . . getdirentries(2)
grodvi: convert groff output to TeX dvi format. . . . . grodvi(1)
groff_out: groff intermediate output format. . . . . groff_out(5)
ranlib: archive (library) table-of-contents format. . . . . ranlib.5(5)
tar: tape archive file format. . . . . tarformat(5)
vis: display non-printable characters in a visual format. . . . . vis(1)
indent: indent and format C program source. . . . . indent(1)
fscanf, sscanf, vscanf, vsscanf, vfscanf: input format conversion. scanf, ... scanf(3)
strftime: format date and time. . . . . strftime(3)
format: how to format disks and tapes. . . . . format(8)
troff: format documents. . . . . troff(1)
UTF2: Universal character set Transformation Format encoding of runes. . . . . utf2(4)
eqn: format equations for troff. . . . . eqn(1)
format: how to format disks and tapes. . . . . format(8)
uuencode: format of an encoded uuencode file. . . . . uuencode.format(5)
a.out: format of executable binary files. . . . . a.out(5)
fs, inode: format of file system volume. . . . . fs(5)
groff_font: format of groff device and font description files. . . . . . groff_font(5)
rcsfile: format of RCS file. . . . . rcsfile(5)
group: format of the group permissions file. . . . . group(5)
passwd: format of the password file. . . . . passwd(5)
scsiformat: format SCSI disks and show SCSI parameters. . . . . . . scsiformat(8)

tbl:	format tables for troff.	tbl(1)
pfbtops: translate a PostScript font in .pfb	format to ASCII.	pfbtops(1)
err, verr, errx, verrx, warn, vwarn, warnx, vwarnx:	formatted error messages.	err(3)
printf:	formatted output.	printf(1)
snprintf, vprintf, vfprintf, vsprintf, vsnprintf:	formatted output conversion. /fprintf, sprintf, ...	printf(3)
bib, listrefs, bibinc, bib2tib: bibliographic	formatter.	bib(1)
fmt: simple text	formatter.	fmt(1)
setlocale, localeconv: natural language	formatting for C.	setlocale(3)
ms: text	formatting macros.	ms(7)
me: macros for	formatting papers.	me(7)
groff: front end for the groff document	formatting system.	groff(1)
fpr: print	Fortran file.	fpr(1)
fsplit: split a multi-routine	Fortran file into individual files.	fsplit(1)
struct: structure	Fortran programs.	struct(1)
adage.	fortune: print a random, hopefully interesting, ...	fortune(6)
route: kernel packet	forwarding database.	route(4)
memccpy: copy string until character	found.	memccpy(3)
pathconf,	fpathconf: get configurable pathname variables.	pathconf(2)
	fpr: print Fortran file.	fpr(1)
vsprintf, vsnprintf: formatted output/ printf,	fprintf, sprintf, snprintf, vprintf, vfprintf, ...	printf(3)
fflush,	fpurge: flush a stream.	fflush(3)
word to a stream.	fputc, putc, putchar, putw: output a character or	putc(3)
	fputs, puts: output a line to a stream.	fputs(3)
frexp: convert floating-point number to	fractional and integral components.	frexp(3)
modf: extract signed integral and	fractional values from floating-point number.	modf(3)
bwtwo: monochromatic	frame buffer.	bwtwo(4)
cgsix: accelerated 8-bit color	frame buffer.	cgsix(4)
cgthree: 8-bit color	frame buffer.	cgthree(4)
grf: HP graphics	frame buffer device interface.	grf(4)
	fread, fwrite: binary stream input/output.	fread(3)
df: display	free disk space.	df(1)
or realloc.	free: free up memory allocated with malloc, calloc	free(3)
allocation operations. malloc,	free, realloc, calloc, alloca: general memory	memory(3)
realloc. free:	free up memory allocated with malloc, calloc or	free(3)
RCS. rcsfreeze:	freeze a configuration of sources checked in under	rcsfreeze(1)
fopen, fdopen,	freopen: stream open functions.	fopen(3)
update: flush internal filesystem caches to disk	frequently.	update(8)
and integral components.	frexp: convert floating-point number to fractional	frexp(3)
groff:	front end for the groff document formatting system. . . .	groff(1)
sccs:	front end for the SCCS subsystem.	sccs(1)
funopen,	fropen, fwopen: open a stream.	funopen(3)
	fs, inode: format of file system volume.	fs(5)
format conversion. scanf,	fscanf, sscanf, vscanf, vsscanf, vfscanf: input	scanf(3)
repair.	fsck: filesystem consistency check and interactive	fsck(8)
	fsdb: file system debugger.	fsdb(8)
fgetpos,	fseek, fsetpos, ftell, rewind: reposition a stream.	fseek(3)
fgetpos, fseek,	fsetpos, ftell, rewind: reposition a stream.	fseek(3)
information.	fsinfo: co-ordinate site-wide filesystem	fsinfo(8)
individual files.	fsplit: split a multi-routine Fortran file into	fsplit(1)
	fstab: static information about the filesystems.	fstab(5)
	fstat: file status.	fstat(1)
stat, lstat,	fstat: get file status.	stat(2)
on disk.	fsync: synchronize a file's in-core state with that	fsync(2)
fgetpos, fseek, fsetpos,	ftell, rewind: reposition a stream.	fseek(3)
	ftime: get date and time.	ftime(3)
	ftp: ARPANET file transfer program.	ftp(1)
	ftpd: Internet File Transfer Protocol server.	ftpd(8)
truncate,	ftruncate: truncate a file to a specified length.	truncate(2)
	fts: traverse a file hierarchy.	fts(3)
shutdown: shut down part of a	full-duplex connection.	shutdown(2)
tn3270:	full-screen remote login to IBM VM/CMS.	tn3270(1)
abs: integer absolute value	function.	abs(3)
acos: arc cosine	function.	acos(3)
acosh: inverse hyperbolic cosine	function.	acosh(3)
asin: arc sine	function.	asin(3)
asinh: inverse hyperbolic sine	function.	asinh(3)
atanh: inverse hyperbolic tangent	function.	atanh(3)
cos: cosine	function.	cos(3)
cosh: hyperbolic cosine	function.	cosh(3)
fabs: floating-point absolute value	function.	fabs(3)
fmod: floating-point remainder	function.	fmod(3)
lgamma gamma: log gamma function, gamma	function.	lgamma(3)

malloc,: general memory allocation function. . . . . malloc(3)
realloc: reallocation of memory function. . . . . realloc(3)
sin: sine function. . . . . sin(3)
sinh: hyperbolic sine function. . . . . sinh(3)
tan: tangent function. . . . . tan(3)
tanh: hyperbolic tangent .function. . . . . tanh(3)
valloc: aligned memory allocation function. . . . . valloc(3)
lgamma gamma: log gamma function, gamma function. . . . . lgamma(3)
atan: arc tangent function of one variable. . . . . atan(3)
atan2: arc tangent function of two variables. . . . . atan2(3)
erf, erfc: error function operators. . . . . erf(3)
atexit: register a function to be called on exit. . . . . atexit(3)
log10, log1p, pow: exponential, logarithm, power functions. exp, expm1, log, ... exp(3)
fopen, fdopen, freopen: stream open functions. . . . . fopen(3)
putenv, setenv, unsetenv: environment variable functions. getenv, ... getenv(3)
cabs: euclidean distance and complex absolute value functions. hypot, ... hypot(3)
math: introduction to mathematical library functions. . . . . math(3)
qsort, heapsort, mergesort: sort functions. . . . . qsort(3)
rint: round-to-closest integer functions. . . . . rint(3)
cbrt, sqrt: cube root and square root functions. . . . . sqrt(3)
stdio: standard input/output library functions. . . . . stdio(3)
tcsendbreak, tcdrain, tcflush, tcflow: line control functions. . . . . tcsendbreak(3)
j0, j1, jn, y0, y1, yn: bessel functions of first and second kind. . . . . j0(3)
curses: screen functions with "optimal" cursor motion. . . . . . . curses(3)
funopen, fropen, fwopen: open a stream. . . . . funopen(3)
funopen, fropen, fwopen: open a stream. . . . . funopen(3)
fread, fwrite: binary stream input/output. . . . . fread(3)
preliminary). cc, g++: GNU project C and C++ Compiler (v2 . . . . cc(1)
g++: GNU project C++ Compiler (v2 preliminary). . . . . . g++(1)
adventure: an exploration game. . . . . adventure(6)
atc: air traffic controller game. . . . . atc(6)
battlestar: a tropical adventure game. . . . . battlestar(6)
boggle: word search game. . . . . boggle(6)
hunt: a multi-player multi-terminal game. . . . . hunt(6)
huntd: hunt daemon, back-end for hunt game. . . . . huntd(6)
monop: Monopoly game. . . . . monop(6)
phantasia: an interterminal fantasy game. . . . . phantasia(6)
snake, snscore: display chase game. . . . . snake(6)
trek: trekkie game. . . . . trek(6)
worm: play the growing worm game. . . . . worm(6)
canfield, cfscores: the solitaire card game canfield. . . . . canfield(6)
cribbage: the card game cribbage. . . . . cribbage(6)
backgammon: the game of backgammon. . . . . backgammon(6)
hangman: the game of hangman. . . . . hangman(6)
tetris: the game of tetris. . . . . tetris(6)
lgamma gamma: log gamma function, gamma function. . . . . lgamma(3)
lgamma gamma: log gamma function, gamma function. . . . . lgamma(3)
lgamma gamma: log gamma function, gamma function. . . . . lgamma(3)
lfs_cleanerd: garbage collect a log-structured file system. . . . . . lfs_cleanerd(8)
gb: HP98700 "Gatorbox" device interface. . . . . gb(4)
gb: HP98700 "Gatorbox" device interface. . . . . gb(4)
min, mout, move, msqrt, msub, mult,/ fmin, fmout, gcd, invert, itom m_in, m_out, madd, mcmp, mdiv, mp(3)
gcore: get core images of running process. . . . . gcore(1)
ecvt, fcvt, gcvt: output conversion. . . . . ecvt(3)
gdb: the GNU debugger. . . . . gdb(1)
buffers. kgmon: generate a dump of the operating system's profile . . . . . kgmon(8)
make_keypair: generate Kerberos host key pair. . . . . make_keypair(8)
lptest: generate lineprinter ripple pattern. . . . . lptest(1)
ncheck: generate names from i-numbers. . . . . ncheck(8)
glob, globfree: generate pathnames matching a pattern. . . . . glob(3)
factor, primes: factor a number, generate primes. . . . . factor(6)
ctermid: generate terminal pathname. . . . . ctermid(3)
pwd_mkdb: generate the password databases. . . . . pwd_mkdb(8)
mh-gen: generating the MH system. . . . . mh-gen(8)
lex: fast lexical analyzer generator. . . . . lex(1)
rand, srand: bad random number generator. . . . . rand(3)
yacc: an LALR(1) parser generator. . . . . yacc(1)
/srandom, initstate, setstate: better random number generator; routines for changing generators. . . . . random(3)
random number generator; routines for changing generators. /srandom, initstate, setstate: better . . . . . random(3)
getdiskbyname: get generic disk description by its name. . . . . getdiskbyname(3)
getbsize: get user block size. . . . . getbsize(3)
from input stream. fgetc, getc, getchar, getw: get next character or word . . . . getc(3)

input stream. fgetc, getc,	getchar, getw: get next character or word from	getc(3)
	getcwd: get working directory pathname.	getcwd(3)
filesystem independent format.	getdirentries: get directory entries in a	getdirentries(2)
name.	getdiskbyname: get generic disk description by its	getdiskbyname(3)
	getdtablesize: get descriptor table size.	getdtablesize(2)
getgid,	getegid: get group process identification.	getgid(2)
variable functions.	getenv, putenv, setenv, unsetenv: environment	getenv(3)
getuid,	geteuid: get user identification.	getuid(2)
	getfh: get file handle.	getfh(2)
get file system descriptor file entry.	getfsent, getfsspec, getfsfile, setfsent, endfsent:	getfsent(3)
descriptor file entry. getfsent, getfsspec,	getfsfile, setfsent, endfsent: get file system	getfsent(3)
system descriptor file entry. getfsent,	getfsspec, getfsfile, setfsent, endfsent: get file	getfsent(3)
	getfsstat: get list of all mounted filesystems.	getfsstat(2)
	getgid, getegid: get group process identification.	getgid(2)
setgrfile, setgrent, endgrent: group database/	getgrent, getgrnam, getgrgid, setgroupent, .Nm	getgrent(3)
endgrent: group database/ getgrent, getgrnam,	getgrgid, setgroupent, .Nm setgrfile, setgrent,	getgrent(3)
setgrent, endgrent: group database/ getgrent,	getgrnam, getgrgid, setgroupent, .Nm setgrfile,	getgrent(3)
	getgrouplist: calculate group access list.	getgrouplist(3)
	getgroups: get group access list.	getgroups(2)
herror: get network host entry. gethostbyname,	gethostbyaddr, gethostent, sethostent, endhostent,	gethostbyname(3)
sethostent, endhostent, herror: get network host/	gethostbyname, gethostbyaddr, gethostent,	gethostbyname(3)
network host entry. gethostbyname, gethostbyaddr,	gethostent, sethostent, endhostent, herror: get	gethostbyname(3)
current host.	gethostid, sethostid: get/set unique identifier of	gethostid(3)
host.	gethostname, sethostname: get/set name of current	gethostname(3)
timer.	getitimer, setitimer: get/set value of interval	getitimer(2)
	getloadavg: get system load averages.	getloadavg(3)
	getlogin, setlogin: get/set login name.	getlogin(2)
systems.	getmntinfo: get information about mounted file	getmntinfo(3)
	getmntopts: scan mount options.	getmntopts(3)
	getmode, setmode: modify mode bits.	setmode(3)
get network entry. getnetent,	getnetbyaddr, getnetbyname, setnetent, endnetent:	getnetent(3)
entry. getnetent, getnetbyaddr,	getnetbyname, setnetent, endnetent: get network	getnetent(3)
endnetent: get network entry.	getnetent, getnetbyaddr, getnetbyname, setnetent,	getnetent(3)
netgroup database operations.	getnetgrent, innetgr, setnetgrent, endnetgrent:	getnetgrent(3)
argument list.	getopt: get option character from command line	getopt(3)
	getpagesize: get system page size.	getpagesize(3)
	getpass: get a password.	getpass(3)
	getpeername: get name of connected peer.	getpeername(2)
	getpgrp: get process group.	getpgrp(2)
identification.	getpid, getppid: get parent or calling process	getpid(2)
identification. getpid,	getppid: get parent or calling process	getpid(2)
scheduling priority.	getpriority, setpriority: get/set program	getpriority(2)
protocol entry. getprotobyname, getprotobynumber,	getprotoent, setprotoent, endprotoent: get	getprotoent(3)
endprotoent: get protocol entry. getprotoent,	getprotobynumber, getprotobyname, setprotoent,	getprotoent(3)
setprotoent, endprotoent: get protocol entry.	getprotoent, getprotobynumber, getprotobyname,	getprotoent(3)
	getpw: get name from uid.	getpw(3)
endpwent: password database operations.	getpwent, getpwnam, getpwuid, setpassent, setpwent,	getpwent(3)
password database operations. getpwent,	getpwnam, getpwuid, setpassent, setpwent, endpwent:	getpwent(3)
database operations. getpwent, getpwnam,	getpwuid, setpassent, setpwent, endpwent: password	getpwent(3)
resource consumption.	getrlimit, setrlimit: control maximum system	getrlimit(2)
utilization.	getrusage: get information about resource	getrusage(2)
fgets,	gets: get a line from a stream.	fgets(3)
entry. getservent, getservbyport,	getservbyname, setservent, endservent: get service	getservent(3)
endservent: get service entry. getservent,	getservbyport, getservbyname, setservent,	getservent(3)
setservent, endservent: get service entry.	getservent, getservbyport, getservbyname,	getservent(3)
gettimeofday, settimeofday:	get/set date and time.	gettimeofday(2)
getlogin, setlogin:	get/set login name.	getlogin(2)
gethostname, sethostname:	get/set name of current host.	gethostname(3)
getpriority, setpriority:	get/set program scheduling priority.	getpriority(2)
gethostid, sethostid:	get/set unique identifier of current host.	gethostid(3)
getitimer, setitimer:	get/set value of interval timer.	getitimer(2)
	getsockname: get socket name.	getsockname(2)
sockets.	getsockopt, setsockopt: get and set options on	getsockopt(2)
	getsubopt: get sub options from an argument.	getsubopt(3)
	gettimeofday, settimeofday: get/set date and time.	gettimeofday(2)
ttys file entry.	getttyent, getttynam, setttyent, endttyent: get	getttyent(3)
entry. getttyent,	getttynam, setttyent, endttyent: get ttys file	getttyent(3)
	getty: set terminal mode.	getty(8)
	gettytab: terminal configuration data base.	gettytab(5)
	getuid, geteuid: get user identification.	getuid(2)
user shells.	getusershell, setusershell, endusershell: get legal	getusershell(3)
fgetc, getc, getchar,	getw: get next character or word from input stream.	getc(3)

madvise:	give advise about use of memory.	madvise(2)
look: display lines beginning with a	given string.	look(1)
at: schedule execution of commands 'at' a	given time.	at(1)
shutdown: close down the system at a	given time.	shutdown(8)
	glob: filename expand argument list.	csh(1)
pattern.	glob, globfree: generate pathnames matching a	glob(3)
glob,	globfree: generate pathnames matching a pattern.	glob(3)
and time value to ASCII. asctime, ctime, difftime,	gmtime, localtime, mktime: transform binary date	ctime(3)
cccp, cpp: the	GNU C-compatible compiler preprocessor.	cpp(1)
chess:	GNU chess.	chess(6)
gdb: the	GNU debugger.	gdb(1)
cc, g++:	GNU project C and C++ Compiler (v2 preliminary).	cc(1)
g++:	GNU project C++ Compiler (v2 preliminary).	g++(1)
emacs:	GNU project Emacs.	emacs(1)
fish: play	"Go Fish".	fish(6)
	goto: command transfer.	csh(1)
	gprof: display call graph profile data.	gprof(1)
graph: draw a	graph.	graph(1)
tsort: topological sort of a directed	graph.	tsort(1)
	graph: draw a graph.	graph(1)
gprof: display call	graph profile data.	gprof(1)
plot:	graphics filters.	plot(1)
grf: HP	graphics frame buffer device interface.	grf(4)
arc, move, cont, point, linemod, space, closepl:	graphics interface. /erase, label, line, circle,	plot(3)
plot:	graphics interface.	plot(5)
ceil: smallest integral value not	greater than x.	ceil(3)
floor: largest integral value not	greater than x.	floor(3)
	grep: file pattern searcher.	grep(1)
	grf: HP graphics frame buffer device interface.	grf(4)
vgrind:	grind nice listings of programs.	vgrind(1)
	grodvi: convert groff output to TeX dvi format.	grodvi(1)
add information to troff font files for use with	groff. addftinfo:	addftinfo(1)
grops: PostScript driver for	groff.	grops(1)
nroff: emulate nroff command with	groff.	nroff(1)
refer: preprocess bibliographic references for	groff.	refer(1)
groff_char:	groff character names.	groff_char(7)
grog: guess options for	groff command.	grog(1)
groff_font: format of	groff device and font description files.	groff_font(5)
groff: front end for the	groff document formatting system.	groff(1)
grotty:	groff driver for typewriter-like devices.	grotty(1)
system.	groff: front end for the groff document formatting	groff(1)
groff_out:	groff intermediate output format.	groff_out(5)
mm:	groff mm macros.	mm(7)
grodvi: convert	groff output to TeX dvi format.	grodvi(1)
tfmtodit: create font files for use with	groff -Tdvi.	tfmtodit(1)
afmtodit: create font files for use with	groff -Tps.	afmtodit(1)
	groff_char: groff character names.	groff_char(7)
description files.	groff_font: format of groff device and font	groff_font(5)
	groff_out: groff intermediate output format.	groff_out(5)
	grog: guess options for groff command.	grog(1)
	grops: PostScript driver for groff.	grops(1)
	grotty: groff driver for typewriter-like devices.	grotty(1)
chgrp: change	group.	chgrp(1)
chown: change file owner and	group.	chown(8)
getpgrp: get process	group.	getpgrp(2)
killpg: send signal to a process	group.	killpg(2)
setpgid, setpgrp: set process	group.	setpgid(2)
getgrouplist: calculate	group access list.	getgrouplist(3)
getgroups: get	group access list.	getgroups(2)
initgroups: initialize	group access list.	initgroups(3)
setgroups: set	group access list.	setgroups(2)
setgroupent, .Nm setgrfile, setgrent, endgrent:	group database operations. /getgrnam, getgrgid,	getgrent(3)
pwcache: cache password and	group entries.	pwcache(3)
	group: format of the group permissions file.	group(5)
setregid: set real and effective	group ID.	setregid(2)
setruid, setrgid: set user and	group ID.	setruid(3)
setsid: create session and set process	group ID.	setsid(2)
setuid, seteuid, setgid, setegid,: set user and	group ID.	setuid(2)
tcgetpgrp: get foreground process	group ID.	tcgetpgrp(3)
tcsetpgrp: set foreground process	group ID.	tcsetpgrp(3)
groups: show	group memberships.	groups(1)
chown, fchown: change owner and	group of a file.	chown(2)

group: format of the   group permissions file. . . . .   group(5)
getgid, getegid: get   group process identification. . . . .   getgid(2)
netgroup: defines network   groups.   netgroup(5)
                         groups: show group memberships. . . . .   groups(1)
worm: play the   growing worm game. . . . .   worm(6)
stty,   gtty: set and get terminal state (defunct). . . . . .   stty(3)
grog: guess options for groff command. . . . .   grog(1)
mdoc: quick reference   guide for the −mdoc macro package. . . . .   mdoc(7)
gzip,   gunzip, zcat: compress or expand files. . . . . . .   gzip(1)
zforce: force a   '.gz' extension on all gzip files. . . . .   zforce(1)
zforce: force a '.   gz' extension on all gzip files. . . . .   zforce(1)
znew: recompress .Z files to .   gz files.   znew(1)
                         gzexe: compress executable files in place. . . . .   gzexe(1)
zforce: force a '.gz' extension on all   gzip files. . . . .   zforce(1)
                         gzip, gunzip, zcat: compress or expand files. . . . . .   gzip(1)
                         hack: exploring The Dungeons of Doom. . . . .   hack(6)
stop: halt a job or process. . . . .   csh(1)
reboot: reboot system or   halt processor. . . . .   reboot(2)
reboot,   halt: stopping and restarting the system. . . . . . .   reboot(8)
getfh: get file   handle. . . . .   getfh(2)
rmail: handle remote mail received via uucp. . . . . .   rmail(8)
ansitape: ANSI standard tape   handler.   ansitape(1)
mh: Message   Handler.   mh(1)
re_comp, re_exec: regular expression   handler.   re_comp(3)
regexec, regsub, regerror: regular expression   handlers. regcomp, ...   regexp(3)
symlink: symbolic link   handling.   symlink(7)
hangman: the game of   hangman. . . . .   hangman(6)
                         hangman: the game of hangman. . . . .   hangman(6)
nohup: run command immune to   hangups.   csh(1)
nohup: invoke a command immune to   hangups.   nohup(1)
link: make a   hard file link. . . . .   link(2)
intro: introduction to special files and   hardware support. . . . .   intro(4)
hash: hash database access method. . . . .   hash(3)
                         hash: hash database access method. . . . .   hash(3)
rehash: recompute command   hash table. . . . .   csh(1)
unhash: discard command   hash table. . . . .   csh(1)
hashstat: print command   hashing statistics. . . . .   csh(1)
                         hashstat: print command hashing statistics. . . . . . .   csh(1)
from: print names of those who   have sent mail. . . . .   from(1)
leave: remind you when you   have to leave. . . . .   leave(1)
qsort,   heapsort, mergesort: sort functions. . . . . . .   qsort(3)
klist: list currently   held Kerberos tickets. . . . .   klist(1)
vacation: return "I am not   here" indication. . . . .   vacation(1)
gethostbyaddr, gethostent, sethostent, endhostent,   herror: get network host entry. gethostbyname, ...   gethostbyname(3)
od: octal, decimal,   hex, ascii dump. . . . .   od(1)
ascii: octal,   hexadecimal and decimal ASCII character sets. . . . . . .   ascii(7)
.hexdump: ascii, decimal,   hexadecimal, octal dump. . . . .   hexdump(1)
isxdigit: hexadecimal-digit character test. . . . .   isxdigit(3)
                         hexdump: ascii, decimal, hexadecimal, octal dump. . . . . .   hexdump(1)
xroach: cockroaches   hide under your windows. . . . .   xroach(6)
                         hier: layout of filesystems. . . . .   hier(7)
read and write file archives and copy directory   hierarchies. pax: . . . .   pax(1)
find: walk a file   hierarchy.   find(1)
fts: traverse a file   hierarchy.   fts(3)
mtree: map a directory   hierarchy.   mtree(8)
                         hil: Human Interface Link device driver. . . . . .   hil(4)
history: print   history event list. . . . .   csh(1)
                         history: print history event list. . . . .   csh(1)
fortune: print a random,   hopefully interesting, adage. . . . .   fortune(6)
sethostid: get/set unique identifier of current   host. gethostid, ...   gethostid(3)
gethostname, sethostname: get/set name of current   host. . . . .   gethostname(3)
showmount: show remote nfs mounts on   host. . . . .   showmount(8)
traceroute: print the route packets take to network   host. . . . .   traceroute(8)
uusend: send a file to a remote   host. . . . .   uusend(1)
htonl, htons, ntohl, ntohs: convert values between   host and network byte order. . . . .   byteorder(3)
L.sys: UUCP remote   host description file. . . . .   L.sys(5)
remote: remote   host description file. . . . .   remote(5)
sethostent, endhostent, herror: get network   host entry. /gethostbyaddr, gethostent, ...   gethostbyname(3)
make_keypair: generate Kerberos   host key pair. . . . .   make_keypair(8)
hosts: host name data base. . . . .   hosts(5)
hostname: host name resolution description. . . . .   hostname(7)
rhost: look up   host names using domain server. . . . .   host(1)

phones: remote	host phone number data base.	phones(5)
ruptime: show	host status of local machines.	ruptime(1)
hostname: set or print name of current	host system.	hostname(1)
/etc/kerberosIV/krb.realms:	host to Kerberos realm translation file.	krb.realms(5)
L.aliases: UUCP	hostname alias file.	L.aliases(5)
	hostname: host name resolution description.	hostname(7)
	hostname: set or print name of current host system.	hostname(1)
ping: send ICMP ECHO_REQUEST packets to network	hosts.	ping(8)
uuname: list names of UUCP	hosts.	uuname(1)
	hosts: host name data base.	hosts(5)
uptime: show	how long system has been running.	uptime(1)
format:	how to format disks and tapes.	format(8)
dcl:	HP 98628A communications link.	dcl(4)
dcm:	HP 98642A communications multiplexer.	dcm(4)
dca:	HP 98644A communications interface.	dca(4)
le:	HP AMD 7990 LANCE Ethernet interface.	le(4)
grf:	HP graphics frame buffer device interface.	grf(4)
ite:	HP Internal Terminal Emulator.	ite(4)
rbootd:	HP remote boot server.	rbootd(8)
cons:	HP300 console interface.	cons(4)
interface. tc:	HP98544 98550 ''Topcat'' and ''Catseye'' device	tc(4)
gb:	HP98700 ''Gatorbox'' device interface.	gb(4)
rb:	HP98720 ''Renaissance'' device interface.	rb(4)
dv:	HP98730 ''DaVinci'' device interface.	dv(4)
ppi:	HP-IB printer/plotter interface.	ppi(4)
host and network byte order.	htonl, htons, ntohl, ntohs: convert values between	byteorder(3)
and network byte order. htonl,	htons, ntohl, ntohs: convert values between host	byteorder(3)
hil:	Human Interface Link device driver.	hil(4)
	hunt: a multi-player multi-terminal game.	hunt(6)
	hunt daemon, back-end for hunt game.	huntd(6)
huntd: hunt daemon, back-end for	hunt game.	huntd(6)
wump:	hunt the wumpus in an underground cave.	wump(6)
	huntd: hunt daemon, back-end for hunt game.	huntd(6)
acosh: inverse	hyperbolic cosine function.	acosh(3)
cosh:	hyperbolic cosine function.	cosh(3)
asinh: inverse	hyperbolic sine function.	asinh(3)
sinh:	hyperbolic sine function.	sinh(3)
atanh: inverse	hyperbolic tangent function.	atanh(3)
tanh:	hyperbolic tangent function.	tanh(3)
absolute value functions.	hypot, cabs: euclidean distance and complex	hypot(3)
vacation: return	''I am not here'' indication.	vacation(1)
mset: retrieve ASCII to	IBM 3270 keyboard map.	mset(1)
map3270: database for mapping ascii keystrokes into	IBM 3270 keys.	map3270(5)
tn3270: full-screen remote login to	IBM VM/CMS.	tn3270(1)
	icheck: file system storage consistency check.	icheck(8)
ping: send	ICMP ECHO_REQUEST packets to network hosts.	ping(8)
	icmp: Internet Control Message Protocol.	icmp(4)
setregid: set real and effective group	ID.	setregid(2)
setruid, setrgid: set user and group	ID.	setruid(3)
setsid: create session and set process group	ID.	setsid(2)
seteuid, setgid, setegid,: set user and group	ID. setuid, ...	setuid(2)
tcgetpgrp: get foreground process group	ID.	tcgetpgrp(3)
tcsetpgrp: set foreground process group	ID.	tcsetpgrp(3)
whoami: display effective user	id.	whoami(1)
	id: return user identity.	id(1)
	ident: identify files.	ident(1)
getgid, getegid: get group process	identification.	getgid(2)
getpid, getppid: get parent or calling process	identification.	getpid(2)
getuid, geteuid: get user	identification.	getuid(2)
uname: get system	identification.	uname(3)
gethostid, sethostid: get/set unique	identifier of current host.	gethostid(3)
file:	identify file content.	file(1)
ident:	identify files.	ident(1)
id: return user	identity.	id(1)
su: substitute user	identity.	su(1)
	idp: Xerox Internet Datagram Protocol.	idp(4)
setreuid: set real and effective user	ID's.	setreuid(2)
copysign, drem, finite, logb, scalb:	IEEE 754 floating point support.	ieee(3)
	if: conditional statement.	csh(1)
biff: be notified	if mail arrives and who it is from.	biff(1)
	ifconfig: configure network interface parameters.	ifconfig(8)
unifdef: remove	ifdef'ed lines.	unifdef(1)

strcasecmp: compare strings, ignoring case. . . . . strcasecmp(3)
pig: eformatray inputway asway Igpay Atinlay. pig(6)
retrieve symbol table names from a kernel image. kvm_nlist: . . . . kvm_nlist(3)
core: memory image file format. . . . . core(5)
end, etext, edata: end boundaries of image segments. . . . . end(3)
gcore: get core images of running process. . . . . gcore(1)
notify: request immediate notification. . . . . csh(1)
nohup: run command immune to hangups. . . . . csh(1)
nohup: invoke a command immune to hangups. . . . . nohup(1)
xstr: extract strings from C programs to implement shared strings. . . . . xstr(1)
named-xfer: ancillary agent for inbound zone transfers. . . . . named-xfer(8)
which: locate a program file including aliases and paths. . . . . which(1)
isprint: printing character test (space character inclusive). . . . . isprint(3)
fsync: synchronize a file's in-core state with that on disk. . . . . fsync(2)
sync: synchronize disk block in-core status with that on disk. . . . . sync(2)
dump, dumpdates: incremental dump format. . . . . dump(5)
indent: indent and format C program source. . . . . indent(1)
indent: indent and format C program source. . . . . indent(1)
get directory entries in a filesystem independent format. getdirentries: . . . . getdirentries(2)
tgetnum, tgetflag, tgetstr, tgoto, tputs: terminal independent operation routines. tgetent, ... termcap(3)
invert, lookup: create and access an inverted index. . . . . invert(1)
ptx: permuted index. . . . . ptx(1)
L-dialcodes: UUCP phone number index file. . . . . L-dialcodes(5)
indxbib: make inverted index for bibliographic databases. . . . . indxbib(1)
index: locate character in string. . . . . index(3)
strpbrk, strsep, strspn, strcspn, strstr, strtok, index, rindex: string specifi /strerror, strlen, ... string(3)
last: indicate last logins of users and ttys. . . . . last(1)
vacation: return "I am not here" indication. . . . . vacation(1)
syscall, __syscall: indirect system call. . . . . syscall(2)
fsplit: split a multi-routine Fortran file into individual files. . . . . fsplit(1)
databases. indxbib: make inverted index for bibliographic . . . . indxbib(1)
inet: Internet protocol family. . . . . inet(4)
inet_lnaof, inet_netof: Internet/ inet_aton, inet_addr, inet_network, inet_ntoa, inet_makeaddr, ... inet(3)
inet_makeaddr, inet_lnaof, inet_netof: Internet/ inet_aton, inet_addr, inet_network, inet_ntoa, ... inet(3)
inetd: internet super-server. . . . . inetd(8)
/inet_addr, inet_network, inet_ntoa, inet_makeaddr, inet_lnaof, inet_netof: Internet address/ . . . . inet(3)
inet_aton, inet_addr, inet_network, inet_ntoa, inet_makeaddr, inet_lnaof, inet_netof: Internet/ . . . . inet(3)
/inet_network, inet_ntoa, inet_makeaddr, inet_lnaof, inet_netof: Internet address manipulation routines. . . . . inet(3)
inet_netof: Internet address/ inet_aton, inet_addr, inet_network, inet_ntoa, inet_makeaddr, inet_lnaof, ... inet(3)
Internet/ inet_aton, inet_addr, inet_network, inet_ntoa, inet_makeaddr, inet_lnaof, inet_netof: . . . . . inet(3)
isinf, isnan: test for infinity or not-a-number. . . . . isinf(3)
on a VAX (temporary). infnan: signals invalid floating-point operations . . . . . infnan(3)
bad144: read/write dec standard 144 bad sector information. . . . . bad144(8)
chpass: add or change user database information. . . . . chpass(1)
dumpfs: dump file system information. . . . . dumpfs(8)
dumplfs: dump file system information. . . . . dumplfs(8)
fsinfo: co-ordinate site-wide filesystem information. . . . . fsinfo(8)
pac: printer/plotter accounting information. . . . . pac(8)
sysctl: get or set system information. . . . . sysctl(3)
ttys: terminal initialization information. . . . . ttys(5)
tzfile: time zone information. . . . . tzfile(5)
tzset, tzsetwall: initialize time conversion information. . . . . tzset(3)
getmntinfo: get information about mounted file systems. . . . . . getmntinfo(3)
rlog: print log messages and other information about RCS files. . . . . rlog(1)
getrusage: get information about resource utilization. . . . . getrusage(2)
vtimes: get information about resource utilization. . . . . vtimes(3)
fstab: static information about the filesystems. . . . . fstab(5)
uname: display information about the system. . . . . uname(1)
strip: remove unnecessary information from executable files. . . . . strip(1)
strmode: convert inode status information into a symbolic string. . . . . strmode(3)
finger: user information lookup program. . . . . finger(1)
intro: miscellaneous information pages. . . . . intro(7)
XNSrouted: NS Routing Information Protocol daemon. . . . . XNSrouted(8)
fingerd: remote user information server. . . . . fingerd(8)
addftinfo: add information to troff font files for use with groff. . . . . . addftinfo(1)
init: process control initialization. . . . . init(8)
initgroups: initialize group access list. . . . . initgroups(3)
init: process control initialization. . . . . init(8)
tset: terminal initialization. . . . . tset(1)
ttys: terminal initialization information. . . . . ttys(5)
initgroups: initialize group access list. . . . . initgroups(3)
database. kdb_init: initialize Kerberos key distribution center . . . . kdb_init(8)

kvm_open, kvm_openfiles, kvm_close: initialize kernel virtual memory access. . . . . kvm_open(3)
tzset, tzsetwall: initialize time conversion information. . . . . tzset(3)
calloc: allocate clean memory (zero initialized space). calloc(3)
connect: initiate a connection on a socket. . . . . connect(2)
generator; routines for changing/ random, srandom, initstate, setstate: better random number . . . . random(3)
database operations. getnetgrent, innetgr, setnetgrent, endnetgrent: netgroup . . . . getnetgrent(3)
clri: clear an inode. . . . . clri(8)
fs, inode: format of file system volume. . . . . fs(5)
strmode: convert inode status information into a symbolic string. . . . . strmode(3)
col: filter reverse line feeds from input. . . . . col(1)
read, readv: read input. . . . . read(2)
soelim: eliminate .so's from nroff input. . . . . soelim(1)
bcd, ppt, morse: reformat input as punch cards, paper tape or morse code. . . . . bcd(6)
scanf, fscanf, sscanf, vscanf, vsscanf, vfscanf: input format conversion. . . . . scanf(3)
getchar, getw: get next character or word from input stream. fgetc, getc, ... getc(3)
ungetc: un-get character from input stream. . . . . ungetc(3)
fread, fwrite: binary stream input/output. . . . . fread(3)
stdio: standard input/output library functions. . . . . stdio(3)
pig: eformatray inputway asway Igpay Atinlay. . . . . pig(6)
insque, remque: insert/remove element from a queue. . . . . insque(3)
insque, remque: insert/remove element from a queue. . . . . insque(3)
install: install binaries. . . . . install(1)
install: install binaries. . . . . install(1)
learn: computer aided instruction about. . . . . learn(1)
number. modf: extract signed integral and fractional values from floating-point . . . . . . modf(3)
convert floating-point number to fractional and integral components. frexp: . . . . frexp(3)
ldexp: multiply floating-point number by integral power of 2. . . . . ldexp(3)
ceil: smallest integral value not greater than x. . . . . ceil(3)
floor: largest integral value not greater than x. . . . . floor(3)
fsck: filesystem consistency check and interactive repair. . . . . fsck(8)
nslookup: query Internet name servers interactively. . . . . nslookup(8)
network address conversion routines for Open System Interconnection. iso_addr, iso_ntoa: elementary . . . . . iso_addr(3)
fortune: print a random, hopefully interesting, adage. . . . . fortune(6)
cons: HP300 console interface. . . . . cons(4)
ct: CS/80 cartridge tape interface. . . . . ct(4)
dca: HP 98644A communications interface. . . . . dca(4)
dv: HP98730 "DaVinci" device interface. . . . . dv(4)
gb: HP98700 "Gatorbox" device interface. . . . . gb(4)
grf: HP graphics frame buffer device interface. . . . . grf(4)
kvm: kernel memory interface. . . . . : . . . . kvm(3)
le: HP AMD 7990 LANCE Ethernet interface. . . . . le(4)
le: SPARC AMD 7990 LANCE ethernet interface. . . . . le(4)
lo: software loopback network interface. . . . . lo(4)
openprom: OPENPROM and EEPROM interface. . . . . openprom(4)
cont, point, linemod, space, closepl: graphics interface. /erase, label, line, circle, arc, move, ... plot(3)
plot: graphics interface. . . . . plot(5)
ppi: HP-IB printer/plotter interface. . . . . ppi(4)
rb: HP98720 "Renaissance" device interface. . . . . rb(4)
rd: CS/80 disk interface. . . . . rd(4)
sliplogin: attach a serial line network interface. . . . . sliplogin(8)
stty: set the options for a terminal device interface. . . . . stty(1)
HP98544 98550 "Topcat" and "Catseye" device interface. tc: . . . . tc(4)
tput: terminal capability interface. . . . . tput(1)
tty: general terminal interface. . . . . tty(4)
nsip: software network interface encapsulating NS packets in IP packets. . . . . . . nsip(4)
hil: Human Interface Link device driver. . . . . hil(4)
ifconfig: configure network interface parameters. . . . . ifconfig(8)
telnet: user interface to the TELNET protocol. . . . . telnet(1)
slattach: attach serial lines as network interfaces. . . . . slattach(8)
swapon: add a swap device for interleaved paging/swapping. . . . . swapon(2)
groff_out: groff intermediate output format. . . . . groff_out(5)
es-is: End System to Intermediate System Routing Protocol. . . . . esis(4)
update: flush internal filesystem caches to disk frequently. . . . . update(8)
ite: HP Internal Terminal Emulator. . . . . ite(4)
sendmail: send mail over the internet. . . . . sendmail(8)
/inet_ntoa, inet_makeaddr, inet_lnaof, inet_netof: Internet address manipulation routines. . . . . inet(3)
icmp: Internet Control Message Protocol. . . . . icmp(4)
idp: Xerox Internet Datagram Protocol. . . . . idp(4)
named: Internet domain name server. . . . . named(8)
ftpd: Internet File Transfer Protocol server. . . . . ftpd(8)
nslookup: query Internet name servers interactively. . . . . nslookup(8)
ip: Internet Protocol. . . . . ip(4)

inet: Internet protocol family. . . . .   inet(4)
inetd: internet super-server. . . . .   inetd(8)
tcp: Internet Transmission Control Protocol. . . . .   tcp(4)
tftpd: Internet Trivial File Transfer Protocol server. . . . .   tftpd(8)
udp: Internet User Datagram Protocol. . . . .   udp(4)
whois: Internet user name directory service. . . . .   whois(1)
spline: interpolate smooth curve. . . . .   spline(1)
uuxqt: UUCP execution file interpreter. . . . .   uuxqt(8)
sh: command interpreter (shell). . . . .   sh(1)
csh: a shell (command interpreter) with C-like syntax. . . . .   csh(1)
pipe: create descriptor pair for interprocess communication. . . . .   pipe(2)
atomically release blocked signals and wait for interrupt. sigpause: . . . .   sigpause(2)
atomically release blocked signals and wait for interrupt. sigsuspend: . . . .   sigsuspend(2)
siginterrupt: allow signals to interrupt system calls. . . . .   siginterrupt(3)
onintr: process interrupts in command scripts. . . . .   csh(1)
phantasia: an interterminal fantasy game. . . . .   phantasia(6)
utilities). intro: introduction to general commands (tools and . . . .   intro(1)
math: introduction to mathematical library functions. . . . .   math(3)
networking: introduction to networking facilities. . . . .   netintro(4)
rcsintro: introduction to RCS commands. . . . .   rcsintro(1)
intro: introduction to special files and hardware support. . . . . . .   intro(4)
intro: introduction to system calls and error numbers. . . . . . .   intro(2)
commands. intro: introduction to system maintenance and operation . . . . .   intro(8)
intro: introduction to the C libraries. . . . .   intro(3)
kerberos: introduction to the Kerberos system. . . . .   kerberos(1)
ncheck: generate names from i-numbers. . . . .   ncheck(8)
(temporary). infnan: signals invalid floating–point operations on a VAX . . . .   infnan(3)
acosh: inverse hyperbolic cosine function. . . . .   acosh(3)
asinh: inverse hyperbolic sine function. . . . .   asinh(3)
atanh: inverse hyperbolic tangent function. . . . .   atanh(3)
mout, move, msqrt, msub, mult,/ fmin, fmout, gcd, invert, itom m_in, m_out, madd, mcmp, mdiv, min, ...   mp(3)
index. invert, lookup: create and access an inverted . . . . .   invert(1)
invert, lookup: create and access an inverted index. . . . .   invert(1)
indxbib: make inverted index for bibliographic databases. . . . .   indxbib(1)
nohup: invoke a command immune to hangups. . . . .   nohup(1)
popen, pclose: process I/O. . . . .   popen(3)
select: synchronous I/O multiplexing. . . . .   select(2)
nfsiod: local NFS asynchronous I/O server.   nfsiod(8)
iostat: report I/O statistics. . . . .   iostat(8)
ioctl: control device. . . . .   ioctl(2)
iostat: report I/O statistics. . . . .   iostat(8)
ip: Internet Protocol. . . . .   ip(4)
network interface encapsulating NS packets in IP packets. nsip: software . . . .   nsip(4)
sail: multi-user wooden ships and iron men. . . . .   sail(6)
isalnum: alphanumeric character test. . . . .   isalnum(3)
isdigit, isgraph, islower, isprint, ispunct,/ isalnum, isalpha, isascii, isblank, iscntrl, ...   ctype(3)
isalpha: alphabetic character test. . . . .   isalpha(3)
isgraph, islower, isprint, ispunct,/ isalnum, isalpha, isascii, isblank, iscntrl, isdigit, ...   ctype(3)
islower, isprint, ispunct,/ isalnum, isalpha, isascii, isblank, iscntrl, isdigit, isgraph, ...   ctype(3)
isascii: test for ASCII character. . . . .   isascii(3)
(tty) from file descriptor. ttyname, isatty, ttyslot: get name of associated terminal . . . .   ttyname(3)
isprint, ispunct,/ isalnum, isalpha, isascii, isblank, iscntrl, isdigit, isgraph, islower, ...   ctype(3)
isblank: space or tab character test. . . . .   isblank(3)
iscntrl: control character test. . . . .   iscntrl(3)
ispunct,/ isalnum, isalpha, isascii, isblank, iscntrl, isdigit, isgraph, islower, isprint, ...   ctype(3)
isdigit: decimal-digit character test. . . . .   isdigit(3)
isalnum, isalpha, isascii, isblank, iscntrl, isdigit, isgraph, islower, isprint, ispunct,/ . . . .   ctype(3)
/isalpha, isascii, isblank, iscntrl, isdigit, isgraph, islower, isprint, ispunct, isspace,/ . . . .   ctype(3)
exclusive). isgraph: printing character test (space character . . . . . .   isgraph(3)
isinf, isnan: test for infinity or not-a-number. . . . .   isinf(3)
/isascii, isblank, iscntrl, isdigit, isgraph, islower, isprint, ispunct, isspace, isupper,/ . . . .   ctype(3)
islower: lower-case character test. . . . .   islower(3)
isinf, isnan: test for infinity or not-a-number. . . . .   isinf(3)
cltp: ISO Connectionless Transport Protocol. . . . .   cltp(4)
iso: ISO protocol family. . . . .   iso(4)
iso: ISO protocol family. . . . .   iso(4)
TP: ISO Transport Protocol. . . . .   tp(4)
mount_cd9660: mount an ISO-9660 filesystem. . . . .   mount_cd9660(8)
conversion routines for Open System/ iso_addr, iso_ntoa: elementary network address . . . . . .   iso_addr(3)
routines for Open System/ iso_addr, iso_ntoa: elementary network address conversion . . . . .   iso_addr(3)
/isblank, iscntrl, isdigit, isgraph, islower, isprint, ispunct, isspace, isupper, isxdigit,/ . . . .   ctype(3)
inclusive). isprint: printing character test (space character . . . . . .   isprint(3)

/iscntrl, isdigit, isgraph, islower, isprint,   ispunct, isspace, isupper, isxdigit, toascii/ . . . . ctype(3)

ispunct: punctuation character test. . . . . ispunct(3)

/isdigit, isgraph, islower, isprint, ispunct,   isspace, isupper, isxdigit, toascii tolower,/ . . . . ctype(3)

isspace: white-space character test. . . . . isspace(3)

/isgraph, islower, isprint, ispunct, isspace,   isupper, isxdigit, toascii tolower, toupper,:/ . . . . ctype(3)

isupper: upper-case character test. . . . . isupper(3)

isxdigit: hexadecimal-digit character test. . . . . isxdigit(3)

/islower, isprint, ispunct, isspace, isupper,   isxdigit, toascii tolower, toupper,: character/ . . . . . . ctype(3)

ite: HP Internal Terminal Emulator. . . . . ite(4)

move, msqrt, msub, mult,/ fmin, fmout, gcd, invert,   itom m_in, m_out, madd, mcmp, mdiv, min, mout, ... mp(3)

and second kind.   j0, j1, jn, y0, y1, yn: bessel functions of first . . . . j0(3)

second kind. j0,   j1, jn, y0, y1, yn: bessel functions of first and . . . . . . j0(3)

second kind. j0, j1,   jn, y0, y1, yn: bessel functions of first and . . . . . . j0(3)

bg: place   job in background. . . . . csh(1)

fg: bring   job into foreground. . . . . csh(1)

jobs: print current   job list. . . . . csh(1)

stop: halt a   job or process. . . . . csh(1)

atq: display the at(1)   job queue. . . . . atq(1)

kill: kill   jobs and processes. . . . . csh(1)

lprm: remove   jobs from the line printer spooling queue. . . . . lprm(1)

jobs: print current job list. . . . . csh(1)

atrm: remove   jobs spooled by at(1). . . . . atrm(1)

join: relational database operator. . . . . join(1)

jot: print sequential or random data. . . . . jot(1)

longjmp, _setjmp, _longjmp longjmperror: non-local   jumps. sigsetjmp, siglongjmp, setjmp, ... setjmp(3)

msgs: system messages and   junk mail program. . . . . msgs(1)

center database.   kdb_destroy: destroy Kerberos key distribution . . . . . . kdb_destroy(8)

editing utility.   kdb_edit: Kerberos key distribution center database . . . . kdb_edit(8)

center database.   kdb_init: initialize Kerberos key distribution . . . . kdb_init(8)

utility.   kdb_util: Kerberos key distribution center database . . . . kdb_util(8)

kdestroy: destroy Kerberos tickets. . . . . kdestroy(1)

kdump: display kernel trace data. . . . . kdump(1)

register: register with   Kerberos. . . . . register(1)

krb_rd_safe, krb_mk_err, krb_rd_err, krb_ck_repl: Kerberos authentication library. /krb_mk_safe, ... krb(3)

/etc/kerberosIV/krb.conf: Kerberos configuration file. . . . . krb.conf(5)

make_keypair: generate   Kerberos host key pair. . . . . make_keypair(8)

kerberos: introduction to the Kerberos system. . . . . . . kerberos(1)

ext_srvtab: extract service key files from   Kerberos key distribution center database. . . . . ext_srvtab(8)

kdb_destroy: destroy   Kerberos key distribution center database. . . . . kdb_destroy(8)

kdb_init: initialize   Kerberos key distribution center database. . . . . kdb_init(8)

utility. kdb_edit: Kerberos key distribution center database editing . . . . . kdb_edit(8)

key. kstash: stash   Kerberos key distribution center database master . . . . . kstash(8)

kdb_util: Kerberos key distribution center database utility. . . . . . kdb_util(8)

kinit: Kerberos login utility. . . . . kinit(1)

kpasswdd: Kerberos password changing daemon. . . . . kpasswdd(8)

/etc/kerberosIV/krb.realms: host to   Kerberos realm translation file. . . . . krb.realms(5)

registerd: Kerberos registration daemon. . . . . registerd(8)

network/ /krb_recvauth, krb_net_write, krb_net_read: Kerberos routines for sending authentication via . . . . . krb_sendauth(3)

krb_set_tkt_string: set   Kerberos ticket cache file name. . . . . krb_set_tkt_string(3)

tf_get_cred, tf_close: routines for manipulating a   Kerberos ticket file. /tf_get_pname, tf_get_pinst, ... tf_util(3)

key. ksrvtgt: fetch and store   Kerberos ticket-granting-ticket using a service . . . . . . ksrvtgt(1)

kdestroy: destroy   Kerberos tickets. . . . . kdestroy(1)

klist: list currently held   Kerberos tickets. . . . . klist(1)

krb_get_admhst, krb_get_lrealm: additional   Kerberos utility routines. /krb_get_krbhst, ... krb_realmofhost(3)

kuserok: Kerberos version of ruserok. . . . . kuserok(3)

mount_kernfs: mount the   /kern file system. . . . . mount_kernfs(8)

config.new: build   kernel compilation directories. . . . . config.new(8)

kvm_mkdb: create   kernel database. . . . . kvm_mkdb(8)

kvm_nlist: retrieve symbol table names from a   kernel image. . . . . kvm_nlist(3)

kvm: kernel memory interface. . . . . kvm(3)

route: kernel packet forwarding database. . . . . route(4)

ktrace: enable   kernel process tracing. . . . . ktrace(1)

sysctl: get or set   kernel state. . . . . sysctl(8)

kdump: display   kernel trace data. . . . . kdump(1)

kvm_read, kvm_write: read or write   kernel virtual memory. . . . . kvm_read(3)

kvm_open, kvm_openfiles, kvm_close: initialize   kernel virtual memory access. . . . . kvm_open(3)

chkey: change your encryption   key. chkey(1)

keylogin: decrypt and store secret   key. keylogin(1)

Kerberos ticket-granting-ticket using a service   key. ksrvtgt: fetch and store . . . . ksrvtgt(1)

Kerberos key distribution center database master   key. kstash: stash . . . . kstash(8)

publickey: public   key database. . . . . publickey(5)

ext_srvtab: extract service key files from Kerberos   key distribution center database. . . . .   ext_srvtab(8)
kdb_destroy: destroy Kerberos   key distribution center database. . . . .   kdb_destroy(8)
kdb_init: initialize Kerberos   key distribution center database. . . . .   kdb_init(8)
kdb_edit: Kerberos   key distribution center database editing utility. . . . . . .   kdb_edit(8)
kstash: stash Kerberos   key distribution center database master key. . . . .   kstash(8)
kdb_util: Kerberos   key distribution center database utility. . . . .   kdb_util(8)
database. ext_srvtab: extract service   key files from Kerberos key distribution center . . . . . .   ext_srvtab(8)
make_keypair: generate Kerberos host   key pair. . . . .   make_keypair(8)
mset: retrieve ASCII to IBM 3270   keyboard map.   mset(1)
   keylogin: decrypt and store secret key. . . . .   keylogin(1)
database for mapping ascii keystrokes into IBM 3270   keys. map3270: . . . .   map3270(5)
makekey: make encrypted   keys or passwords. . . . .   makekey(8)
map3270: database for mapping ascii   keystrokes into IBM 3270 keys. . . . .   map3270(5)
apropos: locate commands by   keyword lookup.   apropos(1)
profile buffers.   kgmon: generate a dump of the operating system's . . . .   kgmon(8)
kill: kill jobs and processes. . . . .   csh(1)
   kill: kill jobs and processes. . . . .   csh(1)
   kill: send signal to a process. . . . .   kill(2)
   kill: terminate or signal a process. . . . .   kill(1)
   killpg: send signal to a process group. . . . .   killpg(2)
y0, y1, yn: bessel functions of first and second   kind. j0, j1, jn, ...   j0(3)
   kinit: Kerberos login utility. . . . .   kinit(1)
   klist: list currently held Kerberos tickets. . . . .   klist(1)
mem,   kmem: main memory. . . . .   mem(4)
mem,   kmem: main memory. . . . .   mem(4)
   kpasswdd: Kerberos password changing daemon. . . . . . .   kpasswdd(8)
/krb_mk_safe, krb_rd_safe, krb_mk_err, krb_rd_err,   krb_ck_repl: Kerberos authentication library. . . . . . .   krb(3)
krb_realmofhost, krb_get_phost, krb_get_krbhst,   krb_get_admhst, krb_get_lrealm: additional Kerberos/ . . . .   krb_realmofhost(3)
krb_mk_req, krb_rd_req, krb_kntoln, krb_set_key,   krb_get_cred, krb_mk_priv, krb_rd_priv,/ . . . .   krb(3)
additional/ krb_realmofhost, krb_get_phost,   krb_get_krbhst, krb_get_admhst, krb_get_lrealm: . . . . . .   krb_realmofhost(3)
/krb_get_phost, krb_get_krbhst, krb_get_admhst,   krb_get_lrealm: additional Kerberos utility/ . . . .   krb_realmofhost(3)
krb_get_lrealm: additional/ krb_realmofhost,   krb_get_phost, krb_get_krbhst, krb_get_admhst, ...   krb_realmofhost(3)
krb_rd_priv, krb_mk_safe,/ krb_mk_req, krb_rd_req,   krb_kntoln, krb_set_key, krb_get_cred, krb_mk_priv, ...   krb(3)
/krb_mk_priv, krb_rd_priv, krb_mk_safe, krb_rd_safe,   krb_mk_err, krb_rd_err, krb_ck_repl: Kerberos/ . . . .   krb(3)
/krb_rd_req, krb_kntoln, krb_set_key, krb_get_cred,   krb_mk_priv, krb_rd_priv, krb_mk_safe, krb_rd_safe,/ . . . .   krb(3)
krb_get_cred, krb_mk_priv, krb_rd_priv,/   krb_mk_req, krb_rd_req, krb_kntoln, krb_set_key, ...   krb(3)
/krb_get_cred, krb_mk_priv, krb_rd_priv,   krb_mk_safe, krb_rd_safe, krb_mk_err, krb_rd_err,/ . . . .   krb(3)
krb_sendauth, krb_recvauth, krb_net_write,   krb_net_read: Kerberos routines for sending/ . . . .   krb_sendauth(3)
sending authentication/ krb_sendauth, krb_recvauth,   krb_net_write, krb_net_read: Kerberos routines for . . . .   krb_sendauth(3)
/krb_rd_err, krb_mk_safe, krb_rd_safe, krb_mk_err,   krb_rd_err, krb_ck_repl: Kerberos authentication/ . . . .   krb(3)
/krb_kntoln, krb_set_key, krb_get_cred, krb_mk_priv,   krb_rd_priv, krb_mk_safe, krb_rd_safe, krb_mk_err,/ . . . .   krb(3)
krb_mk_priv, krb_rd_priv, krb_mk_safe,/ krb_mk_req,   krb_rd_req, krb_kntoln, krb_set_key, krb_get_cred, ...   krb(3)
Kerberos/ /krb_mk_priv, krb_rd_priv, krb_mk_safe,   krb_rd_safe, krb_mk_err, krb_rd_err, krb_ck_repl: . . . .   krb(3)
krb_get_admhst, krb_get_lrealm: additional/   krb_realmofhost, krb_get_phost, krb_get_krbhst, ...   krb_realmofhost(3)
routines for sending authentication/ krb_sendauth,   krb_recvauth, krb_net_write, krb_net_read: Kerberos . . . .   krb_sendauth(3)
krb_net_read: Kerberos routines for sending/   krb_sendauth, krb_recvauth, krb_net_write, ...   krb_sendauth(3)
krb_rd_priv,/ krb_mk_req, krb_rd_req, krb_kntoln,   krb_set_key, krb_get_cred, krb_mk_priv, ...   krb(3)
name.   krb_set_tkt_string: set Kerberos ticket cache file . . . . .   krb_set_tkt_string(3)
ticket-granting-ticket using a service key.   ksrvtgt: fetch and store Kerberos . . . .   ksrvtgt(1)
database master key.   kstash: stash Kerberos key distribution center . . . .   kstash(8)
   ktrace: enable kernel process tracing. . . . .   ktrace(1)
   ktrace: process tracing. . . . .   ktrace(2)
   kuserok: Kerberos version of ruserok. . . . .   kuserok(3)
kvm_geterr: get error message on   kvm descriptor. . . . .   kvm_geterr(3)
kvm_getloadavg: get error message on   kvm descriptor. . . . .   kvm_getloadavg(3)
   kvm: kernel memory interface. . . . .   kvm(3)
kvm_open, kvm_openfiles,   kvm_close: initialize kernel virtual memory access. . . . .   kvm_open(3)
state. kvm_getprocs,   kvm_getargv, kvm_getenvv: access user process . . . . .   kvm_getprocs(3)
kvm_getprocs, kvm_getargv,   kvm_getenvv: access user process state. . . . .   kvm_getprocs(3)
   kvm_geterr: get error message on kvm descriptor. . . . . .   kvm_geterr(3)
   kvm_getfiles: survey open files. . . . .   kvm_getfiles(3)
descriptor.   kvm_getloadavg: get error message on kvm . . . .   kvm_getloadavg(3)
process state.   kvm_getprocs, kvm_getargv, kvm_getenvv: access user . . .   kvm_getprocs(3)
   kvm_mkdb: create kernel database. . . . .   kvm_mkdb(8)
kernel image.   kvm_nlist: retrieve symbol table names from a . . . . . .   kvm_nlist(3)
kernel virtual memory access.   kvm_open, kvm_openfiles, kvm_close: initialize . . . .   kvm_open(3)
memory access. kvm_open,   kvm_openfiles, kvm_close: initialize kernel virtual . . . .   kvm_open(3)
memory.   kvm_read, kvm_write: read or write kernel virtual . . . . .   kvm_read(3)
kvm_read,   kvm_write: read or write kernel virtual memory. . . . . .   kvm_read(3)
disklabel: disk pack   label. . . . .   disklabel.5(5)
disklabel: read and write disk pack   label. . . . .   disklabel(8)
linemod, space, closepl:/ plot: openpl, erase,   label, line, circle, arc, move, cont, point, ...   plot(3)

labs: return the absolute value of a long integer. . . . . . . labs(3)
L.aliases: UUCP hostname alias file. . . . . L.aliases(5)
yacc: an LALR(1) parser generator. . . . . yacc(1)
lam: laminate files. . . . . lam(1)
lam: laminate files. . . . . lam(1)
le: HP AMD 7990 LANCE Ethernet interface. . . . . le(4)
le: SPARC AMD 7990 LANCE ethernet interface. . . . . le(4)
awk: pattern scanning and processing language. . . . . awk(1)
perl: practical extraction and report language. . . . . perl(1)
bc: arbitrary-precision arithmetic language and calculator. . . . . bc(1)
vgrindefs: language definition data base for vgrind(1). . . . . vgrindefs(5)
setlocale, localeconv: natural language formatting for C. . . . . setlocale(3)
m4: macro language preprocessor for ratfor(1) and pascal(1). . . . . . m4(1)
floor: largest integral value not greater than x. . . . . floor(3)
larn: exploring the caverns of Larn. . . . . larn(6)
larn: exploring the caverns of Larn. . . . . larn(6)
order. lastcomm: show last commands executed in reverse . . . . . lastcomm(1)
utmp, wtmp, lastlog: login records. . . . . utmp(5)
demonstrate the use of a null file system layer. mount_null: . . . . mount_null(8)
mount_umap: sample file system layer. . . . . mount_umap(8)
hier: layout of filesystems. . . . . hier(7)
mklocale: make LC_CTYPE locale files. . . . . mklocale(1)
L.cmds: UUCP remote command permissions file. . . . . . L.cmds(5)
ld: link editor. . . . . ld(1)
L-devices: UUCP device description file. . . . . L-devices(5)
power of 2. ldexp: multiply floating-point number by integral . . . . . . ldexp(3)
L-dialcodes: UUCP phone number index file. . . . . L-dialcodes(5)
ldiv: return quotient and remainder from division. . . . . . . ldiv(3)
le: HP AMD 7990 LANCE Ethernet interface. . . . . . . le(4)
le: SPARC AMD 7990 LANCE ethernet interface. . . . . . le(4)
learn: computer aided instruction about. . . . . learn(1)
leave: remind you when you have to leave. . . . . leave(1)
leave: remind you when you have to leave. . . . . leave(1)
exit: leave shell. . . . . csh(1)
getusershell, setusershell, endusershell: get legal user shells. . . . . getusershell(3)
truncate, ftruncate: truncate a file to a specified length. . . . . truncate(2)
strlen: find length of string. . . . . strlen(3)
tolower: upper case to lower case letter conversion. . . . . tolower(3)
toupper: lower case to upper case letter conversion. . . . . toupper(3)
elementary address specification routines for link level access. link_addr, link_ntoa: . . . . linkaddr(3)
lex: fast lexical analyzer generator. . . . . lex(1)
lex: fast lexical analyzer generator. . . . . lex(1)
lsearch, lfind,: linear searching routines. . . . . lsearch(3)
newlfs: construct a new LFS file system. . . . . newlfs(8)
system. lfs_cleanerd: garbage collect a log-structured file . . . . . lfs_cleanerd(8)
lgamma gamma: log gamma function, gamma function. . . . lgamma(3)
intro: introduction to the C libraries. . . . . intro(3)
ranlib: table-of-contents for archive libraries. . . . . ranlib(1)
krb_rd_err, krb_ck_repl: Kerberos authentication library. /krb_mk_safe, krb_rd_safe, krb_mk_err, ... krb(3)
regexec, regerror, regfree: regular-expression library. regcomp, ... regex(3)
ar: create and maintain library archives. . . . . ar(1)
ar: archive (library) file format. . . . . ar.5(5)
math: introduction to mathematical library functions. . . . . math(3)
stdio: standard input/output library functions. . . . . stdio(3)
ranlib: archive (library) table-of-contents format. . . . . ranlib.5(5)
limit: alter per-process resource limitations. . . . . csh(1)
limit: alter per-process resource limitations. . . . . csh(1)
unlimit: remove resource limitations. . . . . csh(1)
quota: display disk usage and limits. . . . . quota(1)
wc: word, line, and byte count. . . . . wc(1)
getopt: get option character from command line argument list. . . . . getopt(3)
acucntrl: turn around tty line between dialin and dialout. . . . . acucntrl(8)
space, closepl:/ plot: openpl, erase, label, line, circle, arc, move, cont, point, linemod, ... plot(3)
tcsendbreak, tcdrain, tcflush, tcflow: line control functions. . . . . tcsendbreak(3)
termios: general terminal line discipline. . . . . termios(4)
col: filter reverse line feeds from input. . . . . col(1)
fgetln: get a line from a stream. . . . . fgetln(3)
fgets, gets: get a line from a stream. . . . . fgets(3)
sliplogin: attach a serial line network interface. . . . . sliplogin(8)
cut: select portions of each line of a file. . . . . cut(1)
ed: line oriented text editor. . . . . ed(1)
lpr: off line print. . . . . lpr(1)

lpc: line printer control program. . . . . lpc(8)
lpd: line printer spooler daemon. . . . . lpd(8)
lprm: remove jobs from the line printer spooling queue. . . . . lprm(1)
fputs, puts: output a line to a stream. . . . . fputs(3)
lsearch, lfind,: linear searching routines. . . . . lsearch(3)
/erase, label, line, circle, arc, move, cont, point, linemod, space, closepl: graphics interface. . . . . plot(3)
lptest: generate lineprinter ripple pattern. . . . . lptest(1)
unifdef: remove ifdef'ed lines. . . . . unifdef(1)
slattach: attach serial lines as network interfaces. . . . . slattach(8)
look: display lines beginning with a given string. . . . . look(1)
comm: select or reject lines common to two files. . . . . comm(1)
fold: fold long lines for finite width output device. . . . . fold(1)
random: random lines from a file or random numbers. . . . . random(6)
uniq: report or filter out repeated lines in a file. . . . . uniq(1)
head: display first lines of a file. . . . . head(1)
rev: reverse lines of a file. . . . . rev(1)
paste: merge corresponding or subsequent lines of files. . . . . paste(1)
dcl: HP 98628A communications link. . . . . dcl(4)
link: make a hard file link. . . . . link(2)
readlink: read value of a symbolic link. . . . . readlink(2)
hil: Human Interface Link device driver. . . . . hil(4)
ld: link editor. . . . . ld(1)
symlink: symbolic link handling. symlink(7)
elementary address specification routines for link level access. link_addr, link_ntoa: . . . . linkaddr(3)
link: make a hard file link. . . . . link(2)
symlink: make symbolic link to a file. . . . . symlink(2)
specification routines for link level access. link_addr, link_ntoa: elementary address . . . . linkaddr(3)
routines for link level access. link_addr, link_ntoa: elementary address specification . . . . linkaddr(3)
ln: make links. . . . . ln(1)
glob: filename expand argument list. . . . . csh(1)
history: print history event list. . . . . csh(1)
jobs: print current job list. . . . . csh(1)
shift: manipulate argument list. . . . . csh(1)
getgrouplist: calculate group access list. getgrouplist(3)
getgroups: get group access list. getgroups(2)
get option character from command line argument list. getopt: . . . . getopt(3)
initgroups: initialize group access list. initgroups(3)
mkdep: construct Makefile dependency list. . . . . mkdep(1)
setgroups: set group access list. setgroups(2)
symorder: rearrange name list. . . . . symorder(1)
users: list current users. . . . . users(1)
klist: list currently held Kerberos tickets. . . . . klist(1)
lorder: list dependencies for object files. . . . . lorder(1)
ls: list directory contents. . . . . ls(1)
nlist: retrieve symbol table name list from an executable file. . . . . nlist(3)
uuname: list names of UUCP hosts. . . . . uuname(1)
getfsstat: get list of all mounted filesystems. . . . . getfsstat(2)
foreach: loop over list of names. . . . . csh(1)
acl_add, acl_delete, acl_initialize: access control list routines. /acl_check, acl_exact_match, ... acl_check(3)
nm: display name list (symbol table). . . . . nm(1)
listen: listen for connections on a socket. . . . . listen(2)
listen: listen for connections on a socket. . . . . listen(2)
LIST_INSERT_AFTER, LIST_INSERT_HEAD, LIST_REMOVE,/ LIST_ENTRY, LIST_HEAD, LIST_INIT, ... queue(3)
LIST_INSERT_HEAD, LIST_REMOVE,/ LIST_ENTRY, LIST_HEAD, LIST_INIT, LIST_INSERT_AFTER, ... queue(3)
vgrind: grind nice listings of programs. . . . . vgrind(1)
LIST_REMOVE, TAILQ_ENTRY,/ LIST_ENTRY, LIST_HEAD, LIST_INIT, LIST_INSERT_AFTER, LIST_INSERT_HEAD, queue(3)
TAILQ_ENTRY,/ LIST_ENTRY, LIST_HEAD, LIST_INIT, LIST_INSERT_AFTER, LIST_INSERT_HEAD, LIST_REMOVE, queue(3)
/LIST_HEAD, LIST_INIT, LIST_INSERT_AFTER, LIST_INSERT_HEAD, LIST_REMOVE, TAILQ_ENTRY,/ . queue(3)
bib, listrefs, bibinc, bib2tib: bibliographic formatter. . . . . . . bib(1)
/LIST_INIT, LIST_INSERT_AFTER, LIST_INSERT_HEAD, LIST_REMOVE, TAILQ_ENTRY, TAILQ_HEAD, TAILQ_INIT,/ queue(3)
column: columnate lists. . . . . column(1)
stdarg: variable argument lists. . . . . stdarg(3)
xargs: construct argument list(s) and execute utility. . . . . xargs(1)
lkbib: search bibliographic databases. . . . . lkbib(1)
ln: make links. . . . . ln(1)
lo: software loopback network interface. . . . . lo(4)
getloadavg: get system load averages. getloadavg(3)
strxfrm: transform a string under locale. . . . . strxfrm(3)
mklocale: make LC_CTYPE locale files. . . . . mklocale(1)
setlocale, localeconv: natural language formatting for C. . . . . setlocale(3)
value to ASCII. asctime, ctime, difftime, gmtime, localtime, mktime: transform binary date and time . . . . . ctime(3)
which: locate a program file including aliases and paths. . . . . . . which(1)

                        strstr: locate a substring in a string. . . . . strstr(3)
                       memchr: locate byte in byte string. . . . . memchr(3)
                        index: locate character in string. . . . . index(3)
                       rindex: locate character in string. . . . . rindex(3)
                       strchr: locate character in string. . . . . strchr(3)
                      strrchr: locate character in string. . . . . strrchr(3)
                      apropos: locate commands by keyword lookup. . . . . apropos(1)
                                locate: find files. . . . . locate(1)
                       strpbrk: locate multiple characters in string. . . . . strpbrk(3)
                      whereis: locate programs. . . . . whereis(1)
    flock: apply or remove an advisory lock on an open file. . . . . flock(2)
                                lock: reserve a terminal. . . . . lock(1)
             mlock, munlock: lock (unlock) physical pages in memory. . . . . mlock(2)
      logger: make entries in the system log. . . . . logger(1)
  openlog, closelog, setlogmask: control system log. syslog, vsyslog, ... syslog(3)
              uulog: display UUCP log entries. . . . . uulog(1)
            lgamma gamma: log gamma function, gamma function. . . . . lgamma(3)
                        login: log into the computer. . . . . login(1)
    power functions. exp, expm1, log, log10, log1p, pow: exponential, logarithm, ... exp(3)
              rlog: print log messages and other information about RCS files. . . . . rlog(1)
                     syslogd: log systems messages. . . . . syslogd(8)
         functions. exp, expm1, log, log10, log1p, pow: exponential, logarithm, power . . . . . exp(3)
      functions. exp, expm1, log, log10, log1p, pow: exponential, logarithm, power . . . . exp(3)
  exp, expm1, log, log10, log1p, pow: exponential, logarithm, power functions. . . . . exp(3)
    copysign, drem, finite, logb, scalb: IEEE 754 floating point support. . . . . ieee(3)
              who: display who is logged in. . . . . who(1)
      rwho: who is logged in on local machines. . . . . rwho(1)
                                logger: make entries in the system log. . . . . logger(1)
      nologin: politely refuse a login. . . . . nologin(8)
             rlogin: remote login. . . . . rlogin(1)
                                login: log into the computer. . . . . login(1)
                                login: login new user. . . . . csh(1)
        getlogin, setlogin: get/set login name. . . . . getlogin(2)
       logname: display user's login name. . . . . logname(1)
                        login: login new user. . . . . csh(1)
        utmp, wtmp, lastlog: login records. . . . . utmp(5)
             rlogind: remote login server. . . . . rlogind(8)
        startslip: dial up and login to a slip server. . . . . startslip(1)
       tn3270: full-screen remote login to IBM VM/CMS. . . . . tn3270(1)
            kinit: Kerberos login utility. . . . . kinit(1)
        last: indicate last logins of users and ttys. . . . . last(1)
                                logname: display user's login name. . . . . logname(1)
                                logout: end session. . . . . csh(1)
    lfs_cleanerd: garbage collect a log-structured file system. . . . . lfs_cleanerd(8)
       mount_lfs: mount a log-structured file system. . . . . mount_lfs(8)
  sigsetjmp, siglongjmp, setjmp, longjmp, _setjmp, _longjmp longjmperror: non-local jumps. . . . . setjmp(3)
    jumps. sigsetjmp, siglongjmp, setjmp, longjmp, _setjmp, _longjmp longjmperror: non-local . . . setjmp(3)
  siglongjmp, setjmp, longjmp, _setjmp, _longjmp longjmperror: non-local jumps. sigsetjmp, ... setjmp(3)
                                look: display lines beginning with a given string. . . . . look(1)
                       rhost: look up host names using domain server. . . . . host(1)
                                lookbib: search bibliographic databases. . . . . lookbib(1)
    apropos: locate commands by keyword lookup. . . . . apropos(1)
                      invert, lookup: create and access an inverted index. . . . . invert(1)
       finger: user information lookup program. . . . . finger(1)
    break: exit while/foreach loop. . . . . csh(1)
        continue: cycle in loop. . . . . csh(1)
           end: terminate loop. . . . . csh(1)
                     foreach: loop over list of names. . . . . csh(1)
             lo: software loopback network interface. . . . . lo(4)
                                lorder: list dependencies for object files. . . . . lorder(1)
    tolower: upper case to lower case letter conversion. . . . . tolower(3)
                     toupper: lower case to upper case letter conversion. . . . . toupper(3)
                     islower: lower-case character test. . . . . islower(3)
                                lpc: line printer control program. . . . . lpc(8)
                                lpd: line printer spooler daemon. . . . . lpd(8)
                                lpq: spool queue examination program. . . . . lpq(1)
                                lpr: off line print. . . . . lpr(1)
                       queue: lprm: remove jobs from the line printer spooling . . . . . lprm(1)
                                lptest: generate lineprinter ripple pattern. . . . . lptest(1)
                                ls: list directory contents. . . . . ls(1)
                                lsearch, lfind,: linear searching routines. . . . . lsearch(3)
                                lseek: reposition read/write file offset. . . . . lseek(2)

stat, lstat, fstat: get file status. . . . . stat(2)
L.sys: UUCP remote host description file. . . . . L.sys(5)
pascal(1). m4: macro language preprocessor for ratfor(1) and . . . . . m4(1)
ruptime: show host status of local machines. ruptime(1)
rwho: who is logged in on local machines. . . . . rwho(1)
assert: expression verification macro. . . . . assert(3)
pascal(1). m4: macro language preprocessor for ratfor(1) and . . . . . . m4(1)
mdoc: quick reference guide for the —mdoc macro package. . . . . mdoc(7)
bitstr_size, bit_test: bit-string manipulation macros. /bit_ffs, bit_nclear, bit_nset, bit_set, . . bitstring(3)
alias: shell macros. . . . . csh(1)
toascii tolower, toupper,: character classification macros. /ispunct, isspace, isupper, isxdigit, ... ctype(3)
mm: groff mm macros. . . . . mm(7)
ms: text formatting macros. . . . . ms(7)
me: macros for formatting papers. . . . . me(7)
man: (deprecated) macros to typeset manual. . . . . man(7)
mult,/ fmin, fmout, gcd, invert, itom m_in, m_out, madd, mcmp, mdiv, min, mout, move, msqrt, msub, ... mp(3)
restore: restore files or file systems from backups made with dump. . . . . restore(8)
madvise: give advise about use of memory. . . . . madvise(2)
tcopy: copy and/or verify mag tapes. . . . . tcopy(1)
mt: magnetic tape manipulating program. . . . . mt(1)
rmt: remote magtape protocol module. . . . . rmt(8)
from: print names of those who have sent mail. . . . . from(1)
mail: send and receive mail. . . . . mail(1)
xsend, xget, enroll: private encrypted mail. . . . . xsend(1)
sendbug: mail a system bug report to 4bsd-bugs. . . . . sendbug(1)
mailaddr: mail addressing description. . . . . mailaddr(7)
newaliases: rebuild the data base for the mail aliases file. . . . . newaliases(1)
biff: be notified if mail arrives and who it is from. . . . . biff(1)
mail.local: store mail in a mailbox. . . . . mail.local(8)
sendmail: send mail over the internet. . . . . sendmail(8)
msgs: system messages and junk mail program. . . . . msgs(1)
mailq: print the mail queue. . . . . mailq(1)
rmail: handle remote mail received via uucp. . . . . rmail(8)
mail: send and receive mail. . . . . mail(1)
mailaddr: mail addressing description. . . . . mailaddr(7)
mail.local: store mail in a mailbox. . . . . mail.local(8)
mail.local: store mail in a mailbox. . . . . mail.local(8)
mailq: print the mail queue. . . . . mailq(1)
mem, kmem: main memory. . . . . mem(4)
mem, kmem: main memory. . . . . mem(4)
ar: create and maintain library archives. . . . . ar(1)
make: maintain program dependencies. . . . . make(1)
intro: introduction to system maintenance and operation commands. . . . . intro(8)
mkdir: make a directory file. . . . . mkdir(2)
mkfifo: make a fifo file. mkfifo(2)
link: make a hard file link. . . . . link(2)
mknod: make a special file node. . . . . mknod(2)
mkdir: make directories. . . . . mkdir(1)
makekey: make encrypted keys or passwords. . . . . makekey(8)
logger: make entries in the system log. . . . . logger(1)
mkfifo: make fifos. . . . . mkfifo(1)
indxbib: make inverted index for bibliographic databases. . . . . . indxbib(1)
mklocale: make LC_CTYPE locale files. . . . . mklocale(1)
ln: make links. . . . . ln(1)
make: maintain program dependencies. . . . . make(1)
symlink: make symbolic link to a file. . . . . symlink(2)
makedev: make system special files. . . . . makedev(8)
mktemp: make temporary file name (unique). . . . . mktemp(3)
script: make typescript of terminal session. . . . . script(1)
MAKEDEV: create system and device special files. . . . . . MAKEDEV(8)
makedev: make system special files. . . . . makedev(8)
mkdep: construct Makefile dependency list. . . . . mkdep(1)
makekey: make encrypted keys or passwords. . . . . makekey(8)
make_keypair: generate Kerberos host key pair. . . . . . . make_keypair(8)
makemap: create database maps for sendmail. . . . . makemap(8)
free: free up memory allocated with malloc, calloc or realloc. . . . . free(3)
memory allocation operations. malloc, free, realloc, calloc, alloca: general . . . . . . memory(3)
malloc,: general memory allocation function. . . . . malloc(3)
man: (deprecated) macros to typeset manual. . . . . man(7)
man: display the on-line manual pages. . . . . man(1)
man.conf: configuration file for man(1). . . . . man.conf(5)
man.conf: configuration file for man(1). . . . . man.conf(5)

```
                         shift:  manipulate argument list.  . . . . . . . . . . . . . .       csh(1)
                   sigprocmask:  manipulate current signal mask.  . . . . . . . . . . . .     sigprocmask(2)
                      quotactl:  manipulate filesystem quotas.  . . . . . . . . . . . . .      quotactl(2)
  sigfillset, sigaddset, sigdelset, sigismember:  manipulate signal sets. sigemptyset,  . . . . . . . . .   sigsetops(3)
                         route:  manually manipulate the routing tables..  . . . . . . . . . . .    route(8)
           uuq:  examine or  manipulate the uucp queue.  . . . . . . . . . . . . . .           uuq(1)
  tf_get_pinst, tf_get_cred, tf_close: routines for  manipulating a Kerberos ticket file. /tf_get_pname,  . . . . .   tf_util(3)
             mt: magnetic tape  manipulating program.  . . . . . . . . . . . . . . .           mt(1)
  cfsetspeed, cfmakeraw, tcgetattr, tcsetattr:  manipulating the termios structure. /cfsetospeed,  . . . . . .   tcsetattr(3)
  bit_set, bitstr_size, bit_test: bit-string  manipulation macros. /bit_nclear, bit_nset,  . . . . . . . .   bitstring(3)
  inet_lnaof, inet_netof: Internet address  manipulation routines. /inet_ntoa, inet_makeaddr,  . . . . .    inet(3)
  man: (deprecated) macros to typeset  manual.  . . . . . . . . . . . . . . . . . . . .         man(7)
           man:  display the on-line  manual pages.  . . . . . . . . . . . . . . . . . .        man(1)
                         route:  manually manipulate the routing tables..  . . . . . . . . .     route(8)
  mdoc.samples: tutorial sampler for writing  manuals with −mdoc.  . . . . . . . . . . . . . . . .   mdoc.samples(7)
             IBM 3270 keys.  map3270: database for mapping ascii keystrokes into  . . . .   map3270(5)
           msync:  synchronize a  mapped region.  . . . . . . . . . . . . . . . . . .          msync(2)
  portmap: DARPA port to RPC program number  mapper.  . . . . . . . . . . . . . . . . . . .         portmap(8)
           munmap: remove a  mapping.  . . . . . . . . . . . . . . . . . . . .                munmap(2)
           map3270: database for  mapping ascii keystrokes into IBM 3270 keys.  . . . . . . .    map3270(5)
  mk-amd-map: create database  maps for Amd.  . . . . . . . . . . . . . . . . .               mk-amd-map(8)
           makemap: create database  maps for sendmail.  . . . . . . . . . . . . . . . .         makemap(8)
  umask: change or display file creation  mask.  . . . . . . . . . . . . . . . . . . . . .        csh(1)
  sigprocmask: manipulate current signal  mask.  . . . . . . . . . . . . . . . . . . . .       sigprocmask(2)
  sigsetmask: set current signal  mask.  . . . . . . . . . . . . . . . . . . . .               sigsetmask(2)
  umask: set file creation mode  mask.  . . . . . . . . . . . . . . . . . . . .                umask(2)
  mkstr: create an error message file by  massaging C source.  . . . . . . . . . . . . . . . .     mkstr(1)
           dm: dungeon  master.  . . . . . . . . . . . . . . . . . . . .                      dm(8)
  stash Kerberos key distribution center database  master key. kstash:  . . . . . . . . . . . . . . . .      kstash(8)
           fnmatch:  match filename or pathname.  . . . . . . . . . . . . . . .              fnmatch(3)
  glob, globfree: generate pathnames  matching a pattern.  . . . . . . . . . . . . . . . .        glob(3)
           functions.  math: introduction to mathematical library  . . . . . . . . .          math(3)
           math:  introduction to  mathematical library functions.  . . . . . . . . . . . . .    math(3)
  getrlimit, setrlimit: control  maximum system resource consumption.  . . . . . . . .        getrlimit(2)
  vlimit: control  maximum system resource consumption.  . . . . . . . .                       vlimit(3)
  multibyte character support for C.  mblen, mbstowcs, mbtowc, wcstombs, wctomb:  . . . . .     multibyte(3)
  mbrune, mbrrune,  mbmb: multibyte rune support for C.  . . . . . . . .                        mbrune(3)
           mbrune,  mbrrune, mbmb: multibyte rune support for C.  . . . . . . .                mbrune(3)
           C.  mbrune, mbrrune, mbmb: multibyte rune support for  . . . .                      mbrune(3)
  character support for C. mblen,  mbstowcs, mbtowc, wcstombs, wctomb: multibyte  . . . . .      multibyte(3)
  support for C. mblen, mbstowcs,  mbtowc, wcstombs, wctomb: multibyte character  . . . . .      multibyte(3)
  fmin, fmout, gcd, invert, itom m_in, m_out, madd,/  mcmp, mdiv, min, mout, move, msqrt, msub, mult,/  . . . . .   mp(3)
  /fmout, gcd, invert, itom m_in, m_out, madd, mcmp,  mdiv, min, mout, move, msqrt, msub, mult, omin,/  . . . . .   mp(3)
  tutorial sampler for writing  manuals with −mdoc. mdoc.samples:  . . . . . . . . . . . . . .    mdoc.samples(7)
  mdoc: quick reference guide for the  −mdoc macro package.  . . . . . . . . . . . . . . .       mdoc(7)
           package.  mdoc: quick reference guide for the −mdoc macro  . . . . . .              mdoc(7)
           with −mdoc.  mdoc.samples: tutorial sampler for writing  manuals  . . . .          mdoc.samples(7)
           me:  macros for formatting papers.  . . . . . . . . . . . . .                       me(7)
           mem, kmem:  main memory.  . . . . . . . . . . . . . . .                            mem(4)
           mem, kmem:  main memory.  . . . . . . . . . . . . . . .                            mem(4)
           groups:  show group  memberships.  . . . . . . . . . . . . . . . . . . .            groups(1)
           memccpy:  copy string until character found.  . . . . . . . .                      memccpy(3)
  byte string operations. bcmp, bcopy, bzero,  memccpy, memchr, memcmp, memcpy, memmove, memset:  . .   bstring(3)
           memchr:  locate byte in byte string.  . . . . . . . . . . .                         memchr(3)
  string operations. bcmp, bcopy, bzero, memccpy,  memchr, memcmp, memcpy, memmove, memset: byte  . . . .   bstring(3)
           memcmp:  compare byte string.  . . . . . . . . . . . . . .                         memcmp(3)
  operations. bcmp, bcopy, bzero, memccpy, memchr,  memcmp, memcpy, memmove, memset: byte string  . . . . .   bstring(3)
           memcpy:  copy byte string.  . . . . . . . . . . . . . .                            memcpy(3)
  bcmp, bcopy, bzero, memccpy, memchr, memcmp,  memcpy, memmove, memset: byte string operations.  . . . .   bstring(3)
           memmove:  copy byte string.  . . . . . . . . . . . . . .                           memmove(3)
  bcopy, bzero, memccpy, memchr, memcmp, memcpy,  memmove, memset: byte string operations. bcmp,  . . . .   bstring(3)
  kvm_read, kvm_write: read or write kernel virtual  memory.  . . . . . . . . . . . . . . . . . . . .       kvm_read(3)
  madvise: give advise about use of  memory.  . . . . . . . . . . . . . . . . . . . .           madvise(2)
           mem, kmem:  main  memory.  . . . . . . . . . . . . . . . . . . . .                  mem(4)
           mem, kmem:  main  memory.  . . . . . . . . . . . . . . . . . . . .                  mem(4)
  mincore: get advise about use of  memory.  . . . . . . . . . . . . . . . . . . . .           mincore(2)
  mlock, munlock: lock (unlock) physical pages in  memory.  . . . . . . . . . . . . . . . . . . . .       mlock(2)
  mmap: map files or devices into  memory.  . . . . . . . . . . . . . . . . . . . .            mmap(2)
  kvm_openfiles, kvm_close: initialize kernel virtual  memory access. kvm_open,  . . . . . . . . . . . . .   kvm_open(3)
           free:  free up  memory allocated with malloc, calloc or realloc.  . . . . . .        free(3)
  malloc,: general  memory allocation function.  . . . . . . . . . . . . .                     malloc(3)
  valloc: aligned  memory allocation function.  . . . . . . . . . . . . .                      valloc(3)
```

malloc, free, realloc, calloc, alloca: general   memory allocation operations.   . . . .   memory(3)
                                     alloca: memory allocator.   . . . .   alloca(3)
                    mpool: shared   memory buffer pool.   . . . .   mpool(3)
   vfork: spawn new process in a virtual   memory efficient way.   . . . .   vfork(2)
         realloc: reallocation of   memory function.   . . . .   realloc(3)
                                     core: memory image file format.   . . . .   core(5)
                       kvm: kernel   memory interface.   . . . .   kvm(3)
          vmstat: report virtual   memory statistics.   . . . .   vmstat(8)
         calloc: allocate clean   memory (zero initialized space).   . . . .   calloc(3)
bzero, memccpy, memchr, memcmp, memcpy, memmove,   memset: byte string operations. bcmp, bcopy, ...   bstring(3)
                                     memset: write a byte to byte string.   . . . .   memset(3)
       sail: multi-user wooden ships and iron   men.   . . . .   sail(6)
            merge: three-way file   merge.   . . . .   merge(1)
                     paste: merge corresponding or subsequent lines of files.   . . . .   paste(1)
                    rcsmerge: merge RCS revisions.   . . . .   rcsmerge(1)
               sort: sort or   merge text files.   . . . .   sort(1)
                                     merge: three-way file merge.   . . . .   merge(1)
         qsort, heapsort,   mergesort: sort functions.   . . . .   qsort(3)
                     users.   mesg: display (do not display) messages from other   . . . . .   mesg(1)
      dmesg: display the system   message buffer.   . . . .   dmesg(8)
            mkstr: create an error   message file by massaging C source.   . . . .   mkstr(1)
  recv, recvfrom, recvmsg: receive a   message from a socket.   . . . .   recv(2)
   send, sendto, sendmsg: send a   message from a socket.   . . . .   send(2)
                     mh: Message Handler.   . . . .   mh(1)
              echo: produce   message in a shell script.   . . . .   echo(1)
    kvm_geterr: get error   message on kvm descriptor.   . . . .   kvm_geterr(3)
kvm_getloadavg: get error   message on kvm descriptor.   . . . .   kvm_getloadavg(3)
    icmp: Internet Control   Message Protocol.   . . . .   icmp(4)
            write: send a   message to another user.   . . . .   write(1)
         wall: write a   message to users.   . . . .   wall(1)
verrx, warn, vwarn, warnx, vwarnx: formatted error   messages. err, verr, errx, ...   err(3)
     error: analyze and disperse compiler error   messages.   . . . .   error(1)
psignal, sys_siglist sys_signame: system signal   messages.   . . . .   psignal(3)
strerror, sys_errlist, sys_nerr: system error   messages. perror, ...   strerror(3)
      syslogd: log systems   messages.   . . . .   syslogd(8)
       msgs: system   messages and junk mail program.   . . . .   msgs(1)
      rlog: print log   messages and other information about RCS files.   . . . .   rlog(1)
   mesg: display (do not display)   messages from other users.   . . . .   mesg(1)
      btree: btree database access   method.   . . . .   btree(3)
         hash: hash database access   method.   . . . .   hash(3)
   recno: record number database access   method.   . . . .   recno(3)
      dbopen: database access   methods.   . . . .   dbopen(3)
               newfs,   mfs: construct a new file system.   . . . .   newfs(8)
                     mh: Message Handler.   . . . .   mh(1)
      mh-gen: generating the   MH system.   . . . .   mh-gen(8)
                     mh-gen: generating the MH system.   . . . .   mh-gen(8)
   usleep: suspend execution for interval of   microseconds.   . . . .   usleep(3)
               mille: play   Mille Bornes.   . . . .   mille(6)
                     mille: play Mille Bornes.   . . . .   mille(6)
msqrt, msub, mult,/ fmin, fmout, gcd, invert, itom   m_in, m_out, madd, mcmp, mdiv, min, mout, move, ...   mp(3)
/gcd, invert, itom m_in, m_out, madd, mcmp, mdiv,   min, mout, move, msqrt, msub, mult, omin, omout,/   . . . . .   mp(3)
                     mincore: get advise about use of memory.   . . . .   mincore(2)
                     intro: miscellaneous information pages.   . . . .   intro(7)
                     mk-amd-map: create database maps for Amd.   . . . . . .   mk-amd-map(8)
                     mkdep: construct Makefile dependency list.   . . . .   mkdep(1)
                     mkdir: make a directory file.   . . . .   mkdir(2)
                     mkdir: make directories.   . . . .   mkdir(1)
                     mkfifo: make a fifo file.   . . . .   mkfifo(2)
                     mkfifo: make fifos.   . . . .   mkfifo(1)
                     mklocale: make LC_CTYPE locale files.   . . . .   mklocale(1)
                     mknod: build special file.   . . . .   mknod(8)
                     mknod: make a special file node.   . . . .   mknod(2)
                     mkproto: construct a prototype file system.   . . . .   mkproto(8)
                 source.   mkstr: create an error message file by massaging C   . . . . .   mkstr(1)
                     mktemp: make temporary file name (unique).   . . . .   mktemp(3)
asctime, ctime, difftime, gmtime, localtime,   mktime: transform binary date and time value to/   . . . . . .   ctime(3)
                 memory.   mlock, munlock: lock (unlock) physical pages in   . . . . .   mlock(2)
                     mm: groff mm macros.   . . . .   mm(7)
            mm: groff   mm macros.   . . . .   mm(7)
                     mmap: map files or devices into memory.   . . . .   mmap(2)
      getty: set terminal   mode.   . . . .   getty(8)
   getmode, setmode: modify   mode bits.   . . . .   setmode(3)

umask: set file creation mode mask. . . . . umask(2)
chmod, fchmod: change mode of file. . . . . chmod(2)
chmod: change file modes. . . . . chmod(1)
from floating-point number. modf: extract signed integral and fractional values   . . . . modf(3)
touch: change file access and modification times. . . . . touch(1)
utimes: set file access and modification times. . . . . utimes(2)
passwd: modify a user's password. . . . . passwd(1)
getmode, setmode: modify mode bits. . . . . setmode(3)
rmt: remote magtape protocol module. . . . . rmt(8)
what: show what versions of object modules were used to construct a file. . . . . what(1)
moncontrol, monstartup: control execution profile. . . . . . moncontrol(3)
bwtwo: monochromatic frame buffer. . . . . bwtwo(4)
monop: Monopoly game. . . . . monop(6)
monop: Monopoly game. . . . . monop(6)
moncontrol, monstartup: control execution profile. . . . . moncontrol(3)
pom: display the phase of the moon. . . . . pom(6)
more: file perusal filter for crt viewing. . . . . more(1)
morse: reformat input as punch cards, paper tape or morse code. bcd, ppt, ... bcd(6)
morse code. bcd, ppt, morse: reformat input as punch cards, paper tape or   . . . . bcd(6)
curses: screen functions with "optimal" cursor motion. . . . . curses(3)
mount_lfs: mount a log-structured file system. . . . . mount_lfs(8)
mount_cd9660: mount an ISO-9660 filesystem. . . . . mount_cd9660(8)
amd: automatically mount file systems. . . . . amd(8)
mount: mount file systems. . . . . mount(8)
mount: mount file systems. . . . . mount(8)
mount_nfs: mount nfs file systems. . . . . mount_nfs(8)
getmntopts: scan mount options. . . . . getmntopts(3)
mount, unmount: mount or dismount a filesystem. . . . . mount(2)
exports: define remote mount points for NFS mount requests. . . . . exports(5)
exports: define remote mount points for NFS mount requests. . . . . exports(5)
mountd: service remote NFS mount requests. . . . . mountd(8)
mount_fdesc: mount the file-descriptor file system. . . . . mount_fdesc(8)
mount_kernfs: mount the /kern file system. . . . . mount_kernfs(8)
mount_portal: mount the portal daemon. . . . . mount_portal(8)
mount_procfs: mount the process file system. . . . . mount_procfs(8)
mount_union: mount union filesystems. . . . . mount_union(8)
mount, unmount: mount or dismount a filesystem. . . . . . mount(2)
mount_cd9660: mount an ISO-9660 filesystem. . . . . . . mount_cd9660(8)
mountd: service remote NFS mount requests. . . . . mountd(8)
getmntinfo: get information about mounted file systems. . . . . getmntinfo(3)
getfsstat: get list of all mounted filesystems. . . . . getfsstat(2)
mount_fdesc: mount the file-descriptor file system. . . . . . mount_fdesc(8)
mount_kernfs: mount the /kern file system. . . . . mount_kernfs(8)
mount_lfs: mount a log-structured file system. . . . . . . mount_lfs(8)
mount_nfs: mount nfs file systems. . . . . mount_nfs(8)
system layer. mount_null: demonstrate the use of a null file   . . . . mount_null(8)
mount_portal: mount the portal daemon. . . . . mount_portal(8)
mount_procfs: mount the process file system. . . . . . . mount_procfs(8)
showmount: show remote nfs mounts on host. showmount(8)
mount_umap: sample file system layer. . . . . mount_umap(8)
mount_union: mount union filesystems. . . . . mount_union(8)
msub, mult,/ fmin, fmout, gcd, invert, itom m_in, m_out, madd, mcmp, mdiv, min, mout, move, msqrt, ... mp(3)
/invert, itom m_in, m_out, madd, mcmp, mdiv, min, mout, move, msqrt, msub, mult, omin, omout, pow,/   . . . . mp(3)
plot: openpl, erase, label, line, circle, arc, move, cont, point, linemod, space, closepl:/   . . . . plot(3)
mv: move files. . . . . mv(1)
/itom m_in, m_out, madd, mcmp, mdiv, min, mout, move, msqrt, msub, mult, omin, omout, pow, rpow,/   . . . . mp(3)
mpool: shared memory buffer pool. . . . . mpool(3)
mprotect: control the protection of pages. . . . . mprotect(2)
ms: text formatting macros. . . . . ms(7)
mset: retrieve ASCII to IBM 3270 keyboard map. . . . . . . mset(1)
msgs: system messages and junk mail program. . . . . . . msgs(1)
/m_in, m_out, madd, mcmp, mdiv, min, mout, move, msqrt, msub, mult, omin, omout, pow, rpow, sdiv,:/   . . . . mp(3)
/m_out, madd, mcmp, mdiv, min, mout, move, msqrt, msub, mult, omin, omout, pow, rpow, sdiv,: multiple/   . . . . mp(3)
msync: synchronize a mapped region. . . . . msync(2)
mt: magnetic tape manipulating program. . . . . mt(1)
mtree: map a directory hierarchy. . . . . mtree(8)
/madd, mcmp, mdiv, min, mout, move, msqrt, msub, mult, omin, omout, pow, rpow, sdiv,: multiple/   . . . . . . mp(3)
mblen, mbstowcs, mbtowc, wcstombs, wctomb: multibyte character support for C. . . . . multibyte(3)
mbrune, mbrrune, mbmb: multibyte rune support for C. . . . . mbrune(3)
hunt: a multi-player multi-terminal game. . . . . hunt(6)
strpbrk: locate multiple characters in string. . . . . strpbrk(3)
msqrt, msub, mult, omin, omout, pow, rpow, sdiv,: multiple precision integer arithmetic. /mout, move, ... mp(3)

dcm: HP 98642A communications multiplexer. . . . . dcm(4)
select: synchronous I/O multiplexing. . . . . select(2)
2. ldexp: multiply floating-point number by integral power of . . . . . ldexp(3)
fsplit: split a multi-routine Fortran file into individual files. . . . . fsplit(1)
hunt: a multi-player multi-terminal game. . . . . hunt(6)
sail: multi-user wooden ships and iron men. . . . . sail(6)
switch: multi-way command branch. . . . . csh(1)
mlock, munlock: lock (unlock) physical pages in memory. . . . . . mlock(2)
munmap: remove a mapping. . . . . munmap(2)
mv: move files. . . . . mv(1)
devname: get device name. . . . . devname(3)
getdiskbyname: get generic disk description by its name. . . . . getdiskbyname(3)
getlogin, setlogin: get/set login name. . . . . getlogin(2)
getsockname: get socket name. . . . . getsockname(2)
krb_set_tkt_string: set Kerberos ticket cache file name. . . . . krb_set_tkt_string(3)
logname: display user's login name. . . . . logname(1)
pwd: return working directory name. . . . . pwd(1)
tty: return user's terminal name. . . . . tty(1)
hosts: host name data base. . . . . hosts(5)
networks: network name data base. . . . . networks(5)
protocols: protocol name data base. . . . . protocols(5)
services: service name data base. . . . . services(5)
whois: Internet user name directory service. . . . . whois(1)
getpw: get name from uid. . . . . getpw(3)
symorder: rearrange name list. . . . . symorder(1)
nlist: retrieve symbol table name list from an executable file. . . . . nlist(3)
nm: display name list (symbol table). . . . . nm(1)
rename: change the name of a file. rename(2)
descriptor. ttyname, isatty, ttyslot: get name of associated terminal (tty) from file . . . . ttyname(3)
getpeername: get name of connected peer. . . . . getpeername(2)
gethostname, sethostname: get/set name of current host. . . . . gethostname(3)
hostname: set or print name of current host system. . . . . hostname(1)
dig: send domain name query packets to name servers. . . . . dig(1)
hostname: host name resolution description. . . . . hostname(7)
named: Internet domain name server. named(8)
named.restart: stop and restart the name server. named.restart(8)
named.reload: cause the name server to synchronize its database. . . . . named.reload(8)
dig: send domain name query packets to name servers. dig(1)
nslookup: query Internet name servers interactively. . . . . nslookup(8)
bind: bind a name to a socket. . . . . bind(2)
mktemp: make temporary file name (unique). mktemp(3)
named: Internet domain name server. . . . . named(8)
its database. named.reload: cause the name server to synchronize . . . . . named.reload(8)
named.restart: stop and restart the name server. . . . . named.restart(8)
transfers. named-xfer: ancillary agent for inbound zone . . . . named-xfer(8)
foreach: loop over list of names. . . . . csh(1)
groff_char: groff character names. . . . . groff_char(7)
term: conventional names for terminals. . . . . term(7)
kvm_nlist: retrieve symbol table names from a kernel image. . . . . kvm_nlist(3)
ncheck: generate names from i-numbers. . . . . ncheck(8)
from: print names of those who have sent mail. . . . . from(1)
uuname: list names of UUCP hosts. . . . . uuname(1)
rhost: look up host names using domain server. . . . . host(1)
setlocale, localeconv: natural language formatting for C. . . . . setlocale(3)
ncheck: generate names from i-numbers. . . . . ncheck(8)
getnetgrent, innetgr, setnetgrent, endnetgrent: netgroup database operations. . . . . getnetgrent(3)
netgroup: defines network groups. . . . . netgroup(5)
netstat: show network status. . . . . netstat(1)
Interconnection. iso_addr, iso_ntoa: elementary network address conversion routines for Open System . . . . iso_addr(3)
ntohl, ntohs: convert values between host and network byte order. htonl, htons, ... byteorder(3)
getnetbyname, setnetent, endnetent: get network entry. getnetent, getnetbyaddr, ... getnetent(3)
netgroup: defines network groups. . . . . netgroup(5)
traceroute: print the route packets take to network host. . . . . traceroute(8)
gethostent, sethostent, endhostent, herror: get network host entry. gethostbyname, gethostbyaddr, ... gethostbyname(3)
ping: send ICMP ECHO_REQUEST packets to network hosts. . . . . ping(8)
lo: software loopback network interface. . . . . lo(4)
sliplogin: attach a serial line network interface. . . . . sliplogin(8)
packets. nsip: software network interface encapsulating NS packets in IP . . . . . . nsip(4)
ifconfig: configure network interface parameters. . . . . ifconfig(8)
slattach: attach serial lines as network interfaces. . . . . slattach(8)
networks: network name data base. . . . . networks(5)
clnp: Connectionless-Mode Network Protocol. . . . . clnp(4)

routed: network routing daemon. . . . . routed(8)
netstat: show network status. . . . . netstat(1)
Kerberos routines for sending authentication via network stream sockets. /krb_net_read: . . . . krb_sendauth(3)
ns: Xerox Network Systems(tm) protocol family. . . . . ns(4)
networking: introduction to networking facilities. . . . . netintro(4)
networking: introduction to networking facilities. . . . . . netintro(4)
networks: network name data base. . . . . networks(5)
config. new: build kernel compilation directories. . . . . config.new(8)
des_pcbc_encrypt, des_cbc_cksum, des_quad_cksum,: (new) DES encryption. /des_cbc_encrypt, ... des_crypt(3)
creat: create a new file. . . . . creat(2)
newfs, mfs: construct a new file system. . . . . newfs(8)
newlfs: construct a new LFS file system. . . . . newlfs(8)
fork: create a new process. . . . . fork(2)
vfork: spawn new process in a virtual memory efficient way. . . . . . . vfork(2)
login: login new user. . . . . csh(1)
adduser: procedure for adding new users. . . . . adduser(8)
aliases file. newaliases: rebuild the data base for the mail . . . . newaliases(1)
newfs, mfs: construct a new file system. . . . . newfs(8)
newlfs: construct a new LFS file system. . . . . newlfs(8)
fgetc, getc, getchar, getw: get next character or word from input stream. . . . . getc(3)
nfsiod: local NFS asynchronous I/O server. . . . . nfsiod(8)
mount_nfs: mount nfs file systems. . . . . mount_nfs(8)
exports: define remote mount points for NFS mount requests. . . . . exports(5)
mountd: service remote NFS mount requests. . . . . mountd(8)
showmount: show remote nfs mounts on host. . . . . showmount(8)
nfsd: remote NFS server. . . . . nfsd(8)
nfssvc: NFS services. . . . . nfssvc(2)
nfsstat: display NFS statistics. . . . . nfsstat(1)
nfsd: remote NFS server. . . . . nfsd(8)
nfsiod: local NFS asynchronous I/O server. . . . . nfsiod(8)
nfsstat: display NFS statistics. . . . . nfsstat(1)
nfssvc: NFS services. . . . . nfssvc(2)
priority. nice: execute a command at a low scheduling . . . . nice(1)
vgrind: grind nice listings of programs. . . . . vgrind(1)
nice: run low priority process. . . . . csh(1)
nice: set program scheduling priority. . . . . nice(3)
executable file. nlist: retrieve symbol table name list from an . . . . nlist(3)
nm: display name list (symbol table). . . . . nm(1)
getgrent, getgrnam, getgrgid, setgroupent, . Nm setgrfile, setgrent, endgrent: group database/ . . . getgrent(3)
mknod: make a special file node. . . . . mknod(2)
nohup: invoke a command immune to hangups. . . . . . . nohup(1)
nohup: run command immune to hangups. . . . . csh(1)
nologin: politely refuse a login. . . . . nologin(8)
setjmp, longjmp, _setjmp, _longjmp longjmperror: non-local jumps. sigsetjmp, siglongjmp, ... setjmp(3)
vis: display non-printable characters in a visual format. . . . . vis(1)
exit: perform normal program termination. . . . . exit(3)
mesg: display (do not display) messages from other users. . . . . mesg(1)
ceil: smallest integral value not greater than x. . . . . ceil(3)
floor: largest integral value not greater than x. . . . . floor(3)
vacation: return "I am not here" indication. . . . . vacation(1)
isinf, isnan: test for infinity or not-a-number. . . . . isinf(3)
notify: request immediate notification. . . . . csh(1)
biff: be notified if mail arrives and who it is from. . . . . biff(1)
notify: request immediate notification. . . . . csh(1)
nroff: emulate nroff command with groff. . . . . nroff(1)
nroff: emulate nroff command with groff. . . . . nroff(1)
soelim: eliminate .so's from nroff input. . . . . soelim(1)
colcrt: filter nroff output for CRT previewing. . . . . colcrt(1)
deroff: remove nroff, troff, tbl and eqn constructs. . . . . deroff(1)
checknr: check nroff/troff files. checknr(1)
ns_addr, ns_ntoa: Xerox NS Ns (tm) address conversion routines. . . . . ns(3)
nsip: software network interface encapsulating NS packets in IP packets. . . . . nsip(4)
XNSrouted: NS Routing Information Protocol daemon. . . . . . . XNSrouted(8)
ns_addr, ns_ntoa: Xerox NS Ns (tm) address conversion routines. . . . . ns(3)
ns: Xerox Network Systems(tm) protocol family. . . . . . . ns(4)
conversion routines. ns_addr, ns_ntoa: Xerox NS Ns (tm) address . . . . ns(3)
packets in IP packets. nsip: software network interface encapsulating NS . . . . . nsip(4)
interactively. nslookup: query Internet name servers . . . . nslookup(8)
routines. ns_addr, ns_ntoa: Xerox NS Ns (tm) address conversion . . . . ns(3)
network byte order. htonl, htons, ntohl, ntohs: convert values between host and . . . . . . byteorder(3)
order. htonl, htons, ntohl, ntohs: convert values between host and network byte . . . . byteorder(3)
null: the null device. . . . . null(4)

mount_null: demonstrate the use of a null file system layer. . . . . mount_null(8)

null: the null device. . . . . null(4)

integral and fractional values from floating-point number. modf: extract signed . . . . modf(3)

ldexp: multiply floating-point number by integral power of 2. . . . . ldexp(3)

number: convert Arabic numerals to English. . . . . number(6)

phones: remote host phone number data base. . . . . phones(5)

rpc: rpc program number data base. . . . . rpc(5)

recno: record number database access method. . . . . recno(3)

factor, primes: factor a number, generate primes. . . . . factor(6)

rand, srand: bad random number generator. . . . . rand(3)

random, srandom, initstate, setstate: better random number generator; routines for changing generators. . . . . . random(3)

L-dialcodes: UUCP phone number index file. . . . . L-dialcodes(5)

portmap: DARPA port to RPC program number mapper. . . . . portmap(8)

frexp: convert floating-point number to fractional and integral components. . . . . frexp(3)

intro: introduction to system calls and error numbers. . . . . intro(2)

random: random lines from a file or random numbers. . . . . random(6)

number: convert Arabic numerals to English. . . . . number(6)

size: display object file segment sizes (text, data and bss). . . . . size(1)

lorder: list dependencies for object files. . . . . lorder(1)

what: show what versions of object modules were used to construct a file. . . . . what(1)

od: octal, decimal, hex, ascii dump. . . . . od(1)

hexdump: ascii, decimal, hexadecimal, octal dump. . . . . hexdump(1)

sets. ascii: octal, hexadecimal and decimal ASCII character . . . . . ascii(7)

od: octal, decimal, hex, ascii dump. . . . . od(1)

lseek: reposition read/write file offset. lseek(2)

/mcmp, mdiv, min, mout, move, msqrt, msub, mult, omin, omout, pow, rpow, sdiv,: multiple precision/ . . . . . mp(3)

/mdiv, min, mout, move, msqrt, msub, mult, omin, omout, pow, rpow, sdiv,: multiple precision integer/ . . . . . mp(3)

atan: arc tangent function of one variable. . . . . atan(3)

onintr: process interrupts in command scripts. . . . . csh(1)

man: display the on-line manual pages. . . . . man(1)

funopen, fropen, fwopen: open a stream. . . . . funopen(3)

flock: apply or remove an advisory lock on an open file. flock(2)

kvm_getfiles: survey open files. kvm_getfiles(3)

fopen, fdopen, freopen: stream open functions. . . . . fopen(3)

open: open or create a file for reading or writing. . . . . . . open(2)

open: open open or create a file for reading or writing. . . . . . . open(2)

elementary network address conversion routines for Open System Interconnection. iso_addr, iso_ntoa: . . . . . iso_addr(3)

closedir, dirfd: directory operations. opendir, readdir, telldir, seekdir, rewinddir, ... directory(3)

syslog, vsyslog, openlog, closelog, setlogmask: control system log. . . . . . syslog(3)

cont, point, linemod, space, closepl:/ plot: openpl, erase, label, line, circle, arc, move, ... plot(3)

openprom: OPENPROM and EEPROM interface. . . . . openprom(4)

eeprom: openprom control utility. . . . . eeprom(8)

openprom: OPENPROM and EEPROM interface. . . . . openprom(4)

savecore: save a core dump of the operating system. . . . . savecore(8)

kgmon: generate a dump of the operating system's profile buffers. . . . . kgmon(8)

intro: introduction to system maintenance and operation commands. . . . . intro(8)

tgetstr, tgoto, tputs: terminal independent operation routines. tgetent, tgetnum, tgetflag, ... termcap(3)

memcmp, memcpy, memmove, memset: byte string operations. bcmp, bcopy, bzero, memccpy, memchr, ... bstring(3)

seekdir, rewinddir, closedir, dirfd: directory operations. opendir, readdir, telldir, ... directory(3)

.Nm setgrfile, setgrent, endgrent: group database operations. /getgrnam, getgrgid, setgroupent, ... getgrent(3)

setnetgrent, endnetgrent: netgroup database operations. getnetgrent, innetgr, ... getnetgrent(3)

setpassent, setpwent, endpwent: password database operations. getpwent, getpwnam, getpwuid, ... getpwent(3)

realloc, calloc, alloca: general memory allocation operations. malloc, free, ... memory(3)

setbuffer, setlinebuf, setvbuf: stream buffering operations. setbuf, ... setbuf(3)

infnan: signals invalid floating-point operations on a VAX (temporary). . . . . infnan(3)

join: relational database operator. join(1)

evaluation. operator: C operator precedence and order of . . . . operator(7)

operator: C operator precedence and order of evaluation. . . . . operator(7)

erf, erfc: error function operators. erf(3)

curses: screen functions with "optimal" cursor motion. . . . . curses(3)

getopt: get option character from command line argument list. . . . . . getopt(3)

getmntopts: scan mount options. getmntopts(3)

stty: set the options for a terminal device interface. . . . . stty(1)

grog: guess options for groff command. . . . . grog(1)

getsubopt: get sub options from an argument. . . . . getsubopt(3)

getsockopt, setsockopt: get and set options on sockets. . . . . getsockopt(2)

ntohs: convert values between host and network byte order. htonl, htons, ntohl, ... byteorder(3)

lastcomm: show last commands executed in reverse order. lastcomm(1)

operator: C operator precedence and order of evaluation. . . . . operator(7)

ed: line oriented text editor. . . . . ed(1)

patch: a program for applying a diff file to an original. patch(1)

revert a visual representation of data back to original form. unvis: . . . . unvis(1)

printf: formatted output. . . . . printf(1)
write, writev: write output. . . . . write(2)
fputc, putc, putchar, putw: output a character or word to a stream. . . . . putc(3)
fputs, puts: output a line to a stream. . . . . fputs(3)
ecvt, fcvt, gcvt: output conversion. . . . . ecvt(3)
vprintf, vfprintf, vsprintf, vsnprintf: formatted output conversion. /fprintf, sprintf, snprintf, ... printf(3)
fold: fold long lines for finite width output device. . . . . fold(1)
colcrt: filter nroff output for CRT previewing. . . . . colcrt(1)
groff_out: groff intermediate output format. groff_out(5)
grodvi: convert groff output to TeX dvi format. . . . . grodvi(1)
foreach: loop over list of names. . . . . csh(1)
sendmail: send mail over the internet. . . . . sendmail(8)
exec: overlay shell with specified command. . . . . csh(1)
chown: change file owner and group. . . . . chown(8)
chown, fchown: change owner and group of a file. . . . . chown(2)
pac: printer/plotter accounting information. . . . . pac(8)
disklabel: disk pack label. . . . . disklabel.5(5)
disklabel: read and write disk pack label. . . . . disklabel(8)
route: kernel packet forwarding database. . . . . route(4)
spp: Xerox Sequenced Packet Protocol. . . . . spp(4)
trsp: transliterate sequenced packet protocol trace. . . . . trsp(8)
network interface encapsulating NS packets in IP packets. nsip: software . . . . . nsip(4)
nsip: software network interface encapsulating NS packets in IP packets. . . . . nsip(4)
traceroute: print the route packets take to network host. . . . . traceroute(8)
dig: send domain name query packets to name servers. . . . . dig(1)
ping: send ICMP ECHO_REQUEST packets to network hosts. . . . . ping(8)
getpagesize: get system page size. . . . . getpagesize(3)
pagesize: print system page size. . . . . pagesize(1)
intro: miscellaneous information pages. . . . . intro(7)
man: display the on-line manual pages. . . . . man(1)
mprotect: control the protection of pages. . . . . mprotect(2)
mlock, munlock: lock (unlock) physical pages in memory. . . . . mlock(2)
pagesize: print system page size. . . . . pagesize(1)
swapon: specify additional device for paging and swapping. . . . . swapon(8)
drum: paging device. . . . . drum(4)
swapon: add a swap device for interleaved paging/swapping. . . . . swapon(2)
make_keypair: generate Kerberos host key pair. . . . . make_keypair(8)
pipe: create descriptor pair for interprocess communication. . . . . pipe(2)
socketpair: create a pair of connected sockets. . . . . socketpair(2)
bcd, ppt, morse: reformat input as punch cards, paper tape or morse code. . . . . bcd(6)
me: macros for formatting papers. . . . . me(7)
ifconfig: configure network interface parameters. . . . . ifconfig(8)
scsiformat: format SCSI disks and show SCSI parameters. . . . . scsiformat(8)
getpid, getppid: get parent or calling process identification. . . . . getpid(2)
yacc: an LALR(1) parser generator. . . . . yacc(1)
diskpart: calculate default disk partition sizes. diskpart(8)
m4: macro language preprocessor for ratfor(1) and pascal(1). . . . . m4(1)
system: pass a command to the shell. . . . . system(3)
passwd: format of the password file. . . . . passwd(5)
passwd: modify a user's password. . . . . passwd(1)
getpass: get a password. . . . . getpass(3)
passwd: modify a user's password. . . . . passwd(1)
pwcache: cache password and group entries. . . . . pwcache(3)
kpasswdd: Kerberos password changing daemon. . . . . kpasswdd(8)
getpwnam, getpwuid, setpassent, setpwent, endpwent: password database operations. getpwent, ... getpwent(3)
pwd_mkdb: generate the password databases. . . . . pwd_mkdb(8)
passwd: format of the password file. . . . . passwd(5)
vipw: edit the password file. . . . . vipw(8)
makekey: make encrypted keys or passwords. . . . . makekey(8)
files. paste: merge corresponding or subsequent lines of . . . . . . paste(1)
original. patch: a program for applying a diff file to an . . . . . . patch(1)
variables. pathconf, fpathconf: get configurable pathname . . . . pathconf(2)
access: check access permissions of a file or pathname. . . . . access(2)
dirname: return filename or directory portion of pathname. basename, ... basename(1)
ctermid: generate terminal pathname. . . . . ctermid(3)
fnmatch: match filename or pathname. . . . . fnmatch(3)
getcwd: get working directory pathname. . . . . getcwd(3)
realpath: returns the canonicalized absolute pathname. . . . . realpath(3)
USERFILE: UUCP pathname permissions file. . . . . USERFILE(5)
pathconf, fpathconf: get configurable pathname variables. . . . . pathconf(2)
glob, globfree: generate pathnames matching a pattern. . . . . glob(3)
which: locate a program file including aliases and paths. . . . . which(1)

glob, globfree: generate pathnames matching a	pattern.	glob(3)
lptest: generate lineprinter ripple	pattern.	lptest(1)
awk:	pattern scanning and processing language.	awk(1)
grep: file	pattern searcher.	grep(1)
	pause: stop until signal.	pause(3)
directory hierarchies.	pax: read and write file archives and copy	pax(1)
popen,	pclose: process I/O.	popen(3)
getpeername: get name of connected	peer.	getpeername(2)
sync: force completion of	pending disk writes (flush cache).	sync(8)
sigpending: get	pending signals.	sigpending(2)
quot: display total block usage	per user for a file system.	quot(8)
exit:	perform normal program termination.	exit(3)
	perl: practical extraction and report language.	perl(1)
group: format of the group	permissions file.	group(5)
L.cmds: UUCP remote command	permissions file.	L.cmds(5)
USERFILE: UUCP pathname	permissions file.	USERFILE(5)
access: check access	permissions of a file or pathname.	access(2)
ptx:	permuted index.	ptx(1)
limit: alter	per-process resource limitations.	csh(1)
error messages.	perror, strerror, sys_errlist, sys_nerr: system	strerror(3)
more: file	perusal filter for crt viewing.	more(1)
zmore: file	perusal filter for crt viewing of compressed text.	zmore(1)
pfbtops: translate a PostScript font in .	pfb format to ASCII.	pfbtops(1)
to ASCII.	pfbtops: translate a PostScript font in .pfb format	pfbtops(1)
	phantasia: an interterminal fantasy game.	phantasia(6)
pom: display the	phase of the moon.	pom(6)
phones: remote host	phone number data base.	phones(5)
L-dialcodes: UUCP	phone number index file.	L-dialcodes(5)
	phones: remote host phone number data base.	phones(5)
mlock, munlock: lock (unlock)	physical pages in memory.	mlock(2)
	pic: compile pictures for troff or TeX.	pic(1)
pic: compile	pictures for troff or TeX.	pic(1)
	pig: eformatray inputway asway Igpay Atinlay.	pig(6)
hosts.	ping: send ICMP ECHO_REQUEST packets to network	ping(8)
communication.	pipe: create descriptor pair for interprocess	pipe(2)
tee:	pipe fitting.	tee(1)
gzexe: compress executable files in	place.	gzexe(1)
bg:	place job in background.	csh(1)
fish:	play "Go Fish".	fish(6)
mille:	play Mille Bornes.	mille(6)
worm:	play the growing worm game.	worm(6)
	plot: graphics filters.	plot(1)
	plot: graphics interface.	plot(5)
move, cont, point, linemod, space, closepl:/	plot: openpl, erase, label, line, circle, arc,	plot(3)
/erase, label, line, circle, arc, move, cont,	point, linemod, space, closepl: graphics interface.	plot(3)
drem, finite, logb, scalb: IEEE 754 floating	point support. copysign,	ieee(3)
exports: define remote mount	points for NFS mount requests.	exports(5)
nologin:	politely refuse a login.	nologin(8)
uupoll:	poll a remote UUCP site.	uupoll(8)
	pom: display the phase of the moon.	pom(6)
mpool: shared memory buffer	pool.	mpool(3)
popd:	pop shell directory stack.	csh(1)
	popd: pop shell directory stack.	csh(1)
	popen, pclose: process I/O.	popen(3)
portmap: DARPA	port to RPC program number mapper.	portmap(8)
mount_portal: mount the	portal daemon.	mount_portal(8)
basename, dirname: return filename or directory	portion of pathname.	basename(1)
cut: select	portions of each line of a file.	cut(1)
	portmap: DARPA port to RPC program number mapper.	portmap(8)
re_format:	POSIX 1003.2 regular expressions.	re_format(7)
zgrep: search	possibly compressed files for a regular expression.	zgrep(1)
psbb: extract bounding box from	PostScript document.	psbb(1)
grops:	PostScript driver for groff.	grops(1)
pfbtops: translate a	PostScript font in .pfb format to ASCII.	pfbtops(1)
exp, expm1, log, log10, log1p,	pow: exponential, logarithm, power functions.	exp(3)
min, mout, move, msqrt, msub, mult, omin, omout,	pow, rpow, sdiv,: multiple precision integer/ /mdiv,	mp(3)
log, log10, log1p, pow: exponential, logarithm,	power functions. exp, expm1,	exp(3)
ldexp: multiply floating-point number by integral	power of 2.	ldexp(3)
	ppi: HP-IB printer/plotter interface.	ppi(4)
tape or morse code. bcd,	ppt, morse: reformat input as punch cards, paper	bcd(6)
	pr: print files.	pr(1)
perl:	practical extraction and report language.	perl(1)

operator: C operator   precedence and order of evaluation.   . . . .   operator(7)
msub, mult, omin, omout, pow, rpow, sdiv,: multiple   precision integer arithmetic. /mout, move, msqrt, ...   mp(3)
cc, g++: GNU project C and C++ Compiler (v2   preliminary).   . . . .   cc(1)
g++: GNU project C++ Compiler (v2   preliminary).   . . . .   g++(1)
refer: preprocess bibliographic references for groff.   . . . .   refer(1)
cccp, cpp: the GNU C-compatible compiler   preprocessor.   . . . .   cpp(1)
m4: macro language   preprocessor for ratfor(1) and pascal(1).   . . . .   m4(1)
w: who   present users are and what they are doing.   . . . .   w(1)
colcrt: filter nroff output for CRT   previewing.   . . . .   colcrt(1)
factor, primes: factor a number, generate   primes.   . . . .   factor(6)
factor,   primes: factor a number, generate primes.   . . . .   factor(6)
lpr: off line   print.   . . . .   lpr(1)
fortune: print a random, hopefully interesting, adage.   . . . .   fortune(6)
hashstat: print command hashing statistics.   . . . .   csh(1)
jobs: print current job list.   . . . .   csh(1)
printenv, env: print out the environment, set and   print environment.   . . . .   printenv(1)
cat: concatenate and   print files.   . . . .   cat(1)
pr: print files.   . . . .   pr(1)
fpr: print Fortran file.   . . . .   fpr(1)
history: print history event list.   . . . .   csh(1)
banner: print large banner on printer.   . . . .   banner(6)
files. rlog: print log messages and other information about RCS   . . . .   rlog(1)
hostname: set or   print name of current host system.   . . . .   hostname(1)
from: print names of those who have sent mail.   . . . .   from(1)
environment. printenv, env: print out the environment, set and print   . . . .   printenv(1)
jot: print sequential or random data.   . . . .   jot(1)
pagesize: print system page size.   . . . .   pagesize(1)
mailq: print the mail queue.   . . . .   mailq(1)
traceroute: print the route packets take to network host.   . . . .   traceroute(8)
diction, explain: print wordy sentences; thesaurus for diction.   . . . .   diction(1)
strings: find   printable strings in a file.   . . . .   strings(1)
    printcap: printer capability data base.   . . . .   printcap(5)
print environment.   printenv, env: print out the environment, set and   . . . . . .   printenv(1)
banner: print large banner on   printer.   . . . .   banner(6)
printcap: printer capability data base.   . . . .   printcap(5)
lpc: line   printer control program.   . . . .   lpc(8)
lpd: line   printer spooler daemon.   . . . .   lpd(8)
lprm: remove jobs from the line   printer spooling queue.   . . . .   lprm(1)
pac: printer/plotter accounting information.   . . . .   pac(8)
ppi: HP-IB   printer/plotter interface.   . . . .   ppi(4)
    printf: formatted output.   . . . .   printf(1)
vfprintf, vsprintf, vsnprintf: formatted output/   printf, fprintf, sprintf, snprintf, vprintf, ...   printf(3)
exclusive). isgraph: printing character test (space character   . . . .   isgraph(3)
inclusive). isprint: printing character test (space character   . . . .   isprint(3)
setpriority: get/set program scheduling   priority. getpriority, ...   getpriority(2)
nice: execute a command at a low scheduling   priority.   . . . .   nice(1)
nice: set program scheduling   priority.   . . . .   nice(3)
renice: alter   priority of running processes.   . . . .   renice(8)
nice: run low   priority process.   . . . .   csh(1)
xsend, xget, enroll: private encrypted mail.   . . . .   xsend(1)
adduser: procedure for adding new users.   . . . .   adduser(8)
boot: system bootstrapping   procedures.   . . . .   boot_hp300(8)
reboot: UNIX bootstrapping   procedures.   . . . .   boot_sparc(8)
nice: run low priority   process.   . . . .   csh(1)
stop: halt a job or   process.   . . . .   csh(1)
_exit: terminate the calling   process.   . . . .   _exit(2)
fork: create a new   process.   . . . .   fork(2)
gcore: get core images of running   process.   . . . .   gcore(1)
kill: terminate or signal a   process.   . . . .   kill(1)
kill: send signal to a   process.   . . . .   kill(2)
raise: send a signal to the current   process.   . . . .   raise(3)
acct: enable or disable   process accounting.   . . . .   acct(2)
wait: await   process completion.   . . . .   wait(1)
init: process control initialization.   . . . .   init(8)
sleep: suspend   process execution for interval of seconds.   . . . .   sleep(3)
mount_procfs: mount the   process file system.   . . . .   mount_procfs(8)
getpgrp: get   process group.   . . . .   getpgrp(2)
killpg: send signal to a   process group.   . . . .   killpg(2)
setpgid, setpgrp: set   process group.   . . . .   setpgid(2)
setsid: create session and set   process group ID.   . . . .   setsid(2)
tcgetpgrp: get foreground   process group ID.   . . . .   tcgetpgrp(3)
tcsetpgrp: set foreground   process group ID.   . . . .   tcsetpgrp(3)

getgid, getegid: get group   process identification.   . . . .   getgid(2)
getpid, getppid: get parent or calling   process identification.   . . . .   getpid(2)
vfork: spawn new   process in a virtual memory efficient way.   . . . .   vfork(2)
onintr: process interrupts in command scripts.   . . . .   csh(1)
popen, pclose: process I/O.   . . . .   popen(3)
profil: control   process profiling.   . . . .   profil(2)
kvm_getprocs, kvm_getargv, kvm_getenvv: access user   process state.   . . . .   kvm_getprocs(3)
ps: process status.   . . . .   ps(1)
wait, waitpid, wait4, wait3: wait for   process termination.   . . . .   wait(2)
times: process times.   . . . .   times(3)
ptrace: process trace.   . . . .   ptrace(2)
ktrace: enable kernel   process tracing.   . . . .   ktrace(1)
ktrace: process tracing.   . . . .   ktrace(2)
kill: kill jobs and   processes.   . . . .   csh(1)
renice: alter priority of running   processes.   . . . .   renice(8)
wait: wait for background   processes to complete.   . . . .   csh(1)
awk: pattern scanning and   processing language.   . . . .   awk(1)
reboot: reboot system or halt   processor.   . . . .   reboot(2)
clock: determine   processor time used.   . . . . . . · · · . . .   clock(3)
echo: produce message in a shell script.   . . . .   echo(1)
profil: control process profiling.   . . . .   profil(2)
moncontrol, monstartup: control execution   profile.   . . . .   moncontrol(3)
kgmon: generate a dump of the operating system's   profile buffers.   . . . .   kgmon(8)
gprof: display call graph   profile data.   . . . .   gprof(1)
profil: control process   profiling.   . . . .   profil(2)
finger: user information lookup   program.   . . . .   finger(1)
ftp: ARPANET file transfer   program.   . . . .   ftp(1)
lpc: line printer control   program.   . . . .   lpc(8)
lpq: spool queue examination   program.   . . . .   lpq(1)
msgs: system messages and junk mail   program.   . . . .   msgs(1)
mt: magnetic tape manipulating   program.   . . . .   mt(1)
rdist: remote file distribution   program.   . . . .   rdist(1)
tftp: trivial file transfer   program.   . . . .   tftp(1)
timedc: timed control   program.   . . . .   timedc(8)
units: conversion   program.   . . . .   units(1)
make: maintain   program dependencies.   . . . .   make(1)
which: locate a   program file including aliases and paths.   . . . .   which(1)
patch: a   program for applying a diff file to an original.   . . . .   patch(1)
rpc: rpc   program number data base.   . . . .   rpc(5)
portmap: DARPA port to RPC   program number mapper.   . . . .   portmap(8)
getpriority, setpriority: get/set   program scheduling priority.   . . . .   getpriority(2)
nice: set   program scheduling priority.   . . . .   nice(3)
indent: indent and format C   program source.   . . . .   indent(1)
abort: cause abnormal   program termination.   . . . .   abort(3)
exit: perform normal   program termination.   . . . .   exit(3)
struct: structure Fortran   programs.   . . . .   struct(1)
vgrind: grind nice listings of   programs.   . . . .   vgrind(1)
whereis: locate   programs.   . . . .   whereis(1)
xstr: extract strings from C   programs to implement shared strings.   . . . .   xstr(1)
cc, g++: GNU   project C and C++ Compiler (v2 preliminary).   . . . .   cc(1)
g++: GNU   project C++ Compiler (v2 preliminary).   . . . .   g++(1)
emacs: GNU   project Emacs.   . . . .   emacs(1)
mprotect: control the   protection of pages.   . . . .   mprotect(2)
clnp: Connectionless-Mode Network   Protocol.   . . . .   clnp(4)
cltp: ISO Connectionless Transport   Protocol.   . . . .   cltp(4)
es-is: End System to Intermediate System Routing   Protocol.   . . . .   esis(4)
icmp: Internet Control Message   Protocol.   . . . .   icmp(4)
idp: Xerox Internet Datagram   Protocol.   . . . .   idp(4)
ip: Internet   Protocol.   . . . .   ip(4)
spp: Xerox Sequenced Packet   Protocol.   . . . .   spp(4)
tcp: Internet Transmission Control   Protocol.   . . . .   tcp(4)
telnet: user interface to the TELNET   protocol.   . . . .   telnet(1)
TP: ISO Transport   Protocol.   . . . .   tp(4)
udp: Internet User Datagram   Protocol.   . . . .   udp(4)
rpcgen: an RPC   protocol compiler.   . . . .   rpcgen(1)
XNSrouted: NS Routing Information   Protocol daemon.   . . . .   XNSrouted(8)
getprotobyname, setprotoent, endprotoent: get   protocol entry. getprotoent, getprotobynumber, ...   getprotoent(3)
inet: Internet   protocol family.   . . . .   inet(4)
iso: ISO   protocol family.   . . . .   iso(4)
ns: Xerox Network Systems(tm)   protocol family.   . . . .   ns(4)
unix: UNIX-domain   protocol family.   . . . .   unix(4)
rmt: remote magtape   protocol module.   . . . .   rmt(8)

protocols: protocol name data base. . . . . protocols(5)
ftpd: Internet File Transfer Protocol server. . . . . ftpd(8)
telnetd: DARPA TELNET protocol server. . . . . telnetd(8)
tftpd: Internet Trivial File Transfer Protocol server. . . . . tftpd(8)
trpt: transliterate protocol trace. . . . . trpt(8)
trsp: transliterate sequenced packet protocol trace. . . . . trsp(8)
protocols: protocol name data base. . . . . protocols(5)
mkproto: construct a prototype file system. . . . . mkproto(8)
ps: process status. . . . . ps(1)
document. psbb: extract bounding box from PostScript . . . . psbb(1)
pty: pseudo terminal driver. . . . . pty(4)
messages. psignal, sys_siglist sys_signame: system signal . . . . . . psignal(3)
pstat: display system data structures. . . . . pstat(8)
ptrace: process trace. . . . . ptrace(2)
ptx: permuted index. . . . . ptx(1)
pty: pseudo terminal driver. . . . . pty(4)
publickey: public key database. . . . . publickey(5)
publickey: public key database. . . . . publickey(5)
bcd, ppt, morse: reformat input as punch cards, paper tape or morse code. . . . . bcd(6)
ispunct: punctuation character test. . . . . ispunct(3)
pushd: push shell directory stack. . . . . csh(1)
pushd: push shell directory stack. . . . . csh(1)
a stream. fputc, putc, putchar, putw: output a character or word to . . . . . . putc(3)
stream. fputc, putc, putchar, putw: output a character or word to a . . . . . . putc(3)
functions. getenv, putenv, setenv, unsetenv: environment variable . . . . . . getenv(3)
fputs, puts: output a line to a stream. . . . . fputs(3)
fputc, putc, putchar, putw: output a character or word to a stream. . . . . putc(3)
pwcache: cache password and group entries. . . . . pwcache(3)
pwd: return working directory name. . . . . pwd(1)
pwd_mkdb: generate the password databases. . . . . pwd_mkdb(8)
qsort, heapsort, mergesort: sort functions. . . . . qsort(3)
strtol, strtoq: convert string value to a long or quad_t integer. . . . . strtol(3)
nslookup: query Internet name servers interactively. . . . . nslookup(8)
dig: send domain name query packets to name servers. . . . . dig(1)
amq: automounter query tool. . . . . amq(8)
atq: display the at(1) job queue. atq(1)
insque, remque: insert/remove element from a queue. insque(3)
lprm: remove jobs from the line printer spooling queue. lprm(1)
mailq: print the mail queue. mailq(1)
uuq: examine or manipulate the uucp queue. uuq(1)
lpq: spool queue examination program. . . . . lpq(1)
uucico, uucpd: transfer files queued by uucp or uux. . . . . uucico(8)
mdoc: quick reference guide for the –mdoc macro package. . . . . . mdoc(7)
arithmetic: quiz on simple arithmetic. . . . . arithmetic(6)
quiz: random knowledge tests. . . . . quiz(6)
system. quot: display total block usage per user for a file . . . . . . quot(8)
quotacheck: filesystem quota consistency checker. . . . . quotacheck(8)
quota: display disk usage and limits. . . . . quota(1)
quotacheck: filesystem quota consistency checker. . . . . . quotacheck(8)
quotactl: manipulate filesystem quotas. . . . . quotactl(2)
quotaon, quotaoff: turn filesystem quotas on and off. . . . . . . quotaon(8)
off. quotaon, quotaoff: turn filesystem quotas on and . . . . quotaon(8)
edquota: edit user quotas. . . . . edquota(8)
quotactl: manipulate filesystem quotas. . . . . quotactl(2)
repquota: summarize quotas for a file system. . . . . repquota(8)
quotaon, quotaoff: turn filesystem quotas on and off. . . . . quotaon(8)
div: return quotient and remainder from division. . . . . div(3)
ldiv: return quotient and remainder from division. . . . . ldiv(3)
radixsort: radix sort. . . . . radixsort(3)
radixsort: radix sort. . . . . radixsort(3)
rain: animated raindrops display. . . . . rain(6)
rain: animated raindrops display. . . . . rain(6)
raise: send a signal to the current process. . . . . raise(3)
rand, srand: bad random number generator. . . . . rand(3)
jot: print sequential or random data. . . . . jot(1)
fortune: print a random, hopefully interesting, adage. . . . . fortune(6)
quiz: random knowledge tests. . . . . quiz(6)
random: random lines from a file or random numbers. . . . . random(6)
rand, srand: bad random number generator. . . . . rand(3)
random, srandom, initstate, setstate: better random number generator; routines for changing/ . . . . . . random(3)
random: random lines from a file or random numbers. . . . . random(6)
random: random lines from a file or random numbers. . . . . random(6)

number generator; routines for changing/	random, srandom, initstate, setstate: better random	random(3)
	ranlib: archive (library) table-of-contents format.	ranlib.5(5)
	ranlib: table-of-contents for archive libraries.	ranlib(1)
m4: macro language preprocessor for	ratfor(1) and pascal(1).	m4(1)
	rb: HP98720 ''Renaissance'' device interface.	rb(4)
	rbootd: HP remote boot server.	rbootd(8)
	rc: command script for auto-reboot and daemons.	rc(8)
stream to a remote command.	rcmd, rresvport, ruserok: routines for returning a	rcmd(3)
	rcp: remote file copy.	rcp(1)
freeze a configuration of sources checked in under	RCS. rcsfreeze:	rcsfreeze(1)
	rcs: change RCS file attributes.	rcs(1)
rcsintro: introduction to	RCS commands.	rcsintro(1)
rcsfile: format of	RCS file.	rcsfile(5)
rcs: change	RCS file attributes.	rcs(1)
print log messages and other information about	RCS files. rlog:	rlog(1)
ci: check in	RCS revisions.	ci(1)
co: check out	RCS revisions.	co(1)
rcsdiff: compare	RCS revisions.	rcsdiff(1)
rcsmerge: merge	RCS revisions.	rcsmerge(1)
	rcsclean: clean up working files.	rcsclean(1)
	rcsdiff: compare RCS revisions.	rcsdiff(1)
	rcsfile: format of RCS file.	rcsfile(5)
checked in under RCS.	rcsfreeze: freeze a configuration of sources	rcsfreeze(1)
	rcsintro: introduction to RCS commands.	rcsintro(1)
	rcsmerge: merge RCS revisions.	rcsmerge(1)
	rd: CS/80 disk interface.	rd(4)
	rdist: remote file distribution program.	rdist(1)
disklabel:	read and write disk pack label.	disklabel(8)
hierarchies. pax:	read and write file archives and copy directory	pax(1)
source:	read commands from file.	csh(1)
read, readv:	read input.	read(2)
kvm_read, kvm_write:	read or write kernel virtual memory.	kvm_read(3)
	read, readv: read input.	read(2)
readlink:	read value of a symbolic link.	readlink(2)
dirfd: directory operations. opendir,	readdir, telldir, seekdir, rewinddir, closedir,	directory(3)
open: open or create a file for	reading or writing.	open(2)
	readlink: read value of a symbolic link.	readlink(2)
read,	readv: read input.	read(2)
bad144:	read/write dec standard 144 bad sector information.	bad144(8)
lseek: reposition	read/write file offset.	lseek(2)
setregid: set	real and effective group ID.	setregid(2)
setreuid: set	real and effective user ID's.	setreuid(2)
free up memory allocated with malloc, calloc or	realloc. free:	free(3)
operations. malloc, free,	realloc, calloc, alloca: general memory allocation	memory(3)
	realloc: reallocation of memory function.	realloc(3)
realloc:	reallocation of memory function.	realloc(3)
/etc/kerberosIV/krb.realms: host to Kerberos	realm translation file.	krb.realms(5)
/etc/kerberosIV/krb.	realms: host to Kerberos realm translation file.	krb.realms(5)
pathname.	realpath: returns the canonicalized absolute	realpath(3)
symorder:	rearrange name list.	symorder(1)
	reboot, halt: stopping and restarting the system.	reboot(8)
	reboot: reboot system or halt processor.	reboot(2)
reboot:	reboot system or halt processor.	reboot(2)
	reboot: UNIX bootstrapping procedures.	boot_sparc(8)
fastboot, fasthalt:	reboot/halt the system without checking the disks.	fastboot(8)
newaliases:	rebuild the data base for the mail aliases file.	newaliases(1)
recv, recvfrom, recvmsg:	receive a message from a socket.	recv(2)
mail: send and	receive mail.	mail(1)
rmail: handle remote mail	received via uucp.	rmail(8)
	recno: record number database access method.	recno(3)
	re_comp, re_exec: regular expression handler.	re_comp(3)
znew:	recompress .Z files to .gz files.	znew(1)
rehash:	recompute command hash table.	csh(1)
recno:	record number database access method.	recno(3)
utmp, wtmp, lastlog: login	records.	utmp(5)
socket.	recv, recvfrom, recvmsg: receive a message from a	recv(2)
recv,	recvfrom, recvmsg: receive a message from a socket.	recv(2)
recv, recvfrom,	recvmsg: receive a message from a socket.	recv(2)
eval:	re-evaluate shell data.	csh(1)
re_comp,	re_exec: regular expression handler.	re_comp(3)
groff.	refer: preprocess bibliographic references for	refer(1)
mdoc: quick	reference guide for the —mdoc macro package.	mdoc(7)

refer: preprocess bibliographic references for groff. . . . . refer(1)
code. bcd, ppt, morse: reformat input as punch cards, paper tape or morse . . . . . bcd(6)
re_format: POSIX 1003.2 regular expressions. . . . . re_format(7)
nologin: politely refuse a login. . . . . nologin(8)
regular-expression library. regcomp, regexec, regerror, regfree: . . . . regex(3)
expression handlers. regcomp, regexec, regsub, regerror: regular . . . . regexp(3)
regcomp, regexec, regerror, regfree: regular-expression library. . . . . regex(3)
regcomp, regexec, regsub, regerror: regular expression handlers. . . . . regexp(3)
library. regcomp, regexec, regerror, regfree: regular-expression . . . . regex(3)
handlers. regcomp, regexec, regsub, regerror: regular expression . . . . regexp(3)
regcomp, regexec, regerror, regfree: regular-expression library. . . . . regex(3)
msync: synchronize a mapped region. . . . . msync(2)
atexit: register a function to be called on exit. . . . . atexit(3)
register: register with Kerberos. . . . . register(1)
register: register with Kerberos. . . . . register(1)
registerd: Kerberos registration daemon. . . . . registerd(8)
registerd: Kerberos registration daemon. . . . . registerd(8)
regcomp, regexec, regsub, regerror: regular expression handlers. . . . . regexp(3)
zgrep: search possibly compressed files for a regular expression. . . . . zgrep(1)
re_comp, re_exec: regular expression handler. . . . . re_comp(3)
regcomp, regexec, regsub, regerror: regular expression handlers. . . . . regexp(3)
re_format: POSIX 1003.2 regular expressions. . . . . re_format(7)
regcomp, regexec, regerror, regfree: regular-expression library. . . . . regex(3)
rehash: recompute command hash table. . . . . csh(1)
comm: select or reject lines common to two files. . . . . comm(1)
join: relational database operator. . . . . join(1)
sigpause: atomically release blocked signals and wait for interrupt. . . . . . . sigpause(2)
sigsuspend: atomically release blocked signals and wait for interrupt. . . . . . . sigsuspend(2)
database. named. reload: cause the name server to synchronize its . . . . . named.reload(8)
div: return quotient and remainder from division. . . . . div(3)
ldiv: return quotient and remainder from division. . . . . ldiv(3)
fmod: floating-point remainder function. . . . . fmod(3)
leave: remind you when you have to leave. . . . . leave(1)
calendar: reminder service. . . . . calendar(1)
rbootd: HP remote boot server. . . . . rbootd(8)
ruserok: routines for returning a stream to a remote command. rcmd, rresvport, ... rcmd(3)
rexec: return stream to a remote command. . . . . rexec(3)
L.cmds: UUCP remote command permissions file. . . . . L.cmds(5)
rexecd: remote execution server. . . . . rexecd(8)
rcp: remote file copy. . . . . rcp(1)
rdist: remote file distribution program. . . . . rdist(1)
uusend: send a file to a remote host. . . . . uusend(1)
L.sys: UUCP remote host description file. . . . . L.sys(5)
remote: remote host description file. . . . . remote(5)
phones: remote host phone number data base. . . . . phones(5)
rlogin: remote login. rlogin(1)
rlogind: remote login server. . . . . rlogind(8)
tn3270: full-screen remote login to IBM VM/CMS. . . . . tn3270(1)
rmt: remote magtape protocol module. . . . . rmt(8)
rmail: handle remote mail received via uucp. . . . . rmail(8)
exports: define remote mount points for NFS mount requests. . . . . exports(5)
mountd: service remote NFS mount requests. . . . . mountd(8)
showmount: show remote nfs mounts on host. . . . . showmount(8)
nfsd: remote NFS server. . . . . nfsd(8)
remote: remote host description file. . . . . remote(5)
rsh: remote shell. . . . . rsh(1)
rshd: remote shell server. . . . . rshd(8)
rstat: remote status display. . . . . rstat(1)
tip, cu: connect to a remote system. . . . . tip(1)
talkd: remote user communication server. . . . . talkd(8)
fingerd: remote user information server. . . . . fingerd(8)
uupoll: poll a remote UUCP site. . . . . uupoll(8)
rmdir: remove a directory file. . . . . rmdir(2)
munmap: remove a mapping. . . . . munmap(2)
unalias: remove aliases. . . . . csh(1)
flock: apply or remove an advisory lock on an open file. . . . . flock(2)
colrm: remove columns from a file. . . . . colrm(1)
rmdir: remove directories. . . . . rmdir(1)
rm: remove directory entries. . . . . rm(1)
remove: remove directory entry. . . . . remove(3)
unlink: remove directory entry. . . . . unlink(2)
unsetenv: remove environment variables. . . . . csh(1)

unifdef: remove ifdef'ed lines. . . . . unifdef(1)

lprm: remove jobs from the line printer spooling queue. . . . . . lprm(1)

atrm: remove jobs spooled by at(1). . . . . atrm(1)

deroff: remove nroff, troff, tbl and eqn constructs. . . . . deroff(1)

remove: remove directory entry. . . . . remove(3)

unlimit: remove resource limitations. . . . . csh(1)

files. strip: remove unnecessary information from executable . . . . . strip(1)

insque, remque: insert/remove element from a queue. . . . . insque(3)

rb: HP98720 "Renaissance" device interface. . . . . rb(4)

rename: change the name of a file. . . . . rename(2)

renice: alter priority of running processes. . . . . renice(8)

fsck: filesystem consistency check and interactive repair. . . . . fsck(8)

while: repeat commands conditionally. . . . . csh(1)

repeat: execute command repeatedly. . . . . csh(1)

uniq: report or filter out repeated lines in a file. . . . . uniq(1)

repeat: execute command repeatedly. . . . . csh(1)

yes: be repetitively affirmative. . . . . yes(1)

iostat: report I/O statistics. . . . . iostat(8)

perl: practical extraction and report language. . . . . perl(1)

uniq: report or filter out repeated lines in a file. . . . . uniq(1)

sendbug: mail a system bug report to 4bsd-bugs. . . . . sendbug(1)

vmstat: report virtual memory statistics. . . . . vmstat(8)

bugfiler: file bug reports in folders automatically. . . . . bugfiler(8)

fgetpos, fseek, fsetpos, ftell, rewind: reposition a stream. . . . . fseek(3)

lseek: reposition read/write file offset. . . . . lseek(2)

repquota: summarize quotas for a file system. . . . . repquota(8)

unvis, strunvis: decode a visual representation of characters. . . . . unvis(3)

unvis: revert a visual representation of data back to original form. . . . . unvis(1)

notify: request immediate notification. . . . . csh(1)

exports: define remote mount points for NFS mount requests. exports(5)

mountd: service remote NFS mount requests. mountd(8)

lock: reserve a terminal. . . . . lock(1)

clearerr, feof, ferror, fileno: check and reset stream status. . . . . ferror(3)

rs: reshape a data array. . . . . rs(1)

res_query, res_search, res_mkquery, res_send, res_init, dn_comp, dn_expand: resolver routines. . . . . . resolver(3)

dn_expand: resolver/ res_query, res_search, res_mkquery, res_send, res_init, dn_comp, ... resolver(3)

hostname: host name resolution description. . . . . hostname(7)

arp: address resolution display and control. . . . . arp(8)

resolver: resolver configuration file. . . . . resolver(5)

resolver: resolver configuration file. . . . . resolver(5)

res_send, res_init, dn_comp, dn_expand: resolver routines. /res_search, res_mkquery, ... resolver(3)

getrlimit, setrlimit: control maximum system resource consumption. . . . . getrlimit(2)

vlimit: control maximum system resource consumption. . . . . vlimit(3)

limit: alter per-process resource limitations. . . . . csh(1)

unlimit: remove resource limitations. . . . . csh(1)

getrusage: get information about resource utilization. . . . . getrusage(2)

vtimes: get information about resource utilization. . . . . vtimes(3)

res_init, dn_comp, dn_expand: resolver routines. res_query, res_search, res_mkquery, res_send, ... resolver(3)

dn_comp, dn_expand: resolver routines. res_query, res_search, res_mkquery, res_send, res_init, ... resolver(3)

routines. res_query, res_search, res_mkquery, res_send, res_init, dn_comp, dn_expand: resolver . . . . . resolver(3)

named. restart: stop and restart the name server. . . . . named.restart(8)

named.restart: stop and restart the name server. . . . . named.restart(8)

reboot, halt: stopping and restarting the system. . . . . reboot(8)

with dump. restore: restore files or file systems from backups made . . . . restore(8)

made with dump. restore: restore files or file systems from backups . . . . . restore(8)

suspend: suspend a shell, resuming its superior. . . . . csh(1)

mset: retrieve ASCII to IBM 3270 keyboard map. . . . . mset(1)

file. nlist: retrieve symbol table name list from an executable . . . . . nlist(3)

kvm_nlist: retrieve symbol table names from a kernel image. . . . . . kvm_nlist(3)

false: return false value. . . . . false(1)

basename, dirname: return filename or directory portion of pathname. . . . . . . basename(1)

sigreturn: return from signal. . . . . sigreturn(2)

vacation: return "I am not here" indication. . . . . vacation(1)

div: return quotient and remainder from division. . . . . div(3)

ldiv: return quotient and remainder from division. . . . . ldiv(3)

rexec: return stream to a remote command. . . . . rexec(3)

labs: return the absolute value of a long integer. . . . . labs(3)

timezone: return the timezone abbreviation. . . . . timezone(3)

true: return true value. . . . . true(1)

id: return user identity. . . . . id(1)

tty: return user's terminal name. . . . . tty(1)

pwd: return working directory name. . . . . pwd(1)

rcmd, rresvport, ruserok: routines for returning a stream to a remote command. . . . . rcmd(3)

realpath: returns the canonicalized absolute pathname. . . . . realpath(3)

rev: reverse lines of a file. . . . . rev(1)

col: filter reverse line feeds from input. . . . . col(1)

rev: reverse lines of a file. . . . . rev(1)

lastcomm: show last commands executed in reverse order. . . . . lastcomm(1)

original form. unvis: revert a visual representation of data back to . . . . unvis(1)

ci: check in RCS revisions. . . . . ci(1)

co: check out RCS revisions. . . . . co(1)

rcsdiff: compare RCS revisions. . . . . rcsdiff(1)

rcsmerge: merge RCS revisions. . . . . rcsmerge(1)

revoke: revoke file access. . . . . revoke(2)

revoke: revoke file access. . . . . revoke(2)

fgetpos, fseek, fsetpos, ftell, rewind: reposition a stream. . . . . fseek(3)

opendir, readdir, telldir, seekdir, rewinddir, closedir, dirfd: directory operations. . . . . directory(3)

rexec: return stream to a remote command. . . . . rexec(3)

rexecd: remote execution server. . . . . rexecd(8)

rhost: look up host names using domain server. . . . . . host(1)

rindex: locate character in string. . . . . rindex(3)

strsep, strspn, strcspn, strstr, strtok, index, rindex: string specifi /strerror, strlen, strpbrk, ... string(3)

rint: round-to-closest integer functions. . . . . rint(3)

lptest: generate lineprinter ripple pattern. . . . . lptest(1)

about RCS files. rlog: print log messages and other information . . . . . . rlog(1)

rlogin: remote login. . . . . rlogin(1)

rlogind: remote login server. . . . . rlogind(8)

rm: remove directory entries. . . . . rm(1)

rmail: handle remote mail received via uucp. . . . . rmail(8)

rmdir: remove a directory file. . . . . rmdir(2)

rmdir: remove directories. . . . . rmdir(1)

rmt: remote magtape protocol module. . . . . rmt(8)

robots: fight off villainous robots. . . . . robots(6)

robots: fight off villainous robots. . . . . robots(6)

rogue: exploring The Dungeons of Doom. . . . . rogue(6)

cbrt, sqrt: cube root and square root functions. . . . . sqrt(3)

chroot: change root directory. . . . . chroot(2)

chroot: change root directory. . . . . chroot(8)

cbrt, sqrt: cube root and square root functions. . . . . sqrt(3)

rint: round-to-closest integer functions. . . . . rint(3)

route: kernel packet forwarding database. . . . . route(4)

route: manually manipulate the routing tables.. . . . . . . route(8)

traceroute: print the route packets take to network host. . . . . traceroute(8)

routed: network routing daemon. . . . . routed(8)

acl_delete, acl_initialize: access control list routines. /acl_check, acl_exact_match, acl_add, ... acl_check(3)

cgetnext, cgetclose: capability database access routines. /cgetnum, cgetstr, cgetustr, cgetfirst, ... getcap(3)

inet_netof: Internet address manipulation routines. /inet_ntoa, inet_makeaddr, inet_lnaof, ... inet(3)

krb_get_lrealm: additional Kerberos utility routines. /krb_get_krbhst, krb_get_admhst, ... krb_realmofhost(3)

lsearch, lfind,: linear searching routines. . . . . lsearch(3)

ns_ntoa: Xerox NS Ns (tm) address conversion routines. ns_addr, ... ns(3)

res_send, res_init, dn_comp, dn_expand: resolver routines. res_query, res_search, res_mkquery, ... resolver(3)

tgoto, tputs: terminal independent operation routines. tgetent, tgetnum, tgetflag, tgetstr, ... termcap(3)

tempnam, tmpfile, tmpnam: temporary file routines. . . . . tmpnam(3)

setstate: better random number generator; routines for changing generators. /initstate, ... random(3)

link_ntoa: elementary address specification routines for link level access. link_addr, ... linkaddr(3)

/tf_get_pname, tf_get_pinst, tf_get_cred, tf_close: routines for manipulating a Kerberos ticket file. . . . . . tf_util(3)

/iso_ntoa: elementary network address conversion routines for Open System Interconnection. . . . . iso_addr(3)

command. rcmd, rresvport, ruserok: routines for returning a stream to a remote . . . . rcmd(3)

/krb_recvauth, krb_net_write, krb_net_read: Kerberos routines for sending authentication via network/ . . . . . krb_sendauth(3)

routed: network routing daemon. . . . . routed(8)

XNSrouted: NS Routing Information Protocol daemon. . . . . XNSrouted(8)

es-is: End System to Intermediate System Routing Protocol. . . . . esis(4)

route: manually manipulate the routing tables.. . . . . route(8)

rpc: rpc program number data base. . . . . rpc(5)

portmap: DARPA port to RPC program number mapper. . . . . portmap(8)

rpcgen: an RPC protocol compiler. . . . . rpcgen(1)

rpc: rpc program number data base. . . . . rpc(5)

rpcgen: an RPC protocol compiler. . . . . rpcgen(1)

/mout, move, msqrt, msub, mult, omin, omout, pow, rpow, sdiv,: multiple precision integer arithmetic. . . . . . . mp(3)

to a remote command. rcmd, rresvport, ruserok: routines for returning a stream . . . . . rcmd(3)

rs: reshape a data array. . . . . rs(1)

rsh: remote shell. . . . . rsh(1)

rshd: remote shell server. . . . . rshd(8)

rstat: remote status display. . . . . rstat(1)

nohup: run command immune to hangups. . . . . csh(1)

daemon: run in the background. . . . . daemon(3)

nice: run low priority process. . . . . csh(1)

mbrune, mbrrune, mbmb: multibyte rune support for C. . . . . mbrune(3)

setrunelocale, setinvalidrune, sgetrune, sputrune: rune support for C. . . . . rune(3)

EUC: EUC encoding of runes. . . . . euc(4)

character set Transformation Format encoding of runes. UTF2: Universal . . . . utf2(4)

uptime: show how long system has been running. . . . . uptime(1)

gcore: get core images of running process. . . . . gcore(1)

renice: alter priority of running processes. . . . . renice(8)

ruptime: show host status of local machines. . . . . ruptime(1)

kuserok: Kerberos version of ruserok. . . . . kuserok(3)

remote command. rcmd, rresvport, ruserok: routines for returning a stream to a . . . . rcmd(3)

rwho: who is logged in on local machines. . . . . rwho(1)

rwhod: system status server. . . . . rwhod(8)

sa, accton: system accounting. . . . . sa(8)

sail: multi-user wooden ships and iron men. . . . . sail(6)

mount_umap: sample file system layer. . . . . mount_umap(8)

mdoc.samples: tutorial sampler for writing manuals with −mdoc. . . . . mdoc.samples(7)

−mdoc. mdoc. samples: tutorial sampler for writing manuals with . . . . mdoc.samples(7)

strdup: save a copy of a string. . . . . strdup(3)

savecore: save a core dump of the operating system. . . . . savecore(8)

savecore: save a core dump of the operating system. . . . . savecore(8)

brk, sbrk: change data segment size. . . . . brk(2)

copysign, drem, finite, logb, scalb: IEEE 754 floating point support. . . . . ieee(3)

scandir, alphasort: scan a directory. . . . . scandir(3)

getmntopts: scan mount options. . . . . getmntopts(3)

scandir, alphasort: scan a directory. . . . . scandir(3)

input format conversion. scanf, fscanf, sscanf, vscanf, vsscanf, vfscanf: . . . . scanf(3)

awk: pattern scanning and processing language. . . . . awk(1)

sccs: front end for the SCCS subsystem. . . . . sccs(1)

sccs: front end for the SCCS subsystem. . . . . sccs(1)

at: schedule execution of commands 'at' a given time. . . . . at(1)

crontab: chronological services schedule file. . . . . crontab(5)

ualarm: schedule signal after specified time. . . . . ualarm(3)

getpriority, setpriority: get/set program scheduling priority. . . . . getpriority(2)

nice: execute a command at a low scheduling priority. . . . . nice(1)

nice: set program scheduling priority. . . . . nice(3)

curses: screen functions with "optimal" cursor motion. . . . . . curses(3)

echo: produce message in a shell script. . . . . echo(1)

rc: command script for auto−reboot and daemons. . . . . rc(8)

script: make typescript of terminal session. . . . . script(1)

onintr: process interrupts in command scripts. . . . . csh(1)

scsiformat: format SCSI disks and show SCSI parameters. . . . . scsiformat(8)

scsiformat: format SCSI disks and show SCSI parameters. . . . . scsiformat(8)

st: CCS SCSI tape driver. . . . . st(4)

parameters. scsiformat: format SCSI disks and show SCSI . . . . scsiformat(8)

/move, msqrt, msub, mult, omin, omout, pow, rpow, sdiv,: multiple precision integer arithmetic. . . . . . . mp(3)

lkbib: search bibliographic databases. . . . . lkbib(1)

lookbib: search bibliographic databases. . . . . lookbib(1)

boggle: word search game. . . . . boggle(6)

bsearch: binary search of a sorted table. . . . . bsearch(3)

expression. zgrep: search possibly compressed files for a regular . . . . . zgrep(1)

grep: file pattern searcher. . . . . grep(1)

lsearch, lfind,: linear searching routines. . . . . lsearch(3)

j1, jn, y0, y1, yn: bessel functions of first and second kind. j0, ... j0(3)

sleep: suspend process execution for interval of seconds. . . . . sleep(3)

keylogin: decrypt and store secret key. . . . . keylogin(1)

bad144: read/write dec standard 144 bad sector information. . . . . bad144(8)

badsect: create files to contain bad sectors. . . . . badsect(8)

sed: stream editor. sed(1)

operations. opendir, readdir, telldir, seekdir, rewinddir, closedir, dirfd: directory . . . . . . directory(3)

brk, sbrk: change data segment size. . . . . brk(2)

size: display object file segment sizes (text, data and bss). . . . . size(1)

end, etext, edata: end boundaries of image segments. . . . . end(3)

comm: select or reject lines common to two files. . . . . comm(1)

cut: select portions of each line of a file. . . . . cut(1)

select: synchronous I/O multiplexing. . . . . select(2)

case: selector in switch. . . . . csh(1)

uusend: send a file to a remote host. . . . . uusend(1)

send, sendto, sendmsg: send a message from a socket. . . . . send(2)

write: send a message to another user. . . . . write(1)

raise: send a signal to the current process. . . . . raise(3)
mail: send and receive mail. . . . . mail(1)
dig: send domain name query packets to name servers. . . . . . . dig(1)
ping: send ICMP ECHO_REQUEST packets to network hosts. . . . ping(8)
sendmail: send mail over the internet. . . . . sendmail(8)
socket. send, sendto, sendmsg: send a message from a . . . . . . send(2)
kill: send signal to a process. . . . . kill(2)
killpg: send signal to a process group. . . . . killpg(2)
sendbug: mail a system bug report to 4bsd-bugs. . . . . . sendbug(1)
/krb_net_write, krb_net_read: Kerberos routines for sending authentication via network stream sockets. . . . . krb_sendauth(3)
aliases: aliases file for sendmail. . . . . aliases(5)
makemap: create database maps for sendmail. . . . . makemap(8)
sendmail: send mail over the internet. . . . . sendmail(8)
send, sendto, sendmsg: send a message from a socket. . . . . send(2)
send, sendto, sendmsg: send a message from a socket. . . . . send(2)
from: print names of those who have sent mail. . . . . from(1)
diction, explain: print wordy sentences; thesaurus for diction. . . . . diction(1)
strsep: separate strings. . . . . strsep(3)
spp: Xerox Sequenced Packet Protocol. . . . . spp(4)
trsp: transliterate sequenced packet protocol trace. . . . . trsp(8)
jot: print sequential or random data. . . . . jot(1)
sliplogin: attach a serial line network interface. . . . . sliplogin(8)
slattach: attach serial lines as network interfaces. . . . . slattach(8)
comsat: biff server. . . . . comsat(8)
fingerd: remote user information server. . . . . fingerd(8)
ftpd: Internet File Transfer Protocol server. . . . . ftpd(8)
rhost: look up host names using domain server. . . . . host(1)
named: Internet domain name server. . . . . named(8)
named.restart: stop and restart the name server. . . . . named.restart(8)
nfsd: remote NFS server. . . . . nfsd(8)
nfsiod: local NFS asynchronous I/O server. . . . . nfsiod(8)
rbootd: HP remote boot server. . . . . rbootd(8)
rexecd: remote execution server. . . . . rexecd(8)
rlogind: remote login server. . . . . rlogind(8)
rshd: remote shell server. . . . . rshd(8)
rwhod: system status server. . . . . rwhod(8)
startslip: dial up and login to a slip server. . . . . startslip(1)
talkd: remote user communication server. . . . . talkd(8)
telnetd: DARPA TELNET protocol server. . . . . telnetd(8)
tftpd: Internet Trivial File Transfer Protocol server. . . . . tftpd(8)
timed: time server daemon. . . . . timed(8)
named.reload: cause the name server to synchronize its database. . . . . named.reload(8)
dig: send domain name query packets to name servers. . . . . dig(1)
nslookup: query Internet name servers interactively. . . . . nslookup(8)
nfssvc: NFS services. . . . . nfssvc(2)
crontab: chronological services schedule file. crontab(5)
services: service name data base. . . . . services(5)
logout: end session. . . . . csh(1)
script: make typescript of terminal session. . . . . script(1)
setsid: create session and set process group ID. . . . . setsid(2)
stty, gtty: set and get terminal state (defunct). . . . . stty(3)
printenv, env: print out the environment, set and print environment. . . . . printenv(1)
sigaltstack: set and/or get signal stack context. . . . . sigaltstack(2)
sigstack: set and/or get signal stack context. . . . . sigstack(2)
set: change value of shell variable. . . . . csh(1)
sigsetmask: set current signal mask. . . . . sigsetmask(2)
date: display or set date and time. . . . . date(1)
utimes: set file access and modification times. . . . . utimes(2)
umask: set file creation mode mask. . . . . umask(2)
chflags, fchflags: set file flags. . . . . chflags(2)
utime: set file times. . . . . utime(3)
tcsetpgrp: set foreground process group ID. . . . . tcsetpgrp(3)
setgroups: set group access list. . . . . setgroups(2)
ffs: find first bit set in a bit string. . . . . ffs(3)
krb_set_tkt_string: set Kerberos ticket cache file name. . . . . krb_set_tkt_string(3)
sysctl: get or set kernel state. . . . . sysctl(8)
apply: apply a command to a set of arguments. . . . . apply(1)
getsockopt, setsockopt: get and set options on sockets. . . . . getsockopt(2)
hostname: set or print name of current host system. . . . . hostname(1)
setpgid, setpgrp: set process group. setpgid(2)
setsid: create session and set process group ID. . . . . setsid(2)
nice: set program scheduling priority. . . . . nice(3)

setregid: set real and effective group ID. . . . . setregid(2)
setreuid: set real and effective user ID's. . . . . setreuid(2)
alarm: set signal timer alarm. . . . . alarm(3)
sysctl: get or set system information. . . . . sysctl(3)
getty: set terminal mode. . . . . getty(8)
stty: set the options for a terminal device interface. . . . . stty(1)
UTF2: Universal character set Transformation Format encoding of runes. . . . . utf2(4)
setruid, setrgid: set user and group ID. . . . . setruid(3)
setuid, seteuid, setgid, setegid,: set user and group ID. . . . . setuid(2)
setenv: set variable in environment. . . . . csh(1)
buffering operations. setbuf, setbuffer, setlinebuf, setvbuf: stream . . . . setbuf(3)
operations. setbuf, setbuffer, setlinebuf, setvbuf: stream buffering . . . . setbuf(3)
setuid, seteuid, setgid, setegid,: set user and group ID. . . . . setuid(2)
setenv: set variable in environment. . . . . csh(1)
getenv, putenv, setenv, unsetenv: environment variable functions. . . . . getenv(3)
setuid, seteuid, setgid, setegid,: set user and group ID. . . . . setuid(2)
entry. getfsent, getfsspec, getfsfile, setfsent, endfsent: get file system descriptor file . . . . . . getfsent(3)
setuid, seteuid, setgid, setegid,: set user and group ID. . . . . setuid(2)
/getgrnam, getgrgid, setgroupent, .Nm setgrfile, setgrent, endgrent: group database operations. . . . . . . getgrent(3)
getgrent, getgrnam, getgrgid, setgroupent, .Nm setgrfile, setgrent, endgrent: group database/ . . . . . . getgrent(3)
group database/ getgrent, getgrnam, getgrgid, setgroupent, .Nm setgrfile, setgrent, endgrent: . . . . . . getgrent(3)
setgroups: set group access list. . . . . setgroups(2)
entry. gethostbyname, gethostbyaddr, gethostent, sethostent, endhostent, herror: get network host . . . . . . gethostbyname(3)
host. gethostid, sethostid: get/set unique identifier of current . . . . gethostid(3)
gethostname, sethostname: get/set name of current host. . . . . gethostname(3)
for C. setrunelocale, setinvalidrune, sgetrune, sputrune: rune support . . . . . . rune(3)
getitimer, setitimer: get/set value of interval timer. . . . . getitimer(2)
sigsetjmp, siglongjmp, setjmp, longjmp, _setjmp, _longjmp longjmperror: non-local jumps. . . setjmp(3)
non-local jumps. sigsetjmp, siglongjmp, setjmp, longjmp, _setjmp, _longjmp longjmperror: . . . . . setjmp(3)
encryption. crypt, setkey, encrypt, des_setkey, des_cipher: DES . . . . crypt(3)
setbuf, setbuffer, setlinebuf, setvbuf: stream buffering operations. . . . . setbuf(3)
for C. setlocale, localeconv: natural language formatting . . . . . . setlocale(3)
getlogin, setlogin: get/set login name. . . . . getlogin(2)
syslog, vsyslog, openlog, closelog, setlogmask: control system log. . . . . syslog(3)
getmode, setmode: modify mode bits. . . . . setmode(3)
getnetent, getnetbyaddr, getnetbyname, setnetent, endnetent: get network entry. . . . . getnetent(3)
operations. getnetgrent, innetgr, setnetgrent, endnetgrent: netgroup database . . . . getnetgrent(3)
operations. getpwent, getpwnam, getpwuid, setpassent, setpwent, endpwent: password database . . . . . . getpwent(3)
setpgid, setpgrp: set process group. . . . . setpgid(2)
setpgid, setpgrp: set process group. . . . . setpgid(2)
getpriority, setpriority: get/set program scheduling priority. . . . . getpriority(2)
getprotoent, getprotobynumber, getprotobyname, setprotoent, endprotoent: get protocol entry. . . . . . getprotoent(3)
getpwent, getpwnam, getpwuid, setpassent, setpwent, endpwent: password database operations. . . . . getpwent(3)
setregid: set real and effective group ID. . . . . setregid(2)
setreuid: set real and effective user ID's. . . . . setreuid(2)
setruid, setrgid: set user and group ID. . . . . setruid(3)
consumption. getrlimit, setrlimit: control maximum system resource . . . . . . getrlimit(2)
setruid, setrgid: set user and group ID. . . . . setruid(3)
rune support for C. setrunelocale, setinvalidrune, sgetrune, sputrune: . . . . . . rune(3)
octal, hexadecimal and decimal ASCII character sets. ascii: . . . . ascii(7)
sigdelset, sigismember: manipulate signal sets. sigemptyset, sigfillset, sigaddset, ... sigsetops(3)
getservent, getservbyport, getservbyname, setservent, endservent: get service entry. . . . . getservent(3)
setsid: create session and set process group ID. . . . . . setsid(2)
getsockopt, setsockopt: get and set options on sockets. . . . . getsockopt(2)
for changing/ random, srandom, initstate, setstate: better random number generator; routines . . . . . random(3)
gettimeofday, settimeofday: get/set date and time. . . . . gettimeofday(2)
getttyent, getttynam, setttyent, endttyent: get ttys file entry. . . . . getttyent(3)
group ID. setuid, seteuid, setgid, setegid,: set user and . . . . . . setuid(2)
getusershell, setusershell, endusershell: get legal user shells. . . . . . . getusershell(3)
setbuf, setbuffer, setlinebuf, setvbuf: stream buffering operations. . . . . setbuf(3)
setrunelocale, setinvalidrune, sgetrune, sputrune: rune support for C. . . . . rune(3)
sh: command interpreter (shell). . . . . sh(1)
shar: create a shell archive of files. . . . . shar(1)
mpool: shared memory buffer pool. . . . . mpool(3)
xstr: extract strings from C programs to implement shared strings. . . . . xstr(1)
exit: leave shell. csh(1)
rsh: remote shell. rsh(1)
sh: command interpreter (shell). sh(1)
system: pass a command to the shell. system(3)
shar: create a shell archive of files. . . . . shar(1)
csh: a shell (command interpreter) with C-like syntax. . . . . . . csh(1)
eval: re-evaluate shell data. csh(1)

shells: shell database. shells(5)
popd: pop shell directory stack. . . . . csh(1)
pushd: push shell directory stack. . . . . csh(1)
alias: shell macros. . . . . csh(1)
suspend: suspend a shell, resuming its superior. . . . . csh(1)
echo: produce message in a shell script. . . . . echo(1)
rshd: remote shell server. . . . . rshd(8)
set: change value of shell variable. . . . . csh(1)
@: arithmetic on shell variables. . . . . csh(1)
unset: discard shell variables. . . . . csh(1)
exec: overlay shell with specified command. . . . . csh(1)
setusershell, endusershell: get legal user shells. getusershell, ... getusershell(3)
shells: shell database. . . . . shells(5)
shift: manipulate argument list. . . . . csh(1)
sail: multi-user wooden ships and iron men. . . . . sail(6)
groups: show group memberships. . . . . groups(1)
ruptime: show host status of local machines. . . . . ruptime(1)
uptime: show how long system has been running. . . . . uptime(1)
lastcomm: show last commands executed in reverse order. . . . . lastcomm(1)
netstat: show network status. . . . . netstat(1)
showmount: show remote nfs mounts on host. . . . . showmount(8)
scsiformat: format SCSI disks and show SCSI parameters. . . . . scsiformat(8)
uusnap: show snapshot of the UUCP system. . . . . uusnap(8)
construct a file. what: show what versions of object modules were used to . . . . what(1)
showmount: show remote nfs mounts on host. . . . . showmount(8)
shutdown: shut down part of a full-duplex connection. . . . . shutdown(2)
shutdown: close down the system at a given time. . . . . . shutdown(8)
connection. shutdown: shut down part of a full-duplex . . . . shutdown(2)
sigaction: software signal facilities. . . . . sigaction(2)
signal sets. sigemptyset, sigfillset, sigaddset, sigdelset, sigismember: manipulate . . . . sigsetops(3)
sigaltstack: set and/or get signal stack context. . . . . . . sigaltstack(2)
sigblock: block signals. . . . . sigblock(2)
sigemptyset, sigfillset, sigaddset, sigdelset, sigismember: manipulate signal sets. . . . . sigsetops(3)
sigismember: manipulate signal sets. sigemptyset, sigfillset, sigaddset, sigdelset, ... sigsetops(3)
manipulate signal sets. sigemptyset, sigfillset, sigaddset, sigdelset, sigismember: . . . . sigsetops(3)
calls. siginterrupt: allow signals to interrupt system . . . . . . siginterrupt(3)
sigemptyset, sigfillset, sigaddset, sigdelset, sigismember: manipulate signal sets. . . . . sigsetops(3)
longjmperror: non-local jumps. sigsetjmp, siglongjmp, setjmp, longjmp, _setjmp, _longjmp . . . . . setjmp(3)
pause: stop until signal. . . . . pause(3)
sigreturn: return from signal. . . . . sigreturn(2)
kill: terminate or signal a process. . . . . kill(1)
ualarm: schedule signal after specified time. . . . . ualarm(3)
sigaction: software signal facilities. . . . . sigaction(2)
signal: simplified software signal facilities. . . . . signal(3)
sigvec: software signal facilities. . . . . sigvec(3)
sigprocmask: manipulate current signal mask. . . . . sigprocmask(2)
sigsetmask: set current signal mask. . . . . sigsetmask(2)
psignal, sys_siglist sys_signame: system signal messages. . . . . psignal(3)
sigaddset, sigdelset, sigismember: manipulate signal sets. sigemptyset, sigfillset, ... sigsetops(3)
signal: simplified software signal facilities. . . . . signal(3)
sigaltstack: set and/or get signal stack context. . . . . sigaltstack(2)
sigstack: set and/or get signal stack context. . . . . sigstack(2)
alarm: set signal timer alarm. . . . . alarm(3)
kill: send signal to a process. . . . . kill(2)
killpg: send signal to a process group. . . . . killpg(2)
raise: send a signal to the current process. . . . . raise(3)
sigblock: block signals. . . . . sigblock(2)
sigpending: get pending signals. . . . . sigpending(2)
sigpause: atomically release blocked signals and wait for interrupt. . . . . sigpause(2)
sigsuspend: atomically release blocked signals and wait for interrupt. . . . . sigsuspend(2)
(temporary). infnan: signals invalid floating-point operations on a VAX . . . . infnan(3)
siginterrupt: allow signals to interrupt system calls. . . . . siginterrupt(3)
floating-point number. modf: extract signed integral and fractional values from . . . . modf(3)
wait for interrupt. sigpause: atomically release blocked signals and . . . . . sigpause(2)
sigpending: get pending signals. . . . . sigpending(2)
sigprocmask: manipulate current signal mask. . . . . sigprocmask(2)
sigreturn: return from signal. . . . . sigreturn(2)
_longjmp longjmperror: non-local jumps. sigsetjmp, siglongjmp, setjmp, longjmp, _setjmp, ... setjmp(3)
sigsetmask: set current signal mask. . . . . sigsetmask(2)
sigstack: set and/or get signal stack context. . . . . sigstack(2)
wait for interrupt. sigsuspend: atomically release blocked signals and . . . . sigsuspend(2)
sigvec: software signal facilities. . . . . sigvec(2)

signal:	simplified software signal facilities.	signal(3)
	sin: sine function.	sin(3)
asin: arc	sine function.	asin(3)
asinh: inverse hyperbolic	sine function.	asinh(3)
sin:	sine function.	sin(3)
sinh: hyperbolic	sine function.	sinh(3)
	sinh: hyperbolic sine function.	sinh(3)
uupoll: poll a remote UUCP	site.	uupoll(8)
fsinfo: co-ordinate	site-wide filesystem information.	fsinfo(8)
brk, sbrk: change data segment	size.	brk(2)
getbsize: get user block	size.	getbsize(3)
getdtablesize: get descriptor table	size.	getdtablesize(2)
getpagesize: get system page	size.	getpagesize(3)
pagesize: print system page	size.	pagesize(1)
and bss).	size: display object file segment sizes (text, data	size(1)
diskpart: calculate default disk partition	sizes.	diskpart(8)
size: display object file segment	sizes (text, data and bss).	size(1)
interfaces.	slattach: attach serial lines as network	slattach(8)
	sleep: suspend execution for an interval of time.	sleep(1)
seconds.	sleep: suspend process execution for interval of	sleep(3)
startslip: dial up and login to a	slip server.	startslip(1)
	sliplogin: attach a serial line network interface.	sliplogin(8)
ceil:	smallest integral value not greater than x.	ceil(3)
spline: interpolate	smooth curve.	spline(1)
snake, snscore:	display chase game.	snake(6)
uusnap: show	snapshot of the UUCP system.	uusnap(8)
formatted output/ printf, fprintf, sprintf,	snprintf, vprintf, vfprintf, vsprintf, vsnprintf:	printf(3)
snake,	snscore: display chase game.	snake(6)
accept: accept a connection on a	socket.	accept(2)
bind: bind a name to a	socket.	bind(2)
connect: initiate a connection on a	socket.	connect(2)
listen: listen for connections on a	socket.	listen(2)
recv, recvfrom, recvmsg: receive a message from a	socket.	recv(2)
send, sendto, sendmsg: send a message from a	socket.	send(2)
	socket: create an endpoint for communication.	socket(2)
getsockname: get	socket name.	getsockname(2)
	socketpair: create a pair of connected sockets.	socketpair(2)
getsockopt, setsockopt: get and set options on	sockets.	getsockopt(2)
for sending authentication via network stream	sockets. /krb_net_read: Kerberos routines	krb_sendauth(3)
socketpair: create a pair of connected	sockets.	socketpair(2)
	soelim: eliminate .so's from nroff input.	soelim(1)
lo:	software loopback network interface.	lo(4)
in IP packets. nsip:	software network interface encapsulating NS packets	nsip(4)
sigaction:	software signal facilities.	sigaction(2)
signal: simplified	software signal facilities.	signal(3)
sigvec:	software signal facilities.	sigvec(2)
canfield, cfscores: the	solitaire card game canfield.	canfield(6)
radixsort: radix	sort.	radixsort(3)
qsort, heapsort, mergesort:	sort functions.	qsort(3)
tsort: topological	sort of a directed graph.	tsort(1)
sort:	sort or merge text files.	sort(1)
	sort: sort or merge text files.	sort(1)
bsearch: binary search of a	sorted table.	bsearch(3)
soelim: eliminate	.so's from nroff input.	soelim(1)
soelim: eliminate .	so's from nroff input.	soelim(1)
indent: indent and format C program	source.	indent(1)
mkstr: create an error message file by massaging C	source.	mkstr(1)
	source: read commands from file.	csh(1)
rcsfreeze: freeze a configuration of	sources checked in under RCS.	rcsfreeze(1)
calloc: allocate clean memory (zero initialized	space).	calloc(3)
df: display free disk	space.	df(1)
isgraph: printing character test	(space character exclusive).	isgraph(3)
isprint: printing character test	(space character inclusive).	isprint(3)
line, circle, arc, move, cont, point, linemod,	space, closepl: graphics interface. /erase, label, ...	plot(3)
isblank:	space or tab character test.	isblank(3)
expand, unexpand: expand tabs to	spaces, and vice versa.	expand(1)
strspn:	span a string.	strspn(3)
strcspn:	span the complement of a string.	strcspn(3)
le:	SPARC AMD 7990 LANCE ethernet interface.	le(4)
way. vfork:	spawn new process in a virtual memory efficient	vfork(2)
strcspn, strstr, strtok, index, rindex: string	specifi /strerror, strlen, strpbrk, strsep, strspn, ...	string(3)
link_addr, link_ntoa: elementary address	specification routines for link level access.	linkaddr(3)

exec: overlay shell with specified command. . . . . csh(1)
truncate, ftruncate: truncate a file to a specified length. . . . . truncate(2)
ualarm: schedule signal after specified time. . . . . ualarm(3)
swapon: specify additional device for paging and swapping. . . . . . swapon(8)
spell, spellin, spellout: find spelling errors. . . . . spell(1)
spell, spellin, spellout: find spelling errors. . . . . spell(1)
spell, spellin, spellout: find spelling errors. . . . . spell(1)
spell, spellin, spellout: find spelling errors. . . . . spell(1)
spline: interpolate smooth curve. . . . . spline(1)
split: split a file into pieces. . . . . split(1)
files. fsplit: split a multi-routine Fortran file into individual . . . . fsplit(1)
split: split a file into pieces. . . . . split(1)
uuclean: uucp spool directory clean-up. . . . . uuclean(8)
lpq: spool queue examination program. . . . . lpq(1)
atrm: remove jobs spooled by at(1). atrm(1)
lpd: line printer spooler daemon. . . . . lpd(8)
lprm: remove jobs from the line printer spooling queue. . . . . lprm(1)
spp: Xerox Sequenced Packet Protocol. . . . . spp(4)
vsnprintf: formatted output/ printf, fprintf, sprintf, snprintf, vprintf, vfprintf, vsprintf, ... printf(3)
setrunelocale, setinvalidrune, sgetrune, sputrune: rune support for C. . . . . rune(3)
cbrt, sqrt: cube root and square root functions. . . . . sqrt(3)
cbrt, sqrt: cube root and square root functions. . . . . sqrt(3)
rand, srand: bad random number generator. . . . . rand(3)
generator; routines for changing/ random, srandom, initstate, setstate: better random number . . . . . random(3)
conversion. scanf, fscanf, sscanf, vscanf, vsscanf, vfscanf: input format . . . . scanf(3)
st: CCS SCSI tape driver. . . . . st(4)
stab: symbol table types. . . . . stab(5)
popd: pop shell directory stack. . . . . csh(1)
pushd: push shell directory stack. . . . . csh(1)
sigaltstack: set and/or get signal stack context. . . . . sigaltstack(2)
sigstack: set and/or get signal stack context. . . . . sigstack(2)
bdes: encrypt/decrypt using the Data Encryption Standard. bdes(1)
bad144: read/write dec standard 144 bad sector information. . . . . bad144(8)
stdio: standard input/output library functions. . . . . stdio(3)
ansitape: ANSI standard tape handler. . . . . ansitape(1)
startslip: dial up and login to a slip server. . . . . startslip(1)
master key. kstash: stash Kerberos key distribution center database . . . . . . kstash(8)
stat, lstat, fstat: get file status. . . . . stat(2)
kvm_getargv, kvm_getenvv: access user process state. kvm_getprocs, ... kvm_getprocs(3)
sysctl: get or set kernel state. . . . . sysctl(8)
stty, gtty: set and get terminal state (defunct). . . . . stty(3)
fsync: synchronize a file's in-core state with that on disk. . . . . fsync(2)
if: conditional statement. csh(1)
statfs: get file system statistics. . . . . statfs(2)
fstab: static information about the filesystems. . . . . fstab(5)
hashstat: print command hashing statistics. . . . . csh(1)
du: display disk usage statistics. . . . . du(1)
iostat: report I/O statistics. . . . . iostat(8)
nfsstat: display NFS statistics. . . . . nfsstat(1)
statfs: get file system statistics. . . . . statfs(2)
vmstat: report virtual memory statistics. . . . . vmstat(8)
systat: display system statistics on a crt. . . . . systat(1)
feof, ferror, fileno: check and reset stream status. clearerr, ... ferror(3)
fstat: file status. . . . . fstat(1)
netstat: show network status. . . . . netstat(1)
ps: process status. . . . . ps(1)
stat, lstat, fstat: get file status. . . . . stat(2)
rstat: remote status display. . . . . rstat(1)
strmode: convert inode status information into a symbolic string. . . . . strmode(3)
ruptime: show host status of local machines. . . . . ruptime(1)
rwhod: system status server. . . . . rwhod(8)
sync: synchronize disk block in-core status with that on disk. . . . . sync(2)
stdarg: variable argument lists. . . . . stdarg(3)
fd, stdin, stdout, stderr: file descriptor files. . . . . fd(4)
fd, stdin, stdout, stderr: file descriptor files. . . . . fd(4)
stdio: standard input/output library functions. . . . . stdio(3)
fd, stdin, stdout, stderr: file descriptor files. . . . . fd(4)
sticky: sticky text and append-only directories. . . . . sticky(8)
sticky: sticky text and append-only directories. . . . . sticky(8)
named.restart: stop and restart the name server. . . . . named.restart(8)
stop: halt a job or process. . . . . csh(1)
pause: stop until signal. . . . . pause(3)

```
            reboot, halt:  stopping and restarting the system. . . . . . . . . . . .  reboot(8)
      icheck: file system  storage consistency check. . . . . . . . . . . . . . .  icheck(8)
service key. ksrvtgt: fetch and  store Kerberos ticket-granting-ticket using a . . . . . . .  ksrvtgt(1)
             mail.local:  store mail in a mailbox. . . . . . . . ' . . . . . . . .  mail.local(8)
keylogin: decrypt and  store secret key. . . . . . . . . . . . . . . . . . .  keylogin(1)
                           strcasecmp: compare strings, ignoring case. . . . . . . .  strcasecmp(3)
strcat, strncat, strchr, strrchr, strcmp, strncmp,  strcasecmp, strncasecmp, strcpy, strncpy, strerror,/ . . . .  string(3)
                           strcat: concatenate strings. . . . . . . . . . . . . . . .  strcat(3)
strcasecmp, strncasecmp, strcpy, strncpy,/  strcat, strncat, strchr, strrchr, strcmp, strncmp, . . . . . .  string(3)
                           strchr: locate character in string. . . . . . . . . . . . .  strchr(3)
strncasecmp, strcpy, strncpy,/  strcat, strncat,  strchr, strrchr, strcmp, strncmp, strcasecmp, . . . . . . .  string(3)
                           strcmp: compare strings. . . . . . . . . . . . . . . . .  strcmp(3)
strncpy,/  strcat, strncat, strchr, strrchr,  strcmp, strncmp, strcasecmp, strncasecmp, strcpy, . . . . .  string(3)
              collation.  strcoll: compare strings according to current . . . . . . . .  strcoll(3)
                           strcpy: copy strings. . . . . . . . . . . . . . . . . . .  strcpy(3)
/strrchr, strcmp, strncmp, strcasecmp, strncasecmp,  strcpy, strncpy, strerror, strlen, strpbrk, strsep,/ . . . . : . .  string(3)
                           strcspn: span the complement of a string. . . . . . . . .  strcspn(3)
/strncpy, strerror, strlen, strpbrk, strsep, strspn,  strcspn, strstr, strtok, index, rindex: string/ . . . . . . . .  string(3)
                           strdup: save a copy of a string. . . . . . . . . . . . .  strdup(3)
          fclose: close a  stream. . . . . . . . . . . . . . . . . . . . . . . . .  fclose(3)
    fflush, fpurge: flush a  stream. . . . . . . . . . . . . . . . . . . . . . . . .  fflush(3)
fgetln: get a line from a  stream. . . . . . . . . . . . . . . . . . . . . . . . .  fgetln(3)
fgets, gets: get a line from a  stream. . . . . . . . . . . . . . . . . . . . . . . . .  fgets(3)
fputs, puts: output a line to a  stream. . . . . . . . . . . . . . . . . . . . . . . . .  fputs(3)
fseek, fsetpos, ftell, rewind: reposition a  stream. fgetpos, . . . . . . . . . . . . . . . . . . . . .  fseek(3)
funopen, fropen, fwopen: open a  stream. . . . . . . . . . . . . . . . . . . . . . . . .  funopen(3)
getw: get next character or word from input  stream. fgetc, getc, getchar, . . . . . . . . . . . . . .  getc(3)
putchar, putw: output a character or word to a  stream. fputc, putc, . . . . . . . . . . . . . . . . . .  putc(3)
ungetc: un-get character from input  stream. . . . . . . . . . . . . . . . . . . . . . . . .  ungetc(3)
setbuf, setbuffer, setlinebuf, setvbuf:  stream buffering operations. . . . . . . . . . . . . .  setbuf(3)
                      sed:  stream editor. . . . . . . . . . . . . . . . . . . . . .  sed(1)
  fread, fwrite: binary  stream input/output. . . . . . . . . . . . . . . . . . .  fread(3)
fopen, fdopen, freopen:  stream open functions. . . . . . . . . . . . . . . . . .  fopen(3)
routines for sending authentication via network  stream sockets. /krb_net_read: Kerberos . . . . . . . . .  krb_sendauth(3)
clearerr, feof, ferror, fileno: check and reset  stream status. . . . . . . . . . . . . . . . . . . . . .  ferror(3)
rcmd, rresvport, ruserok: routines for returning a  stream to a remote command. . . . . . . . . . . . . .  rcmd(3)
            rexec: return  stream to a remote command. . . . . . . . . . . . . .  rexec(3)
/strncmp, strcasecmp, strncasecmp, strcpy, strncpy,  strerror, strlen, strpbrk, strsep, strspn, strcspn,/ . . . . . .  string(3)
        messages. perror,  strerror, sys_errlist, sys_nerr: system error . . . . . . .  strerror(3)
                           strftime: format date and time. . . . . . . . . . . . . .  strftime(3)
      bcmp: compare byte  string. . . . . . . . . . . . . . . . . . . . . . . . .  bcmp(3)
        bcopy: copy byte  string. . . . . . . . . . . . . . . . . . . . . . . . .  bcopy(3)
  bzero: write zeroes to a byte  string. . . . . . . . . . . . . . . . . . . . . . . . .  bzero(3)
  ffs: find first bit set in a bit  string. . . . . . . . . . . . . . . . . . . . . . . . .  ffs(3)
     index: locate character in  string. . . . . . . . . . . . . . . . . . . . . . . . .  index(3)
look: display lines beginning with a given  string. . . . . . . . . . . . . . . . . . . . . . . . .  look(1)
   memchr: locate byte in byte  string. . . . . . . . . . . . . . . . . . . . . . . . .  memchr(3)
    memcmp: compare byte  string. . . . . . . . . . . . . . . . . . . . . . . . .  memcmp(3)
       memcpy: copy byte  string. . . . . . . . . . . . . . . . . . . . . . . . .  memcpy(3)
    memmove: copy byte  string. . . . . . . . . . . . . . . . . . . . . . . . .  memmove(3)
  memset: write a byte to byte  string. . . . . . . . . . . . . . . . . . . . . . . . .  memset(3)
      rindex: locate character in  string. . . . . . . . . . . . . . . . . . . . . . . . .  rindex(3)
      strchr: locate character in  string. . . . . . . . . . . . . . . . . . . . . . . . .  strchr(3)
strcspn: span the complement of a  string. . . . . . . . . . . . . . . . . . . . . . . . .  strcspn(3)
      strdup: save a copy of a  string. . . . . . . . . . . . . . . . . . . . . . . . .  strdup(3)
         strlen: find length of  string. . . . . . . . . . . . . . . . . . . . . . . . .  strlen(3)
convert inode status information into a symbolic  string. strmode: . . . . . . . . . . . . . . . . . . .  strmode(3)
strpbrk: locate multiple characters in  string. . . . . . . . . . . . . . . . . . . . . . . . .  strpbrk(3)
     strrchr: locate character in  string. . . . . . . . . . . . . . . . . . . . . . . . .  strrchr(3)
            strspn: span a  string. . . . . . . . . . . . . . . . . . . . . . . . .  strspn(3)
      strstr: locate a substring in a  string. . . . . . . . . . . . . . . . . . . . . . . . .  strstr(3)
memchr, memcmp, memcpy, memmove, memset: byte  string operations. bcmp, bcopy, bzero, memccpy, . . . . .  bstring(3)
strspn, strcspn, strstr, strtok, index, rindex:  string specifi /strerror, strlen, strpbrk, strsep, . . . . . .  string(3)
strtoul, strtouq: convert a  string to an unsigned long or uquad_t integer. . . . . . . .  strtoul(3)
      atof: convert ASCII  string to double. . . . . . . . . . . . . . . . . . . . .  atof(3)
      strtod: convert ASCII  string to double. . . . . . . . . . . . . . . . . . . . .  strtod(3)
      atoi: convert ASCII  string to integer. . . . . . . . . . . . . . . . . . . . .  atoi(3)
      atol: convert ASCII  string to long integer. . . . . . . . . . . . . . . . . . .  atol(3)
                   strtok:  string tokens. . . . . . . . . . . . . . . . . . . . . . .  strtok(3)
      strxfrm: transform a  string under locale. . . . . . . . . . . . . . . . . . .  strxfrm(3)
       memccpy: copy  string until character found. . . . . . . . . . . . . . .  memccpy(3)
strtol, strtoq: convert  string value to a long or quad_t integer. . . . . . . . . .  strtol(3)
```

strcat: concatenate	strings.	strcat(3)
strcmp: compare	strings.	strcmp(3)
strcpy: copy	strings.	strcpy(3)
strsep: separate	strings.	strsep(3)
extract strings from C programs to implement shared	strings. xstr:	xstr(1)
strcoll: compare	strings according to current collation.	strcoll(3)
	strings: find printable strings in a file.	strings(1)
strings. xstr: extract	strings from C programs to implement shared	xstr(1)
strcasecmp: compare	strings, ignoring case.	strcasecmp(3)
strings: find printable	strings in a file.	strings(1)
confstr: get	string-valued configurable variables.	confstr(3)
executable files. strip: remove unnecessary information from		strip(1)
	strlen: find length of string.	strlen(3)
/strcasecmp, strncasecmp, strcpy, strncpy, strerror,	strlen, strpbrk, strsep, strspn, strcspn, strstr,/	string(3)
symbolic string.	strmode: convert inode status information into a	strmode(3)
/strchr, strrchr, strcmp, strncmp, strcasecmp,	strncasecmp, strcpy, strncpy, strerror, strlen,/	string(3)
strcasecmp, strncasecmp, strcpy, strncpy,/ strcat,	strncat, strchr, strrchr, strcmp, strncmp,	string(3)
strcat, strncat, strchr, strrchr, strcmp,	strncmp, strcasecmp, strncasecmp, strcpy, strncpy,/	string(3)
/strcmp, strncmp, strcasecmp, strncasecmp, strcpy,	strncpy, strerror, strlen, strpbrk, strsep, strspn,/	string(3)
	strpbrk: locate multiple characters in string.	strpbrk(3)
/strncasecmp, strcpy, strncpy, strerror, strlen,	strpbrk, strsep, strspn, strcspn, strstr, strtok,/	string(3)
	strrchr: locate character in string.	strrchr(3)
strcpy, strncpy,/ strcat, strncat, strchr,	strrchr, strcmp, strncmp, strcasecmp, strncasecmp,	string(3)
	strsep: separate strings.	strsep(3)
/strcpy, strncpy, strerror, strlen, strpbrk,	strsep, strspn, strcspn, strstr, strtok, index,/	string(3)
	strspn: span a string.	strspn(3)
/strcpy, strncpy, strerror, strlen, strpbrk, strsep,	strspn, strcspn, strstr, strtok, index, rindex:/	string(3)
	strstr: locate a substring in a string.	strstr(3)
/strerror, strlen, strpbrk, strsep, strspn, strcspn,	strstr, strtok, index, rindex: string specifi	string(3)
	strtod: convert ASCII string to double.	strtod(3)
strlen, strpbrk, strsep, strspn, strcspn, strstr,	strtok, index, rindex: string specifi /strerror,	string(3)
	strtok: string tokens.	strtok(3)
quad_t integer.	strtol, strtoq: convert string value to a long or	strtol(3)
integer. strtol,	strtoq: convert string value to a long or quad_t	strtol(3)
long or uquad_t integer.	strtoul, strtouq: convert a string to an unsigned	strtoul(3)
uquad_t integer. strtoul,	strtouq: convert a string to an unsigned long or	strtoul(3)
	struct: structure Fortran programs.	struct(1)
tcgetattr, tcsetattr: manipulating the termios	structure. /cfsetospeed, cfsetspeed, cfmakeraw,	tcsetattr(3)
struct:	structure Fortran programs.	struct(1)
pstat: display system data	structures.	pstat(8)
characters. unvis,	strunvis: decode a visual representation of	unvis(3)
	strxfrm: transform a string under locale.	strxfrm(3)
	stty, gtty: set and get terminal state (defunct).	stty(3)
interface.	stty: set the options for a terminal device	stty(1)
document.	style: analyze surface characteristics of a	style(1)
	su: substitute user identity.	su(1)
getsubopt: get	sub options from an argument.	getsubopt(3)
paste: merge corresponding or	subsequent lines of files.	paste(1)
su:	substitute user identity.	su(1)
strstr: locate a	substring in a string.	strstr(3)
sccs: front end for the SCCS	subsystem.	sccs(1)
	sum: calculate file checksums and block counts.	sum(1)
repquota:	summarize quotas for a file system.	repquota(8)
suspend: suspend a shell, resuming its	superior.	csh(1)
inetd: internet	super-server.	inetd(8)
drem, finite, logb, scalb: IEEE 754 floating point	support. copysign,	ieee(3)
intro: introduction to special files and hardware	support.	intro(4)
mbrune, mbrrune, mbmb: multibyte rune	support for C.	mbrune(3)
mbtowc, wcstombs, wctomb: multibyte character	support for C. mblen, mbstowcs,	multibyte(3)
setinvalidrune, sgetrune, sputrune: rune	support for C. setrunelocale,	rune(3)
style: analyze	surface characteristics of a document.	style(1)
kvm_getfiles:	survey open files.	kvm_getfiles(3)
suspend:	suspend a shell, resuming its superior.	csh(1)
sleep:	suspend execution for an interval of time.	sleep(1)
usleep:	suspend execution for interval of microseconds.	usleep(3)
sleep:	suspend process execution for interval of seconds.	sleep(3)
	suspend: suspend a shell, resuming its superior.	csh(1)
	swab: swap adjacent bytes.	swab(3)
swab:	swap adjacent bytes.	swab(3)
swapon: add a	swap device for interleaved paging/swapping.	swapon(2)
paging/swapping.	swapon: add a swap device for interleaved	swapon(2)
swapping.	swapon: specify additional device for paging and	swapon(8)

swapon: specify additional device for paging and   swapping.   . . . .   swapon(8)
breaksw: exit from   switch.   . . . .   csh(1)
case: selector in   switch.   . . . .   csh(1)
default: catchall clause in   switch.   . . . .   csh(1)
endsw: terminate   switch.   . . . .   csh(1)
switch: multi-way command branch.   . . . .   csh(1)
nm: display name list   (symbol table).   . . . .   nm(1)
nlist: retrieve   symbol table name list from an executable file.   . . . . .   nlist(3)
kvm_nlist: retrieve   symbol table names from a kernel image.   . . . .   kvm_nlist(3)
stab: symbol table types.   . . . .   stab(5)
readlink: read value of a   symbolic link.   . . . .   readlink(2)
symlink: symbolic link handling.   . . . .   symlink(7)
symlink: make   symbolic link to a file.   . . . .   symlink(2)
strmode: convert inode status information into a   symbolic string.   . . . .   strmode(3)
symlink: make   symbolic link to a file.   . . . .   symlink(2)
symlink: symbolic link handling.   . . . .   symlink(7)
symorder: rearrange name list.   . . . .   symorder(1)
(flush cache).   sync: force completion of pending disk writes   . . . .   sync(8)
that on disk.   sync: synchronize disk block in-core status with   . . . . .   sync(2)
adjtime: correct the time to allow   synchronization of the system clock.   . . . .   adjtime(2)
disk. fsync: synchronize a file's in-core state with that on   . . . .   fsync(2)
msync: synchronize a mapped region.   . . . .   msync(2)
disk. sync: synchronize disk block in-core status with that on   . . . . .   sync(2)
named.reload: cause the name server to   synchronize its database.   . . . .   named.reload(8)
select: synchronous I/O multiplexing.   . . . .   select(2)
csh: a shell (command interpreter) with C-like   syntax.   . . . .   csh(1)
L.   sys: UUCP remote host description file.   . . . .   L.sys(5)
syscall,   __syscall: indirect system call.   . . . .   syscall(2)
syscall, __syscall: indirect system call.   . . . .   syscall(2)
sysconf: get configurable system variables.   . . . . .   sysconf(3)
sysctl: get or set kernel state.   . . . .   sysctl(8)
sysctl: get or set system information.   . . . .   sysctl(3)
perror, strerror,   sys_errlist, sys_nerr: system error messages.   . . . . . .   strerror(3)
control system log.   syslog, vsyslog, openlog, closelog, setlogmask: . . . .   syslog(3)
syslog.conf: syslogd(8) configuration file.   . . . .   syslog.conf(5)
syslogd: log systems messages.   . . . .   syslogd(8)
syslog.conf: syslogd(8) configuration file.   . . . .   syslog.conf(5)
perror, strerror, sys_errlist,   sys_nerr: system error messages.   . . . .   strerror(3)
psignal,   sys_siglist sys_signame: system signal messages.   . . . . . .   psignal(3)
psignal, sys_siglist   sys_signame: system signal messages.   . . . .   psignal(3)
systat: display system statistics on a crt.   . . . .   systat(1)
amd: automatically mount file   systems.   . . . .   amd(8)
getmntinfo: get information about mounted file   systems.   . . . .   getmntinfo(3)
mount: mount file   systems.   . . . .   mount(8)
mount_nfs: mount nfs file   systems.   . . . .   mount_nfs(8)
umount: unmount file   systems.   . . . .   umount(8)
restore: restore files or file   systems from backups made with dump.   . . . .   restore(8)
syslogd: log   systems messages.   . . . .   syslogd(8)
kgmon: generate a dump of the operating   system's profile buffers.   . . . .   kgmon(8)
ns: Xerox Network   Systems(tm) protocol family.   . . . .   ns(4)
isblank: space or   tab character test.   . . . .   isblank(3)
yyfix: extract tables from y.   tab.c.   . . . .   yyfix(1)
bsearch: binary search of a sorted   table.   . . . .   bsearch(3)
rehash: recompute command hash   table.   . . . .   csh(1)
unhash: discard command hash   table.   . . . .   csh(1)
nm: display name list (symbol   table).   . . . .   nm(1)
nlist: retrieve symbol   table name list from an executable file.   . . . .   nlist(3)
kvm_nlist: retrieve symbol   table names from a kernel image.   . . . .   kvm_nlist(3)
getdtablesize: get descriptor   table size.   . . . .   getdtablesize(2)
stab: symbol   table types.   . . . .   stab(5)
ranlib: table-of-contents for archive libraries.   . . . .   ranlib(1)
ranlib: archive (library)   table-of-contents format.   . . . .   ranlib.5(5)
route: manually manipulate the routing   tables..   . . . .   route(8)
tbl: format   tables for troff.   . . . .   tbl(1)
yyfix: extract   tables from y.tab.c.   . . . .   yyfix(1)
expand, unexpand: expand   tabs to spaces, and vice versa.   . . . .   expand(1)
ctags: create a   tags file.   . . . .   ctags(1)
tail: display the last part of a file.   . . . .   tail(1)
LIST_INSERT_AFTER, LIST_INSERT_HEAD, LIST_REMOVE,   TAILQ_ENTRY, TAILQ_HEAD, TAILQ_INIT,/ /LIST_INIT,   queue(3)
/LIST_INSERT_HEAD, LIST_REMOVE, TAILQ_ENTRY,   TAILQ_HEAD, TAILQ_INIT, TAILQ_INSERT_AFTER,/   . .   queue(3)
/LIST_REMOVE, TAILQ_ENTRY, TAILQ_HEAD,   TAILQ_INIT, TAILQ_INSERT_AFTER, TAILQ_INSERT_HEAD,/   queue(3)
/LIST_REMOVE, TAILQ_ENTRY, TAILQ_HEAD, TAILQ_INIT,   TAILQ_INSERT_AFTER, TAILQ_INSERT_HEAD,/   . . . .   queue(3)

/TAILQ_HEAD, TAILQ_INIT, TAILQ_INSERT_AFTER,   TAILQ_INSERT_HEAD, TAILQ_INSERT_TAIL, TAILQ_REMOVE queue(3)
TAILQ_INIT, TAILQ_INSERT_AFTER, TAILQ_INSERT_HEAD,   TAILQ_INSERT_TAIL, TAILQ_REMOVE /TAILQ_HEAD,   queue(3)
TAILQ_INSERT_HEAD, TAILQ_INSERT_TAIL,   TAILQ_REMOVE /TAILQ_INIT, TAILQ_INSERT_AFTER,   queue(3)
traceroute: print the route packets   take to network host. . . . .   traceroute(8)
talk: talk to another user. . . . .   talk(1)
talk: talk to another user. . . . .   talk(1)
talkd: remote user communication server. . . . .   talkd(8)
tan: tangent function. . . . .   tan(3)
atanh: inverse hyperbolic   tangent function. . . . .   atanh(3)
tan: tangent function. . . . .   tan(3)
tanh: hyperbolic   tangent function. . . . .   tanh(3)
atan: arc   tangent function of one variable. . . . .   atan(3)
atan2: arc   tangent function of two variables. . . . .   atan2(3)
tanh: hyperbolic tangent function. . . . .   tanh(3)
tar: tape archive file format. . . . .   tarformat(5)
tar: tape archiver. . . . .   tar(1)
st: CCS SCSI   tape driver. . . . .   st(4)
ansitape: ANSI standard   tape handler. . . . .   ansitape(1)
ct: CS/80 cartridge   tape interface. . . . .   ct(4)
mt: magnetic   tape manipulating program. . . . .   mt(1)
ppt, morse: reformat input as punch cards, paper   tape or morse code. bcd, ...   bcd(6)
format: how to format disks and   tapes. . . . .   format(8)
tcopy: copy and/or verify mag   tapes. . . . .   tcopy(1)
tar: tape archive file format. . . . .   tarformat(5)
tar: tape archiver. . . . .   tar(1)
deroff: remove nroff, troff,   tbl and eqn constructs. . . . .   deroff(1)
tbl: format tables for troff. . . . .   tbl(1)
device interface.   tc: HP98544 98550 "Topcat" and "Catseye" . . . . .   tc(4)
tcsendbreak,   tcdrain, tcflush, tcflow: line control functions. . . . .   tcsendbreak(3)
tcsendbreak, tcdrain, tcflush,   tcflow: line control functions. . . . .   tcsendbreak(3)
tcsendbreak, tcdrain,   tcflush, tcflow: line control functions. . . . .   tcsendbreak(3)
/cfgetospeed, cfsetospeed, cfsetspeed, cfmakeraw,   tcgetattr, tcsetattr: manipulating the termios/ . . . .   tcsetattr(3)
tcgetpgrp: get foreground process group ID. . . . . .   tcgetpgrp(3)
tcopy: copy and/or verify mag tapes. . . . .   tcopy(1)
tcp: Internet Transmission Control Protocol. . . . . .   tcp(4)
functions.   tcsendbreak, tcdrain, tcflush, tcflow: line control . . . .   tcsendbreak(3)
/cfsetospeed, cfsetspeed, cfmakeraw, tcgetattr,   tcsetattr: manipulating the termios structure. . . . .   tcsetattr(3)
tcsetpgrp: set foreground process group ID. . . . . .   tcsetpgrp(3)
tfmtodit: create font files for use with groff   −Tdvi. . . . .   tfmtodit(1)
tee: pipe fitting. . . . .   tee(1)
directory operations. opendir, readdir,   telldir, seekdir, rewinddir, closedir, dirfd: . . . .   directory(3)
telnet: user interface to the   TELNET protocol. . . . .   telnet(1)
telnetd: DARPA   TELNET protocol server. . . . .   telnetd(8)
telnet: user interface to the TELNET protocol. . . . .   telnet(1)
telnetd: DARPA TELNET protocol server. . . . .   telnetd(8)
tempnam, tmpfile, tmpnam: temporary file routines. . . . . .   tmpnam(3)
signals invalid floating−point operations on a VAX   (temporary). infnan: . . . .   infnan(3)
mktemp: make   temporary file name (unique). . . . .   mktemp(3)
tempnam, tmpfile, tmpnam: temporary file routines. . . . .   tmpnam(3)
term: conventional names for terminals. . . . .   term(7)
termcap: terminal capability data base. . . . .   termcap(5)
lock: reserve a   terminal. . . . .   lock(1)
worms: animate worms on a display   terminal. . . . .   worms(6)
termcap: terminal capability data base. . . . .   termcap(5)
tput: terminal capability interface. . . . .   tput(1)
gettytab: terminal configuration data base. . . . .   gettytab(5)
stty: set the options for a   terminal device interface. . . . .   stty(1)
pty: pseudo   terminal driver. . . . .   pty(4)
ite: HP Internal   Terminal Emulator. . . . .   ite(4)
tgetent, tgetnum, tgetflag, tgetstr, tgoto, tputs: terminal independent operation routines. . . . . . .   termcap(3)
tset: terminal initialization. . . . .   tset(1)
ttys: terminal initialization information. . . . .   ttys(5)
tty: general   terminal interface. . . . .   tty(4)
termios: general   terminal line discipline. . . . .   termios(4)
getty: set   terminal mode. . . . .   getty(8)
tty: return user's   terminal name. . . . .   tty(1)
ctermid: generate   terminal pathname. . . . .   ctermid(3)
script: make typescript of   terminal session. . . . .   script(1)
stty, gtty: set and get   terminal state (defunct). . . . .   stty(3)
ttyname, isatty, ttyslot: get name of associated   terminal (tty) from file descriptor. . . . .   ttyname(3)
term: conventional names for   terminals. . . . .   term(7)
endif: terminate conditional. . . . .   csh(1)

```
                          end:  terminate loop.  . . . . . . . . . . . . . . . .   csh(1)
                         kill:  terminate or signal a process.  . . . . . . . . . . . . .   kill(1)
                        endsw:  terminate switch.  . . . . . . . . . . . . . . .   csh(1)
                        _exit:  terminate the calling process.  . . . . . . . . . . . .   _exit(2)
   abort: cause abnormal program  termination. . . . . . . . . . . . . . . . . . . .   abort(3)
     exit: perform normal program  termination. . . . . . . . . . . . . . . . . . . .   exit(3)
  wait, waitpid, wait4, wait3: wait for process  termination. . . . . . . . . . . . . . . . . . . .   wait(2)
                                 termios: general terminal line discipline.  . . . . . . . . . .   termios(4)
 cfmakeraw, tcgetattr, tcsetattr: manipulating the  termios structure. /cfsetospeed, cfsetspeed,  . . . . . . . .   tcsetattr(3)
      isalnum: alphanumeric character  test.  . . . . . . . . . . . . . . . . . . . . . .   isalnum(3)
         isalpha: alphabetic character  test.  . . . . . . . . . . . . . . . . . . . . . .   isalpha(3)
       isblank: space or tab character  test.  . . . . . . . . . . . . . . . . . . . . . .   isblank(3)
            iscntrl: control character  test.  . . . . . . . . . . . . . . . . . . . . . .   iscntrl(3)
        isdigit: decimal-digit character  test.  . . . . . . . . . . . . . . . . . . . . . .   isdigit(3)
          islower: lower-case character  test.  . . . . . . . . . . . . . . . . . . . . . .   islower(3)
        ispunct: punctuation character  test.  . . . . . . . . . . . . . . . . . . . . . .   ispunct(3)
        isspace: white-space character  test.  . . . . . . . . . . . . . . . . . . . . . .   isspace(3)
          isupper: upper-case character  test.  . . . . . . . . . . . . . . . . . . . . . .   isupper(3)
      isxdigit: hexadecimal-digit character  test.  . . . . . . . . . . . . . . . . . . . . . .   isxdigit(3)
                                 test: condition evaluation utility.  . . . . . . . . .   test(1)
                       isascii:  test for ASCII character.  . . . . . . . . . . . .   isascii(3)
                  isinf, isnan:  test for infinity or not-a-number.  . . . . . . . . .   isinf(3)
        isgraph: printing character  test (space character exclusive).  . . . . . . . . . .   isgraph(3)
         isprint: printing character  test (space character inclusive).  . . . . . . . . . .   isprint(3)
         quiz: random knowledge  tests.  . . . . . . . . . . . . . . . . . . . . .   quiz(6)
          tetris: the game of  tetris.  . . . . . . . . . . . . . . . . . . . . .   tetris(6)
                                 tetris: the game of tetris.  . . . . . . . . . . . .   tetris(6)
       pic: compile pictures for troff or  TeX.  . . . . . . . . . . . . . . . . . . . . . .   pic(1)
        grodvi: convert groff output to  TeX dvi format.  . . . . . . . . . . . . . . . .   grodvi(1)
 file perusal filter for crt viewing of compressed  text. zmore:  . . . . . . . . . . . . . . . . . . .   zmore(1)
               sticky: sticky  text and append-only directories.  . . . . . . . . . . .   sticky(8)
  size: display object file segment sizes  (text, data and bss).  . . . . . . . . . . . . . . .   size(1)
              ed: line oriented  text editor.  . . . . . . . . . . . . . . . . . . .   ed(1)
            ex, vi, view:  text editors.  . . . . . . . . . . . . . . . . . . .   vi(1)
           sort: sort or merge  text files.  . . . . . . . . . . . . . . . . . . .   sort(1)
             fmt: simple  text formatter.  . . . . . . . . . . . . . . . . . . .   fmt(1)
                          ms:  text formatting macros.  . . . . . . . . . . . . . .   ms(7)
 tf_init, tf_get_pname, tf_get_pinst, tf_get_cred,  tf_close: routines for manipulating a Kerberos/  . . . . .   tf_util(3)
 Kerberos/ tf_init, tf_get_pname, tf_get_pinst,  tf_get_cred, tf_close: routines for manipulating a  . . . . .   tf_util(3)
 manipulating a Kerberos/ tf_init, tf_get_pname,  tf_get_pinst, tf_get_cred, tf_close: routines for  . . . . .   tf_util(3)
 routines for manipulating a Kerberos/ tf_init,  tf_get_pname, tf_get_pinst, tf_get_cred, tf_close:  . . . . .   tf_util(3)
 tf_close: routines for manipulating a Kerberos/  tf_init, tf_get_pname, tf_get_pinst, tf_get_cred,  . . . . . .   tf_util(3)
                       −Tdvi.  tfmtodit: create font files for use with groff  . . . . . .   tfmtodit(1)
                                 tftp: trivial file transfer program.  . . . . . . . . . . . .   tftp(1)
                      server.  tftpd: Internet Trivial File Transfer Protocol  . . . . . . . .   tftpd(8)
    terminal independent operation routines.  tgetent, tgetnum, tgetflag, tgetstr, tgoto, tputs:  . . . . . . .   termcap(3)
 independent operation routines. tgetent, tgetnum,  tgetflag, tgetstr, tgoto, tputs: terminal  . . . . . . . . . .   termcap(3)
 independent operation routines. tgetent,  tgetnum, tgetflag, tgetstr, tgoto, tputs: terminal  . . . . . . . . . .   termcap(3)
 operation routines. tgetent, tgetnum, tgetflag,  tgetstr, tgoto, tputs: terminal independent  . . . . . . . .   termcap(3)
 routines. tgetent, tgetnum, tgetflag, tgetstr,  tgoto, tputs: terminal independent operation  . . . . . . .   termcap(3)
 ceil: smallest integral value not greater  than x.  . . . . . . . . . . . . . . . . . . . . . .   ceil(3)
 floor: largest integral value not greater  than x.  . . . . . . . . . . . . . . . . . . . . . .   floor(3)
 diction, explain: print wordy sentences;  thesaurus for diction.  . . . . . . . . . . . . .   diction(1)
       from: print names of  those who have sent mail.  . . . . . . . . . . . .   from(1)
               merge:  three-way file merge.  . . . . . . . . . . . . . . .   merge(1)
 krb_set_tkt_string: set Kerberos  ticket cache file name.  . . . . . . . . . . . . . .   krb_set_tkt_string(3)
 tf_close: routines for manipulating a Kerberos  ticket file. /tf_get_pinst, tf_get_cred,  . . . . . . . .   tf_util(3)
 ksrvtgt: fetch and store Kerberos  ticket-granting-ticket using a service key.  . . . . . . .   ksrvtgt(1)
     kdestroy: destroy Kerberos  tickets.  . . . . . . . . . . . . . . . . . . . . .   kdestroy(1)
 klist: list currently held Kerberos  tickets.  . . . . . . . . . . . . . . . . . . . . .   klist(1)
 at: schedule execution of commands 'at' a given  time.  . . . . . . . . . . . . . . . . . . . . . .   at(1)
   date: display or set date and  time.  . . . . . . . . . . . . . . . . . . . . . .   date(1)
      ftime: get date and  time.  . . . . . . . . . . . . . . . . . . . . . .   ftime(3)
 gettimeofday, settimeofday: get/set date and  time.  . . . . . . . . . . . . . . . . . . . . . .   gettimeofday(2)
 shutdown: close down the system at a given  time.  . . . . . . . . . . . . . . . . . . . . . .   shutdown(8)
 sleep: suspend execution for an interval of  time.  . . . . . . . . . . . . . . . . . . . . . .   sleep(1)
        strftime: format date and  time.  . . . . . . . . . . . . . . . . . . . . . .   strftime(3)
 ualarm: schedule signal after specified  time.  . . . . . . . . . . . . . . . . . . . . . .   ualarm(3)
       ac: display connect  time accounting.  . . . . . . . . . . . . . . . . .   ac(8)
              time:  time command.  . . . . . . . . . . . . . . . . . . .   csh(1)
              time:  time command execution.  . . . . . . . . . . . . .   time(1)
 tzset, tzsetwall: initialize  time conversion information.  . . . . . . . . . . . . .   tzset(3)
```

time: get time of day. . . . . time(3)
time: get time of day. . . . . time(3)
timed: time server daemon. . . . . timed(8)
time: time command. . . . . csh(1)
time: time command execution. . . . . time(1)
adjtime: correct the time to allow synchronization of the system clock. . . . . . adjtime(2)
clock: determine processor time used. clock(3)
localtime, mktime: transform binary date and time value to ASCII. /ctime, difftime, gmtime, ... ctime(3)
zic: time zone compiler. . . . . zic(8)
tzfile: time zone information. . . . . tzfile(5)
timedc: timed control program. . . . . timedc(8)
timed: time server daemon. . . . . timed(8)
timedc: timed control program. . . . . timedc(8)
getitimer, setitimer: get/set value of interval timer. . . . . getitimer(2)
alarm: set signal timer alarm. alarm(3)
times: process times. . . . . times(3)
touch: change file access and modification times. . . . . touch(1)
utime: set file times. . . . . utime(3)
utimes: set file access and modification times. . . . . utimes(2)
times: process times. . . . . times(3)
timezone: return the timezone abbreviation. . . . . timezone(3)
timezone: return the timezone abbreviation. . . . . timezone(3)
tip, cu: connect to a remote system. . . . . tip(1)
ns_addr, ns_ntoa: Xerox NS Ns (tm) address conversion routines. . . . . ns(3)
tempnam, tmpfile, tmpnam: temporary file routines. . . . . tmpnam(3)
tempnam, tmpfile, tmpnam: temporary file routines. . . . . tmpnam(3)
tn3270: full-screen remote login to IBM VM/CMS. . . . . . tn3270(1)
toascii: convert a byte to 7-bit ASCII. . . . . toascii(3)
/isprint, ispunct, isspace, isupper, isxdigit, toascii tolower, toupper,: character classification/ . . . . . . ctype(3)
strtok: string tokens. . . . . strtok(3)
/ispunct, isspace, isupper, isxdigit, toascii tolower, toupper,: character classification macros. . . . . . ctype(3)
conversion. tolower: upper case to lower case letter . . . . tolower(3)
amq: automounter query tool. . . . . amq(8)
intro: introduction to general commands (tools and utilities). . . . . intro(1)
tc: HP98544 98550 ''Topcat'' and ''Catseye'' device interface. . . . . tc(4)
tsort: topological sort of a directed graph. . . . . tsort(1)
quot: display total block usage per user for a file system. . . . . . quot(8)
touch: change file access and modification times. . . . . . touch(1)
/isspace, isupper, isxdigit, toascii tolower, toupper,: character classification macros. . . . . . ctype(3)
conversion. toupper: lower case to upper case letter . . . . toupper(3)
TP: ISO Transport Protocol. . . . . tp(4)
afmtodit: create font files for use with groff –Tps. . . . . afmtodit(1)
tput: terminal capability interface. . . . . tput(1)
tgetent, tgetnum, tgetflag, tgetstr, tgoto, tputs: terminal independent operation routines. . . . . . . termcap(3)
tr: translate characters. . . . . tr(1)
ptrace: process trace. . . . . ptrace(2)
trpt: transliterate protocol trace. . . . . trpt(8)
trsp: transliterate sequenced packet protocol trace. . . . . trsp(8)
kdump: display kernel trace data. kdump(1)
host. traceroute: print the route packets take to network . . . . . traceroute(8)
ktrace: enable kernel process tracing. . . . . ktrace(1)
ktrace: process tracing. . . . . ktrace(2)
atc: air traffic controller game. . . . . atc(6)
goto: command transfer. csh(1)
uucico, uucpd: transfer files queued by uucp or uux. . . . . uucico(8)
ftp: ARPANET file transfer program. . . . . ftp(1)
tftp: trivial file transfer program. . . . . tftp(1)
ftpd: Internet File Transfer Protocol server. . . . . ftpd(8)
tftpd: Internet Trivial File Transfer Protocol server. . . . . tftpd(8)
named-xfer: ancillary agent for inbound zone transfers. named-xfer(8)
strxfrm: transform a string under locale. . . . . strxfrm(3)
/ctime, difftime, gmtime, localtime, mktime: transform binary date and time value to ASCII. . . . . . . ctime(3)
UTF2: Universal character set Transformation Format encoding of runes. . . . . utf2(4)
ASCII. pfbtops: translate a PostScript font in .pfb format to . . . . pfbtops(1)
tr: translate characters. . . . . tr(1)
/etc/kerberosIV/krb.realms: host to Kerberos realm translation file. . . . . krb.realms(5)
trpt: transliterate protocol trace. . . . . trpt(8)
trsp: transliterate sequenced packet protocol trace. . . . . trsp(8)
tcp: Internet Transmission Control Protocol. . . . . tcp(4)
cltp: ISO Connectionless Transport Protocol. . . . . cltp(4)
TP: ISO Transport Protocol. . . . . tp(4)
fts: traverse a file hierarchy. . . . . fts(3)

```
                                      trek: trekkie game.  . . . . . . . . . . . . . . . . .  trek(6)
                              trek:   trekkie game.  . . . . . . . . . . . . . . . . .  trek(6)
                              tftp:   trivial file transfer program.  . . . . . . . . . . .  tftp(1)
                   tftpd: Internet   Trivial File Transfer Protocol server.  . . . . . . . . .  tftpd(8)
          eqn: format equations for   troff.  . . . . . . . . . . . . . . . . . . . . . .  eqn(1)
             tbl: format tables for   troff.  . . . . . . . . . . . . . . . . . . . . . .  tbl(1)
          addftinfo: add information to   troff font files for use with groff.  . . . . . . . . .  addftinfo(1)
                                      troff: format documents. . . . . . . . . . . . . . .  troff(1)
           pic: compile pictures for   troff or TeX.  . . . . . . . . . . . . . . . . . .  pic(1)
              deroff: remove nroff,   troff, tbl and eqn constructs.  . . . . . . . . . . .  deroff(1)
                  battlestar: a   tropical adventure game.  . . . . . . . . . . . . . .  battlestar(6)
                                      trpt: transliterate protocol trace.  . . . . . . . . . . .  trpt(8)
                            trace.   trsp: transliterate sequenced packet protocol  . . . . . .  trsp(8)
                                      true: return true value. . . . . . . . . . . . . . . .  true(1)
                 true: return   true value.  . . . . . . . . . . . . . . . . . . . .  true(1)
         truncate, ftruncate:   truncate a file to a specified length.  . . . . . . . . .  truncate(2)
                            length.   truncate, ftruncate: truncate a file to a specified  . . . . . . .  truncate(2)
                                      tset: terminal initialization.  . . . . . . . . . . . .  tset(1)
                                      tsort: topological sort of a directed graph.  . . . . . . . .  tsort(1)
   isatty, ttyslot: get name of associated terminal   (tty) from file descriptor. ttyname,  . . . . . . . . .  ttyname(3)
                                      tty: general terminal interface.  . . . . . . . . . . . .  tty(4)
          acucntrl: turn around   tty line between dialin and dialout.  . . . . . . . . . .  acucntrl(8)
                                      tty: return user's terminal name.  . . . . . . . . . . .  tty(1)
          terminal (tty) from file descriptor.   ttyname, isatty, ttyslot: get name of associated  . . . . . . . .  ttyname(3)
        last: indicate last logins of users and   ttys.  . . . . . . . . . . . . . . . . . . . . .  last(1)
 getttyent, getttynam, setttyent, endttyent: get   ttys file entry.  . . . . . . . . . . . . . . . . . .  getttyent(3)
                                      ttys: terminal initialization information.  . . . . . . . . . .  ttys(5)
   file descriptor.  ttyname, isatty,   ttyslot: get name of associated terminal (tty) from  . . . . . .  ttyname(3)
                            tunefs:   tune up an existing file system.  . . . . . . . . . . .  tunefs(8)
                                      tunefs: tune up an existing file system.  . . . . . . . . .  tunefs(8)
                    mdoc.samples:   tutorial sampler for writing  manuals with –mdoc.  . . . . . .  mdoc.samples(7)
           stab: symbol table   types.  . . . . . . . . . . . . . . . . . . . . . .  stab(5)
          types: system data   types.  . . . . . . . . . . . . . . . . . . . . . .  types(5)
                                      types: system data types.  . . . . . . . . . . . . . .  types(5)
               script: make   typescript of terminal session.  . . . . . . . . . . . . .  script(1)
        man: (deprecated) macros to   typeset manual.  . . . . . . . . . . . . . . . . . .  man(7)
          grotty: groff driver for   typewriter-like devices.  . . . . . . . . . . . . . .  grotty(1)
                     information.   tzfile: time zone information.  . . . . . . . . . . . . .  tzfile(5)
                            tzset,   tzset, tzsetwall: initialize time conversion  . . . . . . . .  tzset(3)
                information.   tzset, tzsetwall: initialize time conversion information.  . . . . . .  tzset(3)
                                      ualarm: schedule signal after specified time.  . . . . . . .  ualarm(3)
                                      udp: Internet User Datagram Protocol.  . . . . . . . . . .  udp(4)
               getpw: get name from   uid.  . . . . . . . . . . . . . . . . . . . . . .  getpw(3)
                                      ul: do underlining.  . . . . . . . . . . . . . . . . . .  ul(1)
                                      umask: change or display file creation mask.  . . . . . . . .  csh(1)
                                      umask: set file creation mode mask.  . . . . . . . . . .  umask(2)
                                      umount: unmount file systems.  . . . . . . . . . . . .  umount(8)
                                      unalias: remove aliases.  . . . . . . . . . . . . . .  csh(1)
                                      uname: display information about the system.  . . . . . . . .  uname(1)
                                      uname: get system identification.  . . . . . . . . . . .  uname(3)
               cat them. compact,   uncompact, ccat: compress and uncompress files, and  . . . .  compact(1)
    compact, uncompact, ccat: compress and   uncompress files, and cat them.  . . . . . . . . . . .  compact(1)
                         compress,   uncompress, zcat: compress and expand data.  . . . . . . . .  compress(1)
        strxfrm: transform a string   under locale.  . . . . . . . . . . . . . . . . . .  strxfrm(3)
  freeze a configuration of sources checked in   under RCS. rcsfreeze:  . . . . . . . . . . . . . . . .  rcsfreeze(1)
          xroach: cockroaches hide   under your windows.  . . . . . . . . . . . . . . . .  xroach(6)
          wump: hunt the wumpus in an   underground cave.  . . . . . . . . . . . . . . . . .  wump(6)
                                      ul: do   underlining.  . . . . . . . . . . . . . . . . . . .  ul(1)
                           expand,   unexpand: expand tabs to spaces, and vice versa.  . . . . . .  expand(1)
                           ungetc:   un-get character from input stream.  . . . . . . . . . .  ungetc(3)
                                      ungetc: un-get character from input stream.  . . . . . . . .  ungetc(3)
                                      unhash: discard command hash table.  . . . . . . . . . .  csh(1)
                                      unifdef: remove ifdef'ed lines.  . . . . . . . . . . . .  unifdef(1)
            mount_union: mount   union filesystems.  . . . . . . . . . . . . . . . . .  mount_union(8)
                            file.   uniq: report or filter out repeated lines in a  . . . . . . . . .  uniq(1)
        mktemp: make temporary file name   (unique).  . . . . . . . . . . . . . . . . . . .  mktemp(3)
         gethostid, sethostid: get/set   unique identifier of current host.  . . . . . . . . . . .  gethostid(3)
                                      units: conversion program.  . . . . . . . . . . . . .  units(1)
         encoding of runes. UTF2:   Universal character set Transformation Format  . . . . . . .  utf2(4)
                           reboot:   UNIX bootstrapping procedures.  . . . . . . . . . . . .  boot_sparc(8)
                 uux: unix to   unix command execution.  . . . . . . . . . . . . . . .  uux(1)
                 uucp: unix to   unix copy.  . . . . . . . . . . . . . . . . . . . . .  uucp(1)
```

crash: UNIX system failures. . . . . crash(8)
uux: unix to unix command execution. . . . . uux(1)
uucp: unix to unix copy. . . . . uucp(1)
unix: UNIX-domain protocol family. . . . . unix(4)
unix: UNIX-domain protocol family. . . . . unix(4)
unlimit: remove resource limitations. . . . . csh(1)
unlink: remove directory entry. . . . . unlink(2)
mlock, munlock: lock (unlock) physical pages in memory. . . . . mlock(2)
umount: unmount file systems. . . . . umount(8)
mount, unmount: mount or dismount a filesystem. . . . . mount(2)
strip: remove unnecessary information from executable files. . . . . . . strip(1)
unset: discard shell variables. . . . . csh(1)
getenv, putenv, setenv, unsetenv: environment variable functions. . . . . getenv(3)
unsetenv: remove environment variables. . . . . csh(1)
strtoul, strtouq: convert a string to an unsigned long or uquad_t integer. . . . . strtoul(3)
to original form. unvis: revert a visual representation of data back . . . . . unvis(1)
characters. unvis, strunvis: decode a visual representation of . . . . . . unvis(3)
tunefs: tune up an existing file system. . . . . tunefs(8)
startslip: dial up and login to a slip server. . . . . startslip(1)
rhost: look up host names using domain server. . . . . host(1)
free: free up memory allocated with malloc, calloc or realloc. . . . . free(3)
rcsclean: clean up working files. . . . . rcsclean(1)
frequently. update: flush internal filesystem caches to disk . . . . . . update(8)
toupper: lower case to upper case letter conversion. . . . . toupper(3)
tolower: upper case to lower case letter conversion. . . . . tolower(3)
isupper: upper-case character test. . . . . isupper(3)
uptime: show how long system has been running. . . . . . . uptime(1)
strtouq: convert a string to an unsigned long or uquad_t integer. strtoul, ... strtoul(3)
quota: display disk usage and limits. . . . . quota(1)
quot: display total block usage per user for a file system. . . . . quot(8)
du: display disk usage statistics. . . . . du(1)
mount_null: demonstrate the use of a null file system layer. . . . . mount_null(8)
madvise: give advise about use of memory. . . . . madvise(2)
mincore: get advise about use of memory. . . . . mincore(2)
addftinfo: add information to troff font files for use with groff. . . . . addftinfo(1)
tfmtodit: create font files for use with groff −Tdvi. . . . . tfmtodit(1)
afmtodit: create font files for use with groff −Tps. . . . . afmtodit(1)
clock: determine processor time used. clock(3)
what: show what versions of object modules were used to construct a file. . . . . what(1)
login: login new user. . . . . csh(1)
talk: talk to another user. . . . . talk(1)
write: send a message to another user. . . . . write(1)
setruid, setrgid: set user and group ID. . . . . setruid(3)
setuid, seteuid, setgid, setegid,: set user and group ID. . . . . setuid(2)
getbsize: get user block size. . . . . getbsize(3)
talkd: remote user communication server. . . . . talkd(8)
chpass: add or change user database information. . . . . chpass(1)
udp: Internet User Datagram Protocol. . . . . udp(4)
environ: user environment. . . . . environ(7)
quot: display total block usage per user for a file system. . . . . quot(8)
whoami: display effective user id. . . . . whoami(1)
getuid, geteuid: get user identification. . . . . getuid(2)
id: return user identity. . . . . id(1)
su: substitute user identity. . . . . su(1)
setreuid: set real and effective user ID's. . . . . setreuid(2)
finger: user information lookup program. . . . . finger(1)
fingerd: remote user information server. . . . . fingerd(8)
telnet: user interface to the TELNET protocol. . . . . telnet(1)
whois: Internet user name directory service. . . . . whois(1)
kvm_getprocs, kvm_getargv, kvm_getenvv: access user process state. . . . . kvm_getprocs(3)
edquota: edit user quotas. . . . . edquota(8)
getusershell, setusershell, endusershell: get legal user shells. . . . . getusershell(3)
USERFILE: UUCP pathname permissions file. . . . . . . USERFILE(5)
adduser: procedure for adding new users. . . . . adduser(8)
mesg: display (do not display) messages from other users. . . . . mesg(1)
users: list current users. . . . . users(1)
wall: write a message to users. . . . . wall(1)
last: indicate last logins of users and ttys. . . . . last(1)
w: who present users are and what they are doing. . . . . w(1)
users: list current users. . . . . users(1)
logname: display user's login name. . . . . logname(1)
passwd: modify a user's password. . . . . passwd(1)

tty: return user's terminal name. . . . . tty(1)
fetch and store Kerberos ticket-granting-ticket using a service key. ksrvtgt: . . . . ksrvtgt(1)
rhost: look up host names using domain server. . . . . host(1)
bdes: encrypt/decrypt using the Data Encryption Standard. . . . . bdes(1)
microseconds. usleep: suspend execution for interval of . . . . usleep(3)
encoding of runes. UTF2: Universal character set Transformation Format . . . . utf2(4)
intro: introduction to general commands (tools and utilities). intro(1)
eeprom: openprom control utility. . . . . eeprom(8)
Kerberos key distribution center database editing utility. kdb_edit: . . . . kdb_edit(8)
kdb_util: Kerberos key distribution center database utility. . . . . kdb_util(8)
kinit: Kerberos login utility. . . . . kinit(1)
test: condition evaluation utility. . . . . test(1)
xargs: construct argument list(s) and execute utility. . . . . xargs(1)
krb_get_admhst, krb_get_lrealm: additional Kerberos utility routines. /krb_get_phost, krb_get_krbhst, ... krb_realmofhost(3)
getrusage: get information about resource utilization. getrusage(2)
vtimes: get information about resource utilization. vtimes(3)
utime: set file times. . . . . utime(3)
utimes: set file access and modification times. . . . . . utimes(2)
utmp, wtmp, lastlog: login records. . . . . utmp(5)
uux. uucico, uucpd: transfer files queued by uucp or . . . . . . uucico(8)
uuclean: uucp spool directory clean-up. . . . . uuclean(8)
rmail: handle remote mail received via uucp. . . . . rmail(8)
L-devices: UUCP device description file. . . . . L-devices(5)
uuxqt: UUCP execution file interpreter. . . . . uuxqt(8)
L.aliases: UUCP hostname alias file. . . . . L.aliases(5)
uuname: list names of UUCP hosts. . . . . uuname(1)
uulog: display UUCP log entries. . . . . uulog(1)
uucico, uucpd: transfer files queued by uucp or uux. . . . . uucico(8)
USERFILE: UUCP pathname permissions file. . . . . USERFILE(5)
L-dialcodes: UUCP phone number index file. . . . . L-dialcodes(5)
uuq: examine or manipulate the uucp queue. . . . . uuq(1)
L.cmds: UUCP remote command permissions file. . . . . L.cmds(5)
L.sys: UUCP remote host description file. . . . . L.sys(5)
uupoll: poll a remote UUCP site. . . . . uupoll(8)
uuclean: uucp spool directory clean-up. . . . . uuclean(8)
uusnap: show snapshot of the UUCP system. uusnap(8)
uucp: unix to unix copy. . . . . uucp(1)
uucico, uucpd: transfer files queued by uucp or uux. . . . . uucico(8)
uuencode, uudecode: encode/decode a binary file. . . . . uuencode(1)
uuencode: format of an encoded uuencode file. . . . . uuencode.format(5)
uuencode: format of an encoded uuencode file. . . . . . . uuencode.format(5)
uuencode, uudecode: encode/decode a binary file. . . . . . uuencode(1)
uulog: display UUCP log entries. . . . . uulog(1)
uuname: list names of UUCP hosts. . . . . uuname(1)
uupoll: poll a remote UUCP site. . . . . uupoll(8)
uuq: examine or manipulate the uucp queue. . . . . . . uuq(1)
uusend: send a file to a remote host. . . . . uusend(1)
uusnap: show snapshot of the UUCP system. . . . . . . uusnap(8)
uucico, uucpd: transfer files queued by uucp or uux. . . . . uucico(8)
uux: unix to unix command execution. . . . . uux(1)
uuxqt: UUCP execution file interpreter. . . . . uuxqt(8)
cc, g++: GNU project C and C++ Compiler (v2 preliminary). cc(1)
g++: GNU project C++ Compiler (v2 preliminary). . . . . g++(1)
vacation: return ''I am not here'' indication. . . . . . . vacation(1)
valloc: aligned memory allocation function. . . . . valloc(3)
false: return false value. . . . . false(1)
true: return true value. . . . . true(1)
abs: integer absolute value function. . . . . abs(3)
fabs: floating-point absolute value function. fabs(3)
cabs: euclidean distance and complex absolute value functions. hypot, ... hypot(3)
ceil: smallest integral value not greater than x. . . . . ceil(3)
floor: largest integral value not greater than x. . . . . floor(3)
labs: return the absolute value of a long integer. . . . . labs(3)
readlink: read value of a symbolic link. . . . . readlink(2)
getitimer, setitimer: get/set value of interval timer. . . . . getitimer(2)
set: change value of shell variable. . . . . csh(1)
strtol, strtoq: convert string value to a long or quad_t integer. . . . . strtol(3)
localtime, mktime: transform binary date and time value to ASCII. asctime, ctime, difftime, gmtime, ... ctime(3)
htonl, htons, ntohl, ntohs: convert values between host and network byte order. . . . . byteorder(3)
modf: extract signed integral and fractional values from floating-point number. . . . . modf(3)
atan: arc tangent function of one variable. . . . . atan(3)
set: change value of shell variable. . . . . csh(1)

stdarg:	variable argument lists.	stdarg(3)
getenv, putenv, setenv, unsetenv: environment	variable functions.	getenv(3)
setenv: set	variable in environment.	csh(1)
atan2: arc tangent function of two	variables.	atan2(3)
confstr: get string-valued configurable	variables.	confstr(3)
@: arithmetic on shell	variables.	csh(1)
unset: discard shell	variables.	csh(1)
unsetenv: remove environment	variables.	csh(1)
pathconf, fpathconf: get configurable pathname	variables.	pathconf(2)
sysconf: get configurable system	variables.	sysconf(3)
signals invalid floating–point operations on a	VAX (temporary). infnan:	infnan(3)
assert: expression	verification macro.	assert(3)
tcopy: copy and/or	verify mag tapes.	tcopy(1)
formatted error messages. err,	verr, errx, verrx, warn, vwarn, warnx, vwarnx:	err(3)
messages. err, verr, errx,	verrx, warn, vwarn, warnx, vwarnx: formatted error	err(3)
expand, unexpand: expand tabs to spaces, and vice	versa.	expand(1)
kuserok: Kerberos	version of ruserok.	kuserok(3)
file. what: show what	versions of object modules were used to construct a	what(1)
efficient way.	vfork: spawn new process in a virtual memory	vfork(2)
printf, fprintf, sprintf, snprintf, vprintf,	vfprintf, vsprintf, vsnprintf: formatted output/	printf(3)
scanf, fscanf, sscanf, vscanf, vsscanf,	vfscanf: input format conversion.	scanf(3)
	vgrind: grind nice listings of programs.	vgrind(1)
vgrindefs: language definition data base for	vgrind(1).	vgrindefs(5)
vgrind(1).	vgrindefs: language definition data base for	vgrindefs(5)
ex,	vi, view: text editors.	vi(1)
Kerberos routines for sending authentication	via network stream sockets. /krb_net_read:	krb_sendauth(3)
rmail: handle remote mail received	via uucp.	rmail(8)
expand, unexpand: expand tabs to spaces, and	vice versa.	expand(1)
ex, vi,	view: text editors.	vi(1)
more: file perusal filter for crt	viewing.	more(1)
zmore: file perusal filter for crt	viewing of compressed text.	zmore(1)
robots: fight off	villainous robots.	robots(6)
	vipw: edit the password file.	vipw(8)
kvm_read, kvm_write: read or write kernel	virtual memory.	kvm_read(3)
kvm_openfiles, kvm_close: initialize kernel	virtual memory access. kvm_open,	kvm_open(3)
vfork: spawn new process in a	virtual memory efficient way.	vfork(2)
vmstat: report	virtual memory statistics.	vmstat(8)
format.	vis: display non-printable characters in a visual	vis(1)
	vis: visually encode characters.	vis(3)
vis: display non-printable characters in a	visual format.	vis(1)
unvis, strunvis: decode a	visual representation of characters.	unvis(3)
form. unvis: revert a	visual representation of data back to original	unvis(1)
vis:	visually encode characters.	vis(3)
consumption.	vlimit: control maximum system resource	vlimit(3)
tn3270: full-screen remote login to IBM	VM/CMS.	tn3270(1)
	vmstat: report virtual memory statistics.	vmstat(8)
fs, inode: format of file system	volume.	fs(5)
output/ printf, fprintf, sprintf, snprintf,	vprintf, vfprintf, vsprintf, vsnprintf: formatted	printf(3)
scanf, fscanf, sscanf,	vscanf, vsscanf, vfscanf: input format conversion.	scanf(3)
sprintf, snprintf, vprintf, vfprintf, vsprintf,	vsnprintf: formatted output conversion. /fprintf,	printf(3)
/fprintf, sprintf, snprintf, vprintf, vfprintf,	vsprintf, vsnprintf: formatted output conversion.	printf(3)
scanf, fscanf, sscanf, vscanf,	vsscanf, vfscanf: input format conversion.	scanf(3)
system log. syslog,	vsyslog, openlog, closelog, setlogmask: control	syslog(3)
	vtimes: get information about resource utilization.	vtimes(3)
err, verr, errx, verrx, warn,	vwarn, warnx, vwarnx: formatted error messages.	err(3)
err, verr, errx, verrx, warn, vwarn, warnx,	vwarnx: formatted error messages.	err(3)
	w: who present users are and what they are doing.	w(1)
	wait: await process completion.	wait(1)
wait:	wait for background processes to complete.	csh(1)
sigpause: atomically release blocked signals and	wait for interrupt.	sigpause(2)
sigsuspend: atomically release blocked signals and	wait for interrupt.	sigsuspend(2)
wait, waitpid, wait4, wait3:	wait for process termination.	wait(2)
	wait: wait for background processes to complete.	csh(1)
termination.	wait, waitpid, wait4, wait3: wait for process	wait(2)
wait, waitpid, wait4,	wait3: wait for process termination.	wait(2)
wait, waitpid,	wait4, wait3: wait for process termination.	wait(2)
termination. wait,	waitpid, wait4, wait3: wait for process	wait(2)
find:	walk a file hierarchy.	find(1)
	wall: write a message to users.	wall(1)
messages. err, verr, errx, verrx,	warn, vwarn, warnx, vwarnx: formatted error	err(3)
err, verr, errx, verrx, warn, vwarn,	warnx, vwarnx: formatted error messages.	err(3)
	wc: word, line, and byte count.	wc(1)

C. mblen, mbstowcs, mbtowc, wcstombs, wctomb: multibyte character support for . . . . . multibyte(3)
mblen, mbstowcs, mbtowc, wcstombs, wctomb: multibyte character support for C. . . . . multibyte(3)
what: show what versions of object modules were used to construct a file. . . . . what(1)
whatis: describe what a command is. . . . . whatis(1)
used to construct a file. what: show what versions of object modules were . . . . . . what(1)
w: who present users are and what they are doing. . . . . w(1)
construct a file. what: show what versions of object modules were used to . . . . what(1)
whatis: describe what a command is. . . . . whatis(1)
leave: remind you when you have to leave. . . . . leave(1)
whereis: locate programs. . . . . whereis(1)
paths. which: locate a program file including aliases and . . . . . . which(1)
while: repeat commands conditionally. . . . . csh(1)
break: exit while/foreach loop. . . . . csh(1)
isspace: white-space character test. . . . . isspace(3)
who: display who is logged in. . . . . who(1)
from: print names of those who have sent mail. . . . . from(1)
who: display who is logged in. . . . . who(1)
rwho: who is logged in on local machines. . . . . rwho(1)
biff: be notified if mail arrives and who it is from. . . . . biff(1)
w: who present users are and what they are doing. . . . . w(1)
whoami: display effective user id. . . . . whoami(1)
whois: Internet user name directory service. . . . . whois(1)
fold: fold long lines for finite width output device. . . . . fold(1)
xneko: cat-and-mouse chase in an X window. . . . . xneko(6)
window: window environment. . . . . window(1)
window: window environment. . . . . window(1)
xroach: cockroaches hide under your windows. . . . . xroach(6)
fastboot, fasthalt: reboot/halt the system without checking the disks. . . . . fastboot(8)
sail: multi-user wooden ships and iron men. . . . . sail(6)
fgetc, getc, getchar, getw: get next character or word from input stream. . . . . getc(3)
wc: word, line, and byte count. . . . . wc(1)
boggle: word search game. . . . . boggle(6)
fputc, putc, putchar, putw: output a character or word to a stream. . . . . putc(3)
diction, explain: print wordy sentences; thesaurus for diction. . . . . diction(1)
cd: change working directory. . . . . cd(1)
chdir, fchdir: change current working directory. . . . . chdir(2)
pwd: return working directory name. . . . . pwd(1)
getcwd: get working directory pathname. . . . . getcwd(3)
rcsclean: clean up working files. . . . . rcsclean(1)
worm: play the growing worm game. . . . . worm(6)
worm: play the growing worm game. . . . . worm(6)
worms: animate worms on a display terminal. . . . . worms(6)
worms: animate worms on a display terminal. . . . . worms(6)
memset: write a byte to byte string. . . . . memset(3)
wall: write a message to users. . . . . wall(1)
disklabel: read and write disk pack label. . . . . disklabel(8)
pax: read and write file archives and copy directory hierarchies. . . . . . . pax(1)
kvm_read, kvm_write: read or write kernel virtual memory. . . . . kvm_read(3)
write, writev: write output. write(2)
write: send a message to another user. . . . . write(1)
write, writev: write output. . . . . write(2)
bzero: write zeroes to a byte string. . . . . bzero(3)
sync: force completion of pending disk writes (flush cache). . . . . sync(8)
write, writev: write output. . . . . write(2)
open: open or create a file for reading or writing. . . . . open(2)
mdoc.samples: tutorial sampler for writing manuals with –mdoc. . . . . mdoc.samples(7)
utmp, wtmp, lastlog: login records. . . . . utmp(5)
wump: hunt the wumpus in an underground cave. . . . . . . wump(6)
wump: hunt wumpus in an underground cave. . . . . wump(6)
ceil: smallest integral value not greater than x. . . . . ceil(3)
floor: largest integral value not greater than x. . . . . floor(3)
xchess: X chess display. . . . . xchess(1)
xneko: cat-and-mouse chase in an X window. . . . . xneko(6)
utility. xargs: construct argument list(s) and execute . . . . xargs(1)
xchess: X chess display. . . . . xchess(1)
idp: Xerox Internet Datagram Protocol. . . . . idp(4)
ns: Xerox Network Systems(tm) protocol family. . . . . ns(4)
ns_addr, ns_ntoa: Xerox NS Ns (tm) address conversion routines. . . . . ns(3)
spp: Xerox Sequenced Packet Protocol. . . . . spp(4)
xsend, xget, enroll: private encrypted mail. . . . . xsend(1)
xneko: cat-and-mouse chase in an X window. . . . . xneko(6)
XNSrouted: NS Routing Information Protocol daemon. . . . XNSrouted(8)

xroach: cockroaches hide under your windows. . . . . . . xroach(6)

xsend, xget, enroll: private encrypted mail. . . . . xsend(1)

shared strings. xstr: extract strings from C programs to implement . . . . . xstr(1)

kind. j0, j1, jn, y0, y1, yn: bessel functions of first and second . . . . . . j0(3)

j0, j1, jn, y0, y1, yn: bessel functions of first and second kind. . . . . . j0(3)

yacc: an LALR(1) parser generator. . . . . yacc(1)

yes: be repetitively affirmative. . . . . yes(1)

j0, j1, jn, y0, y1, yn: bessel functions of first and second kind. . . . . . . j0(3)

yyfix: extract tables from y.tab.c. . . . . yyfix(1)

yyfix: extract tables from y.tab.c. . . . . yyfix(1)

znew: recompress . Z files to .gz files. . . . . znew(1)

compress, uncompress, zcat: compress and expand data. . . . . compress(1)

gzip, gunzip, zcat: compress or expand files. . . . . gzip(1)

zcmp, zdiff: compare compressed files. . . . . zdiff(1)

zcmp, zdiff: compare compressed files. . . . . zdiff(1)

calloc: allocate clean memory (zero initialized space). . . . . calloc(3)

bzero: write zeroes to a byte string. . . . . bzero(3)

zforce: force a '.gz' extension on all gzip files. . . . . zforce(1)

regular expression. zgrep: search possibly compressed files for a . . . . zgrep(1)

zic: time zone compiler. . . . . zic(8)

compressed text. zmore: file perusal filter for crt viewing of . . . . zmore(1)

znew: recompress .Z files to .gz files. . . . . znew(1)

zic: time zone compiler. zic(8)

tzfile: time zone information. . . . . tzfile(5)

named-xfer: ancillary agent for inbound zone transfers. named-xfer(8)

BERKELEY 4.4 SOFTWARE DISTRIBUTION

4.4BSD is the final release of what may be one of the most significant research projects in the history of computing. When Bell Labs originally released UNIX source code to the R&D community, brilliant researchers wrote their own software and added it to UNIX in a spree of creative anarchy that hasn't been equaled since. The Berkeley Software Distribution became the repository of much of that work.

In those years of creative ferment, source code was widely available, so programmers could build on the work of others. As UNIX became commercialized, access to source became increasingly curtailed and original development more difficult.

With this release of 4.4BSD-Lite, you need no longer work at a university or UNIX system development house to have access to UNIX source. The source code included on the 4.4BSD-Lite CD-ROM Companion will provide invaluable information on the design of any modern UNIX or UNIX-like system, and the source code for the utilities and support libraries will greatly enhance any programmer's toolkit. (Note that the 4.4BSD-Lite distribution does not include sources for the complete 4.4BSD system.

The source code for a small number of utilities and files, including a few from the operating system, were removed so that the system could be freely distributed.)

In addition to source code, the CD includes the manual pages, other documentation, and research papers from the University of California, Berkeley's 4.4BSD-Lite distribution.

This documentation is also available in printed form as a five-volume set.

—Tim O'Reilly

4.4BSD-Lite CD Companion

112 pages plus CD-ROM
CD Domestic ISBN 1-56592-081-3
CD International ISBN 1-56592-092-9

This CD is a copy of the University of California, Berkeley's 4.4BSD-Lite release, with additional documentation and enhancements. Access to the source code included here will provide invaluable information on the design of a modern UNIX-like system, and the source code for the utilities and support libraries will greatly enhance any programmer's toolkit. The CD is a source distribution, and does not contain program binaries for any architecture. It will not be possible to compile or run this software without a pre-existing system that is already installed and running. The 4.4BSD-Lite distribution did not include sources for the complete 4.4BSD system. The source code for a small number of utilities and files (including a few from the operating system) were removed so that the system could be freely distributed.

4.4BSD System Manager's Manual

646(est.) pages, ISBN 1-56592-080-5

Man pages for system administration commands and files, plus papers on system administration.

4.4BSD User's Reference Manual

909 pages, ISBN 1-56592-075-9

The famous "man pages" for over 500 utilities.

4.4BSD User's Supplementary Documents

686(est.) pages, ISBN 1-56592-076-7

Papers providing in-depth documentation of complex programs such as the shell, editors, and word processing utilities.

4.4BSD Programmer's Reference Manual

884 pages, ISBN 1-56592-078-3

Man pages for system calls, libraries, and file formats.

4.4BSD Programmer's Supplementary Documents

606(est.) pages, ISBN 1-56592-079-1

The original Bell and BSD research papers providing in-depth documentation of the programming environment.

GLOBAL NETWORK NAVIGATOR

The Global Network Navigator™ (GNN) is a unique kind of information service that makes the Internet easy and enjoyable to use. We organize access to the vast information resources of the Internet so that you can find what you want. We also help you understand the Internet and the many ways you can explore it.

Charting the Internet, the Ultimate Online Service

In GNN you'll find:

- **The Online Whole Internet Catalog**, an interactive card catalog for Internet resources that expands on the catalog in Ed Krol's bestselling book, *The Whole Internet User's Guide & Catalog*.

- **Newsnet**, a news service that keeps you up to date on what's happening on the Net.

- **The Netheads department**, which features profiles of interesting people on the Internet and commentary by Internet experts.

- **GNN Metacenters**, special-interest online magazines aimed at serving the needs of particular audiences. GNN Metacenters not only gather the best Internet resources together in one convenient place, they also introduce new material from a variety of sources. Each Metacenter contains new feature articles, as well as columns, subject-oriented reference guides for using the Internet, and topic-oriented discussion groups. Travel, music, education, and computers are some of the areas that we cover.

All in all, GNN helps you get more value for the time you spend on the Internet.

Subscribe Today

GNN is available over the Internet as a subscription service. To get complete information about subscribing to GNN, send email to **info@gnn.com**. If you have access to a World Wide Web browser such as Mosaic or Lynx, you can use the following URL to register online: `http://gnn.com/`

If you use a browser that does not support online forms, you can retrieve an email version of the registration form automatically by sending email to **form@gnn.com**. Fill this form out and send it back to us by email, and we will confirm your registration.

FOR INFORMATION: **800-998-9938**, *707-829-0515*; NUTS@ORA.COM

BOOK INFORMATION AT YOUR FINGERTIPS

O'Reilly & Associates offers extensive online information through a Gopher server (*gopher.ora.com*). Here you can find detailed information on our entire catalog of books, tapes, and much more.

The O'Reilly Online Catalog

Gopher is basically a hierarchy of menus and files that can easily lead you to a wealth of information. Gopher is also easy to navigate; helpful instructions appear at the bottom of each screen (notice the three prompts in the sample screen below). Another nice feature is that Gopher files can be downloaded, saved, or printed out for future reference. You can also search Gopher files and even email them.

To give you an idea of our Gopher, here's a look at the top, or root, menu:

```
O'Reilly & Associates (The public gopher server)

    1.  News Flash! -- New Products and Projects/

    2.  Feature Articles/

    3.  Product Descriptions/

    4.  Ordering Information/

    5.  Complete Listing of Titles

    6.  Errata for "Learning Perl"

    7.  FTP Archive and Email Information/

    8.  Bibliographies/


   Press ? for Help, q to Quit, u to go up a menu
```

The heart of the O'Reilly Gopher service is the extensive information provided on all ORA products in menu item three, "Product Descriptions." For most books this usually includes title information, a long description, a short author bio, the table of contents, quotes and reviews, a gif image of the book's cover, and even some interesting information about the animal featured on the cover (one of the benefits of a Gopher database is the ability to pack a lot of information in an organized, easy-to-find place).

How to Order

Another important listing is "Ordering Information," where we supply information to those interested in buying our books. Here, you'll find instructions and an application for ordering O'Reilly products online, a listing of distributors (local and international), a listing of bookstores that carry our titles, and much more.

The item that follows, "Complete Listing of Titles," is helpful when it's time to order. This single file, with short one-line listings of all ORA products, quickly provides the essentials for easy ordering: title, ISBN, and price.

And More

One of the most widely read areas of the O'Reilly Gopher is "News Flash!," which focuses on important new products and projects of ORA. Here, you'll find entries on newly published books and audiotapes; announcements of exciting new projects and product lines from ORA; upcoming tradeshows, conferences, and exhibitions of interest; author appearances; contest winners; job openings; and anything else that's timely and topical.

"Feature Articles" contains just that—many of the articles and interviews found here are excerpted from the O'Reilly magazine/catalog *ora.com*.

The "Bibliographies" entries are also very popular with readers, providing critical, objective reviews on the important literature in the field.

"FTP Archive and Email Information" contains helpful ORA email addresses, information about our "ora-news" listproc server, and detailed instructions on how to download ORA book examples via FTP.

Other menu listings are often available. "Errata for 'Learning Perl,'" for example, apprised readers of errata found in the first edition of our book, and responses to this file greatly aided our campaign to ferret out errors and typos for the upcoming corrected edition (a nice example of the mutual benefits of online interactivity).

Come and Explore

Our Gopher is vibrant and constantly in flux. By the time you actually log onto this Gopher, the root menu may well have changed. The goal is to always improve, and to that end we welcome your input (email: **gopher@ora.com**). We invite you to come and explore.

Here are four basic ways to call up our Gopher online.

1) If you have a local Gopher client, type:
   ```
   gopher gopher.ora.com
   ```

2) For Xgopher:
   ```
   xgopher -xrm "xgopher.root\
   Server: gopher.ora.com"
   ```

3) To use telnet (for those without a Gopher client):
   ```
   telnet gopher.ora.com
   ```
   login: **gopher** (no password)

4) For a World Wide Web browser, use this URL:
   ```
   http://gopher.ora.com:70/
   ```

COMPLETE LISTING OF TITLES

from O'Reilly & Associates, Inc.

INTERNET

The Whole Internet User's Guide & Catalog
Connecting to the Internet: An O'Reilly Buyer's Guide
!%@:: A Directory of Electronic Mail Addressing & Networks
Smileys

USING UNIX AND X

UNIX Power Tools (with CD-ROM)
UNIX in a Nutshell: System V Edition
UNIX in a Nutshell: Berkeley Edition
SCO UNIX in a Nutshell
Learning the UNIX Operating System
Learning the vi Editor
Learning GNU Emacs
Learning the Korn Shell
Making TeX Work
sed & awk
MH & xmh: E-mail for Users & Programmers
Using UUCP and Usenet
X Window System User's Guide: Volume 3
X Window System User's Guide, Motif Edition: Volume 3M

SYSTEM ADMINISTRATION

Essential System Administration
sendmail
Computer Security Basics
Practical UNIX Security
System Performance Tuning
TCP/IP Network Administration
Learning Perl
Programming perl
Managing NFS and NIS
Managing UUCP and Usenet
DNS and BIND
termcap & terminfo
X Window System Administrator's Guide: Volume 8
    (available with or without CD-ROM)

UNIX AND C PROGRAMMING

ORACLE Performance Tuning
High Performance Computing
lex & yacc
POSIX Programmer's Guide
Power Programming with RPC
Programming with curses
Managing Projects with make
Software Portability with imake
Understanding and Using COFF
Migrating to Fortran 90
UNIX for FORTRAN Programmers
Using C on the UNIX System
Checking C Programs with lint
Practical C Programming
Understanding Japanese Information Processing

DCE (DISTRIBUTED COMPUTING ENVIRONMENT)

Distributing Applications Across DCE and Windows NT
Guide to Writing DCE Applications
Understanding DCE

BERKELEY 4.4 SOFTWARE DISTRIBUTION

4.4BSD System Manager's Manual
4.4BSD User's Reference Manual
4.4BSD User's Supplementary Documents
4.4BSD Programmer's Reference Manual
4.4BSD Programmer's Supplementary Documents
4.4BSD-Lite CD Companion

X PROGRAMMING

The X Window System in a Nutshell
X Protocol Reference Manual: Volume 0
Xlib Programming Manual: Volume 1
Xlib Reference Manual: Volume 2
X Toolkit Intrinsics Programming Manual: Volume 4
X Toolkit Intrinsics Programming Manual, Motif Edition: Volume 4M
X Toolkit Intrinsics Reference Manual: Volume 5
Motif Programming Manual: Volume 6A
Motif Reference Manual: Volume 6B
XView Programming Manual: Volume 7A
XView Reference Manual: Volume 7B
PEXlib Programming Manual
PEXlib Reference Manual
PHIGS Programming Manual (softcover or hardcover)
PHIGS Reference Manual
Programmer's Supplement for R5 of the X Window System

THE X RESOURCE

A quarterly working journal for X programmers
The X Resource: Issues 0 through 10

OTHER

Building a Successful Software Business
Love Your Job!

TRAVEL

Travelers' Tales Thailand

AUDIOTAPES

Internet Talk Radio's "Geek of the Week" Interviews

The Future of the Internet Protocol, 4 hours
Global Network Operations, 2 hours
Mobile IP Networking, 1 hour
Networked Information and Online Libraries, 1 hour
Security and Networks, 1 hour
European Networking, 1 hour

Notable Speeches of the Information Age

John Perry Barlow, 1.5 hours

INTERNATIONAL DISTRIBUTORS

Customers outside North America can now order O'Reilly & Associates' books through the following distributors. They offer our international customers faster order processing, more bookstores, increased representation at tradeshows worldwide, and the high-quality, responsive service our customers have come to expect.

EUROPE, MIDDLE EAST, AND AFRICA
except Germany, Switzerland, and Austria

INQUIRIES
International Thomson Publishing Europe
Berkshire House
168-173 High Holborn
London WC1V 7AA
United Kingdom
Telephone: 44-71-497-1422
Fax: 44-71-497-1426
Email: danni.dolbear@itpuk.co.uk

ORDERS
International Thomson Publishing Services, Ltd.
Cheriton House, North Way
Andover, Hampshire SP10 5BE
United Kingdom
Telephone: 44-264-342-832 (UK orders)
Telephone: 44-264-342-806 (outside UK)
Fax: 44-264-364418 (UK orders)
Fax: 44-264-342761 (outside UK)

GERMANY, SWITZERLAND, AND AUSTRIA

International Thomson Publishing GmbH
O'Reilly-International Thomson Verlag
Königswinterer Strasse 418
53227 Bonn
Germany
Telephone: 49-228-445171
Fax: 49-228-441342
Email (CompuServe): 100272,2422
Email (Internet): 100272.2422@compuserve.com

ASIA
except Japan

INQUIRIES
International Thomson Publishing Asia
221 Henderson Road
#05 10 Henderson Building
Singapore 0315
Telephone: 65-272-6496
Fax: 65-272-6498

ORDERS
Telephone: 65-268-7867
Fax: 65-268-6727

AUSTRALIA

WoodsLane Pty. Ltd.
Unit 8, 101 Darley Street (P.O. Box 935)
Mona Vale NSW 2103
Australia
Telephone: 61-2-9795944
Fax: 61-2-9973348
Email: woods@tmx.mhs.oz.au

NEW ZEALAND

WoodsLane New Zealand Ltd.
7 Purnell Street (P.O. Box 575)
Wanganui, New Zealand
Telephone: 64-6-3476543
Fax: 64-6-3454840
Email: woods@tmx.mhs.oz.au

THE AMERICAS, JAPAN, AND OCEANIA

O'Reilly & Associates, Inc.
103A Morris Street
Sebastopol, CA 95472 U.S.A.
Telephone: 707-829-0515
Telephone: 800-998-9938 (U.S. & Canada)
Fax: 707-829-0104
Email: order@ora.com

WE WOULD LIKE TO
TELL YOU MORE ABOUT

USENIX is the Unix and advanced computing systems technical and professional membership association founded in 1975.
We would like to send you information about our major conferences and frequent symposia held throughout the United States
and Canada, about our important technical documentation and other publications, and about the benefits of becoming a
member of USENIX and or SAGE, the System Administrators Guild.

Please send me information about:

❑ Joining the USENIX Association

❑ Joining the System Administrators Guild, dedicated to the
advancement of system administration as a profession

❑ The bimonthly newsletter *;login:*, featuring technical
articles, a worldwide calendar of events, SAGE News,
media reviews, reports from USENIX representatives on
various ANSI, IEEE, and ISO standards and much more

❑ The refereed technical quarterly *Computing Systems*,
published with The MIT Press

❑ Proceedings from USENIX conferences and symposia
and other technical publications

❑ The USENIX Association book series published by
The MIT Press. First in the series: *The Evolution of C++:
Language Design in the Marketplace of Ideas*, edited by
Jim Waldo of Sun Microsystems Laboratories

Name/Title

Company/Institution

Mail Address

City   State   Zip/Postal Code   Country

Telephone   FAX   Internet Address

You may receive the catalog of available conference information for the USENIX Winter multi-topic technical conference, the annual Systems
Administration (LISA) conference, and the frequent symposia addressing topics such as Operating System Design, High Speed Networking,
Security, Object-Oriented Technologies, and Mobile Computing, by telephoning the USENIX conference office at 1-714-588-8649 or sending
e-mail to: **info@usenix.org**. In the body of your mail message, send the line: **send conferences catalog**.

O'REILLY WOULD LIKE TO HEAR FROM YOU

Please send me the following:

❑ *ora.com*

O'Reilly's magazine/catalog,
containing behind-the-scenes
articles, interviews on the
technology we write about, and
a complete listing of O'Reilly
books and products.

❑ *Global Network Navigator*™
Subscription information.

Please print legibly

Thank you for purchasing a *Berkeley 4.4 Software Distribution* document.

Where did you buy this book? ❑ Bookstore   ❑ Class/seminar
   ❑ Direct from O'Reilly   ❑ Bundled with hardware/software

What computer system do you use? ❑ UNIX   ❑ PC(DOS/Windows)
   ❑ MAC   ❑ SUN   ❑ Other _____

How do you use computers? ❑ Programmer ❑ SysAdmin
   ❑ End user   ❑ Other _____

Do you have a modem? ❑ yes ❑ no   What speed?_____

Name   Company/Organization

Address

City   State   Zip/Postal Code   Country

Telephone   Internet or other email address (specify network)

USENIX

**THE UNIX AND ADVANCED COMPUTING SYSTEMS
PROFESSIONAL AND TECHNICAL ASSOCIATION**

2560 Ninth Street, Suite 215, Berkeley, CA USA 94710
Telephone 1-510-528-8649, FAX: 1-510-548-5738
Internet: office@usenix.org

NO POSTAGE
NECESSARY IF
MAILED IN THE
UNITED STATES

BUSINESS REPLY MAIL

FIRST CLASS MAIL   PERMIT NO. 80   SEBASTOPOL, CA

Postage will be paid by addressee

O'Reilly & Associates, Inc.
103A Morris Street
Sebastopol, CA 95472-9902